Call of the Night

〈1〉

KOTOYAMA

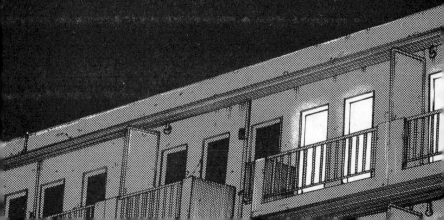

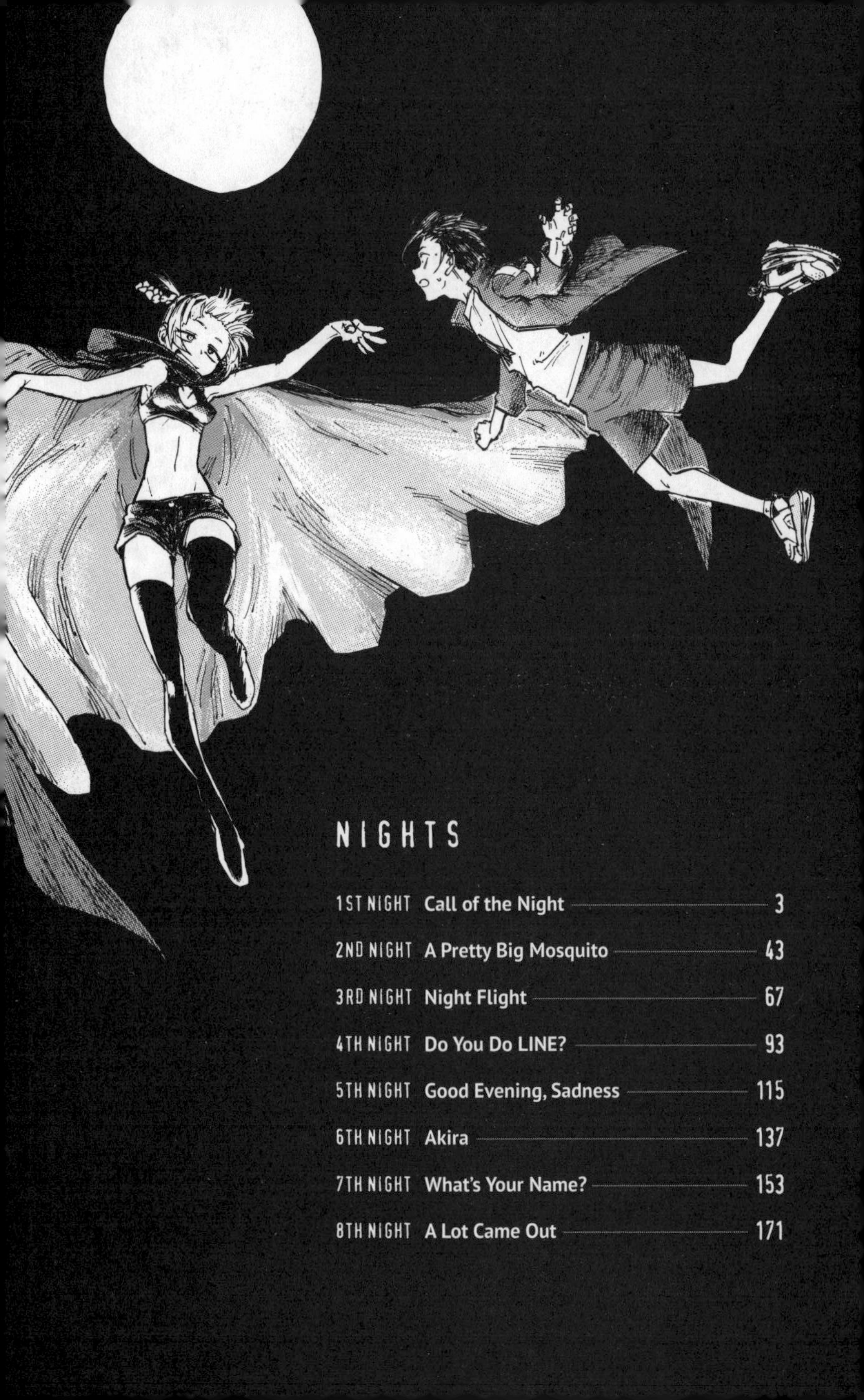

NIGHTS

NIGHT 1: CALL OF THE NIGHT

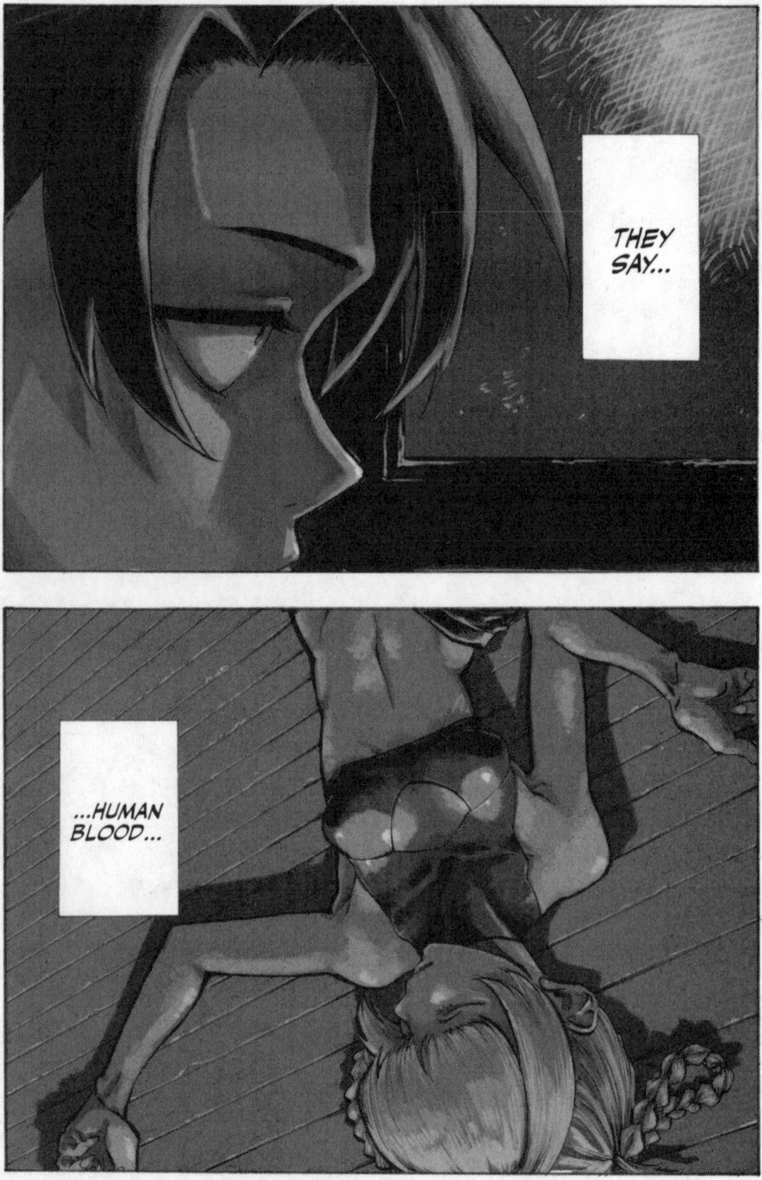
THEY SAY...
...HUMAN BLOOD...

...TASTES BEST AT NIGHT.

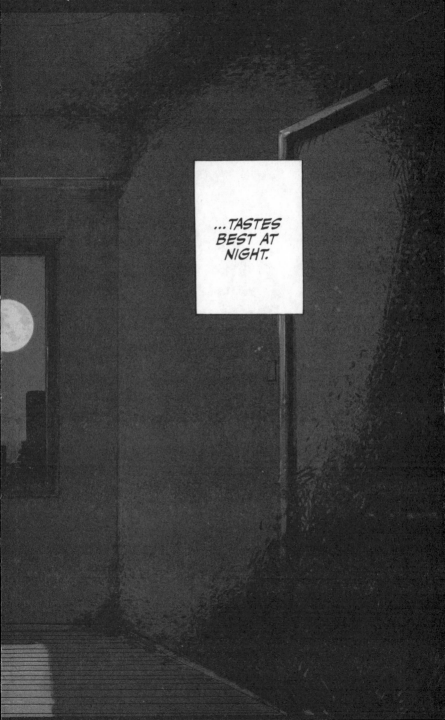

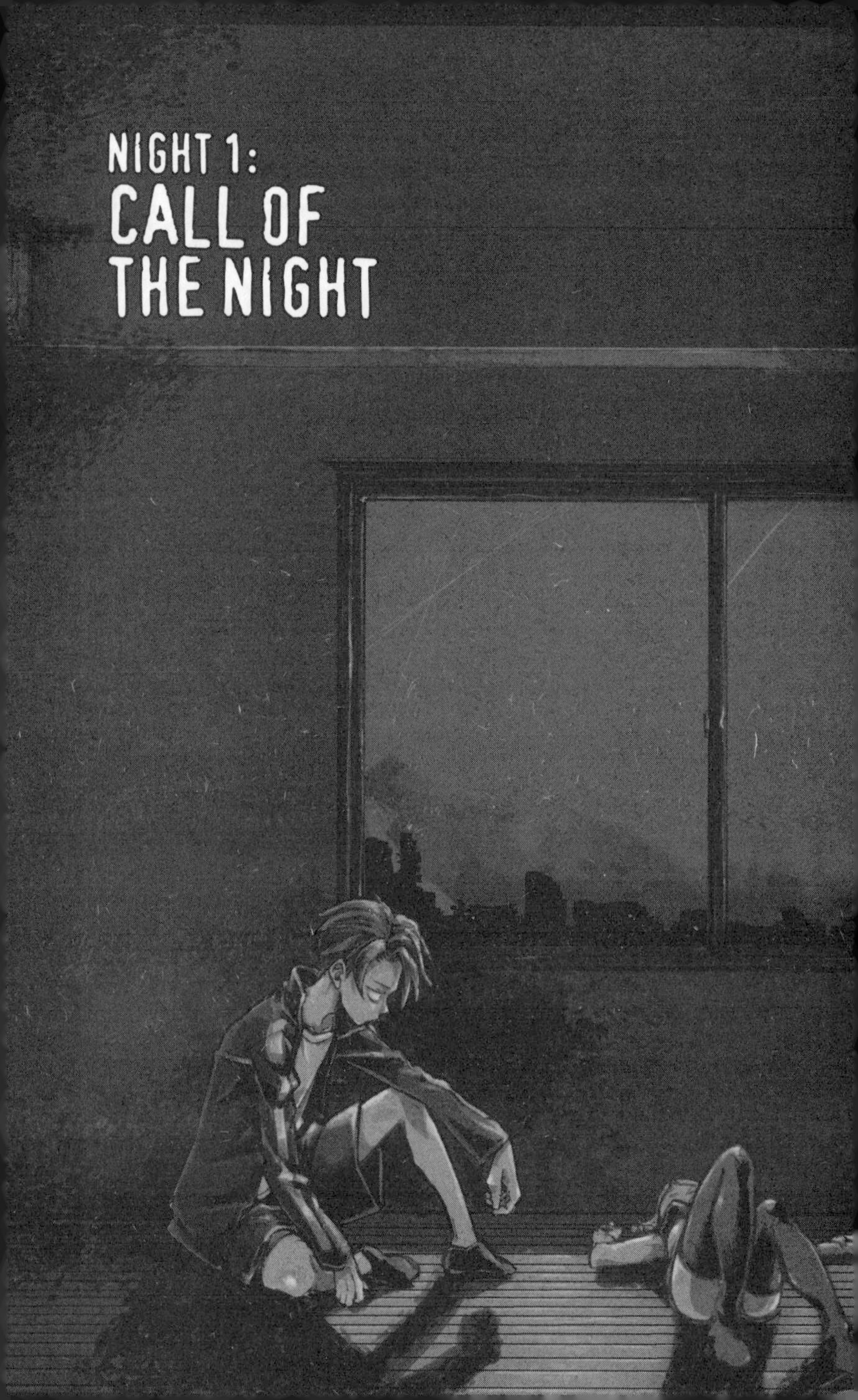
NIGHT 1:
CALL OF
THE NIGHT

Call of the Night

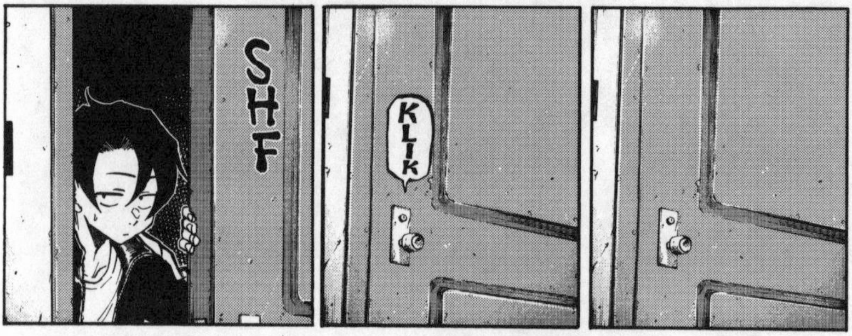
KLIK
SHF

I'M KO YAMORI.

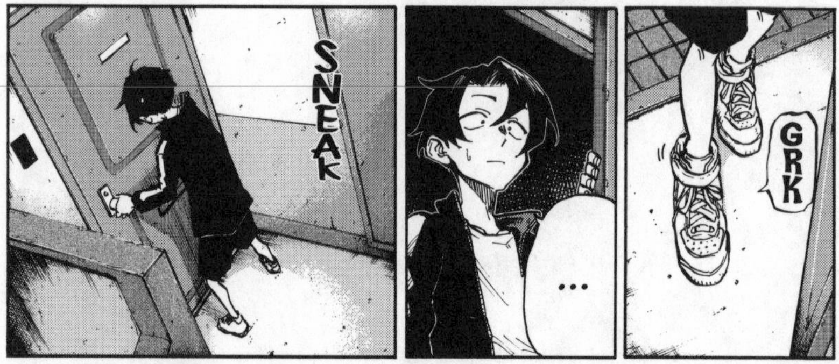
GRK
...
SNEAK

SECOND YEAR OF JUNIOR HIGH. AGE 14.

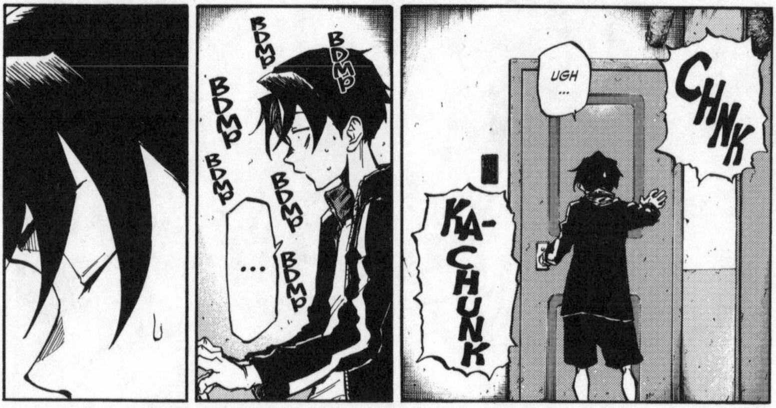
UGH ...
CHNK
KA-CHUNK
BDMP BDMP BDMP BDMP BDMP BDMP BDMP
...

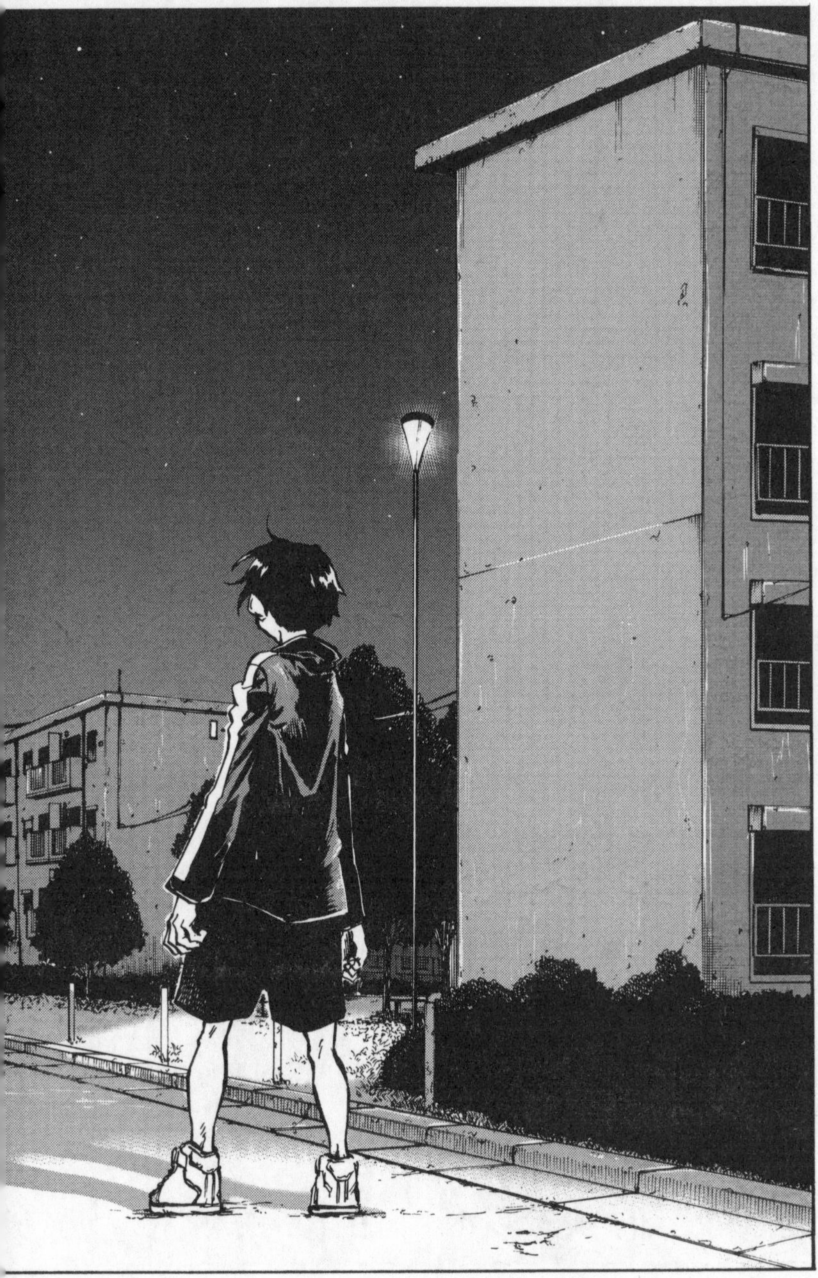

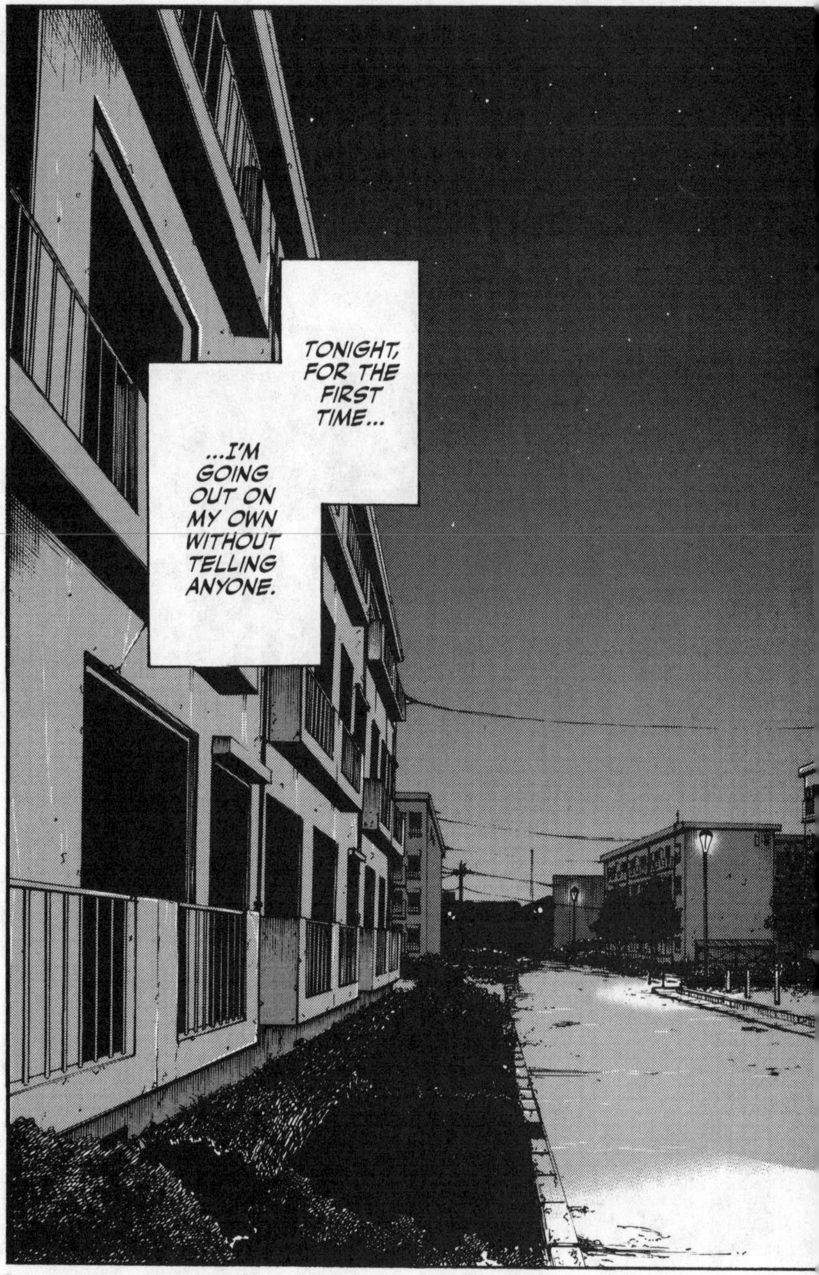
TONIGHT, FOR THE FIRST TIME...
...I'M GOING OUT ON MY OWN WITHOUT TELLING ANYONE.

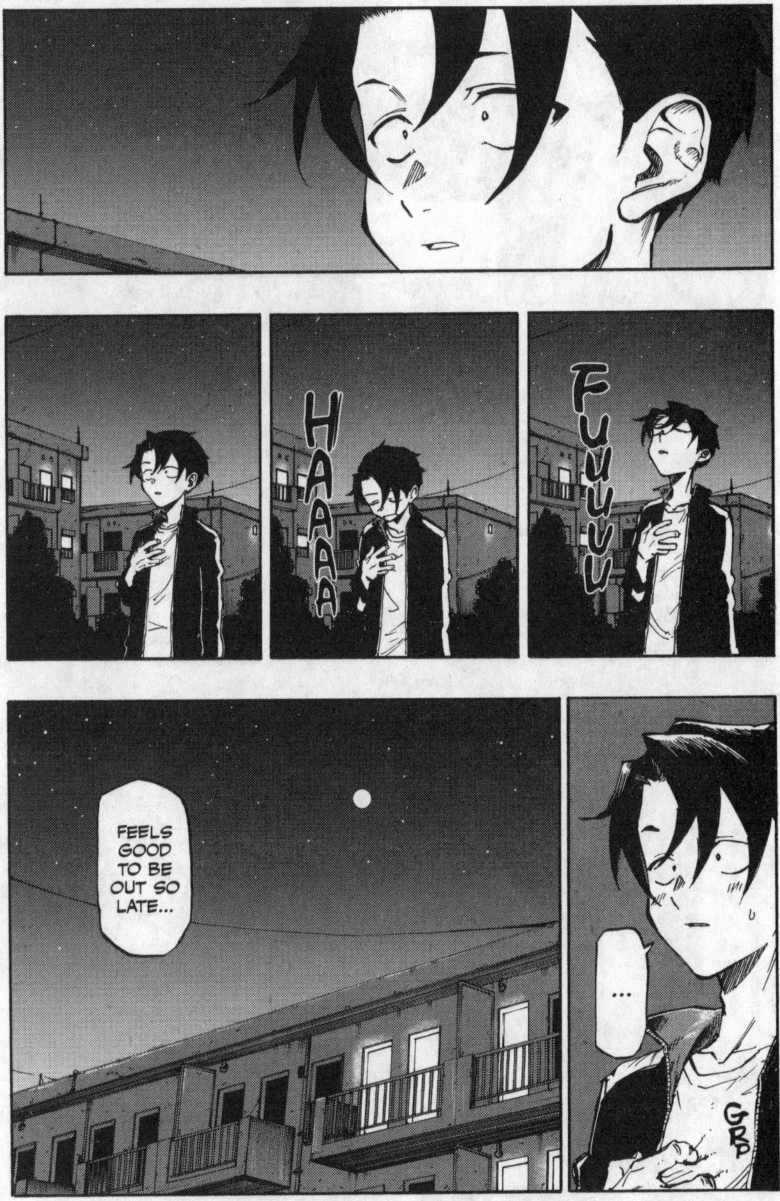
FUUUUUU
HAAAA
...
GRP
FEELS GOOD TO BE OUT SO LATE...

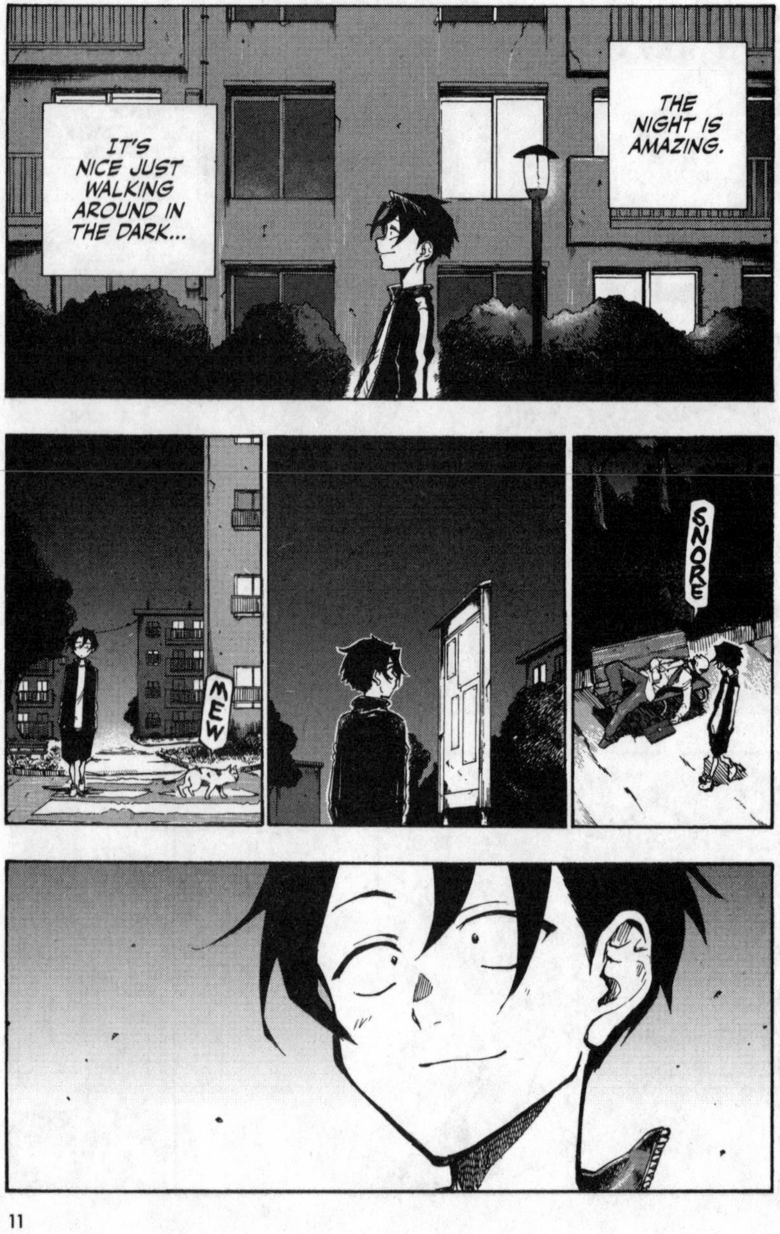
THE NIGHT IS AMAZING.
IT'S NICE JUST WALKING AROUND IN THE DARK...
SNORE
MEW

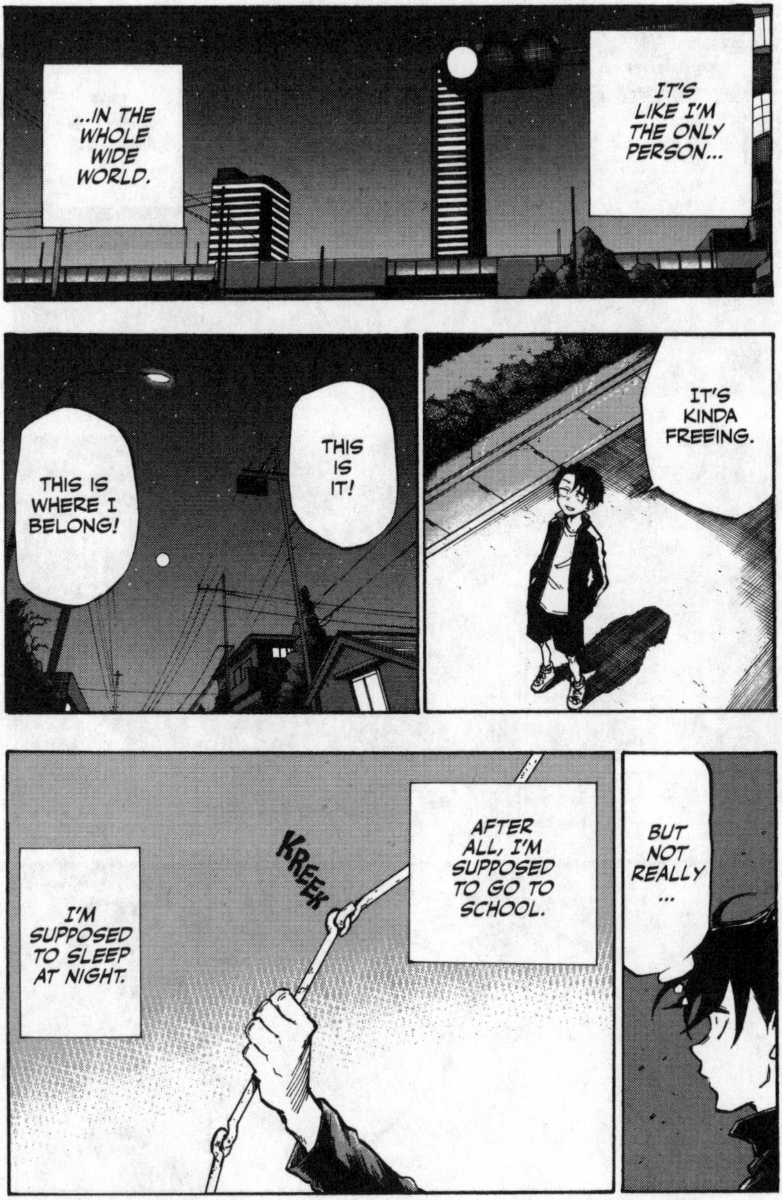
IT'S LIKE I'M THE ONLY PERSON...
...IN THE WHOLE WIDE WORLD.
IT'S KINDA FREEING.
THIS IS IT!
THIS IS WHERE I BELONG!
BUT NOT REALLY ...
AFTER ALL, I'M SUPPOSED TO GO TO SCHOOL.
KREEK
I'M SUPPOSED TO SLEEP AT NIGHT.

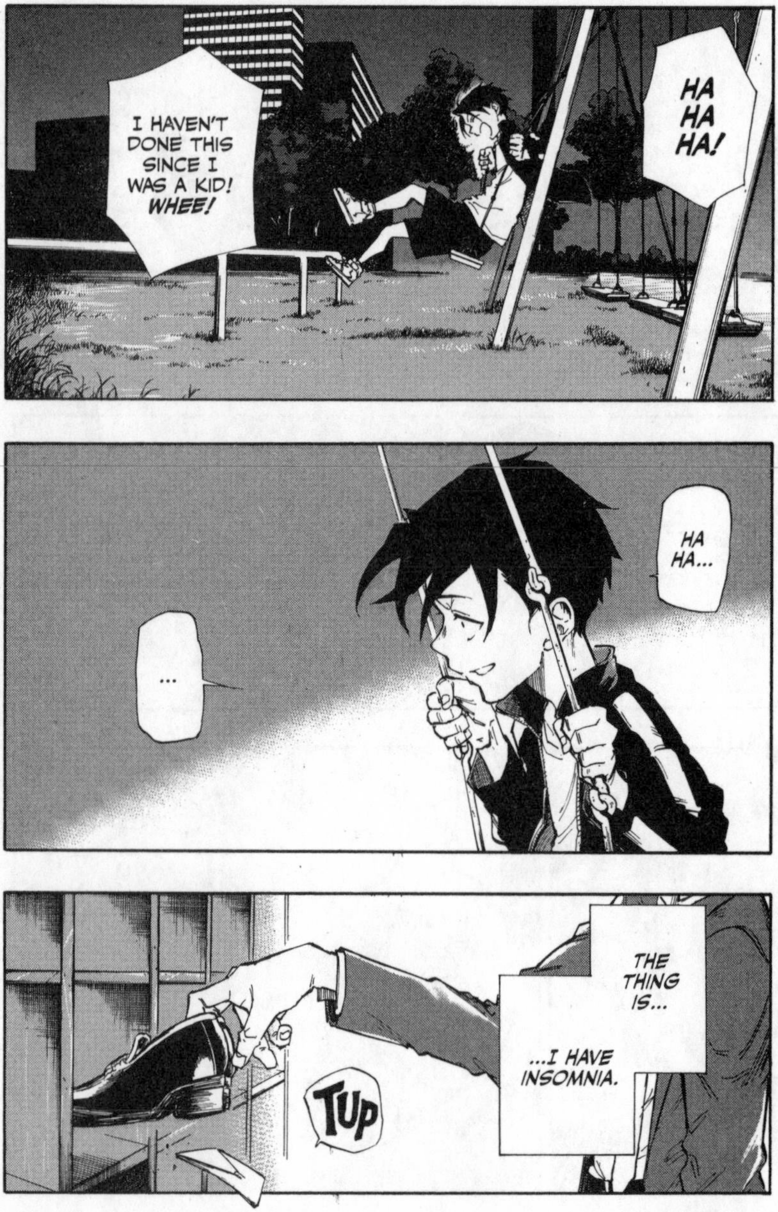
HA HA HA!
I HAVEN'T DONE THIS SINCE I WAS A KID! WHEE!
HA HA...
...
THE THING IS...
...I HAVE INSOMNIA.
TUP

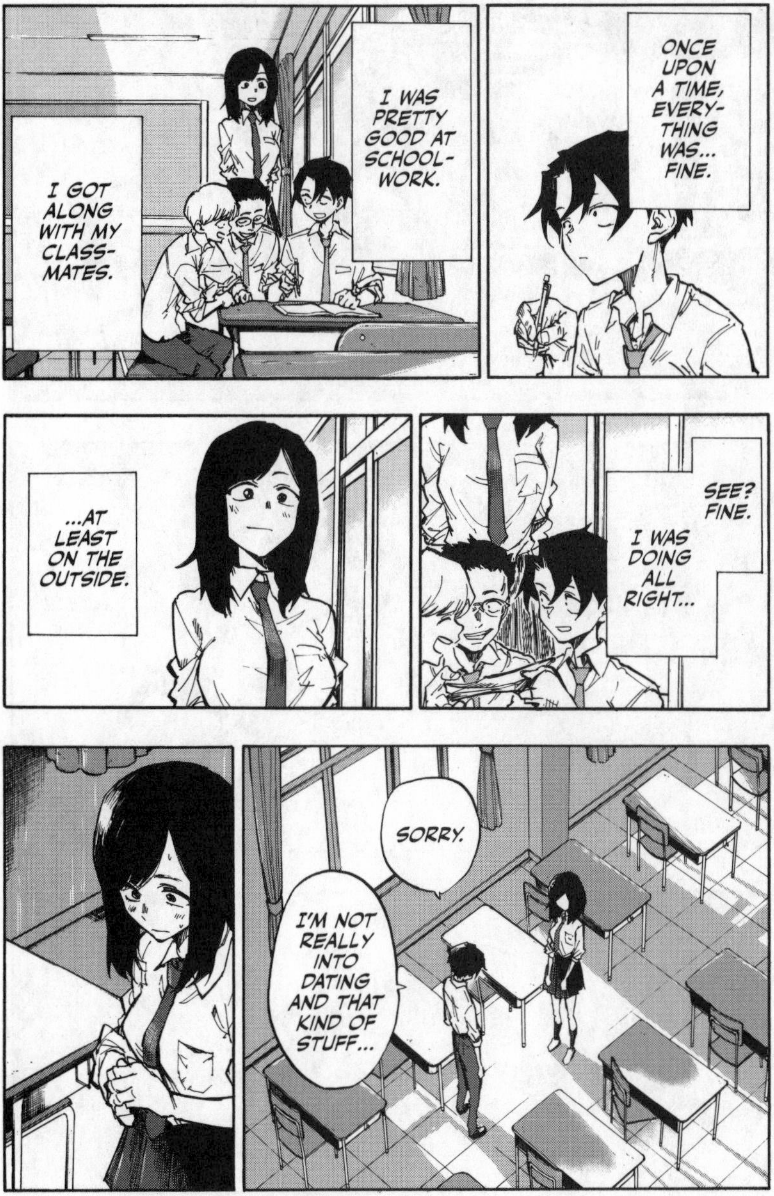
ONCE UPON A TIME, EVERYTHING WAS... FINE.
I WAS PRETTY GOOD AT SCHOOLWORK.
I GOT ALONG WITH MY CLASSMATES.
SEE? FINE.
I WAS DOING ALL RIGHT...
...AT LEAST ON THE OUTSIDE.
SORRY.
I'M NOT REALLY INTO DATING AND THAT KIND OF STUFF...

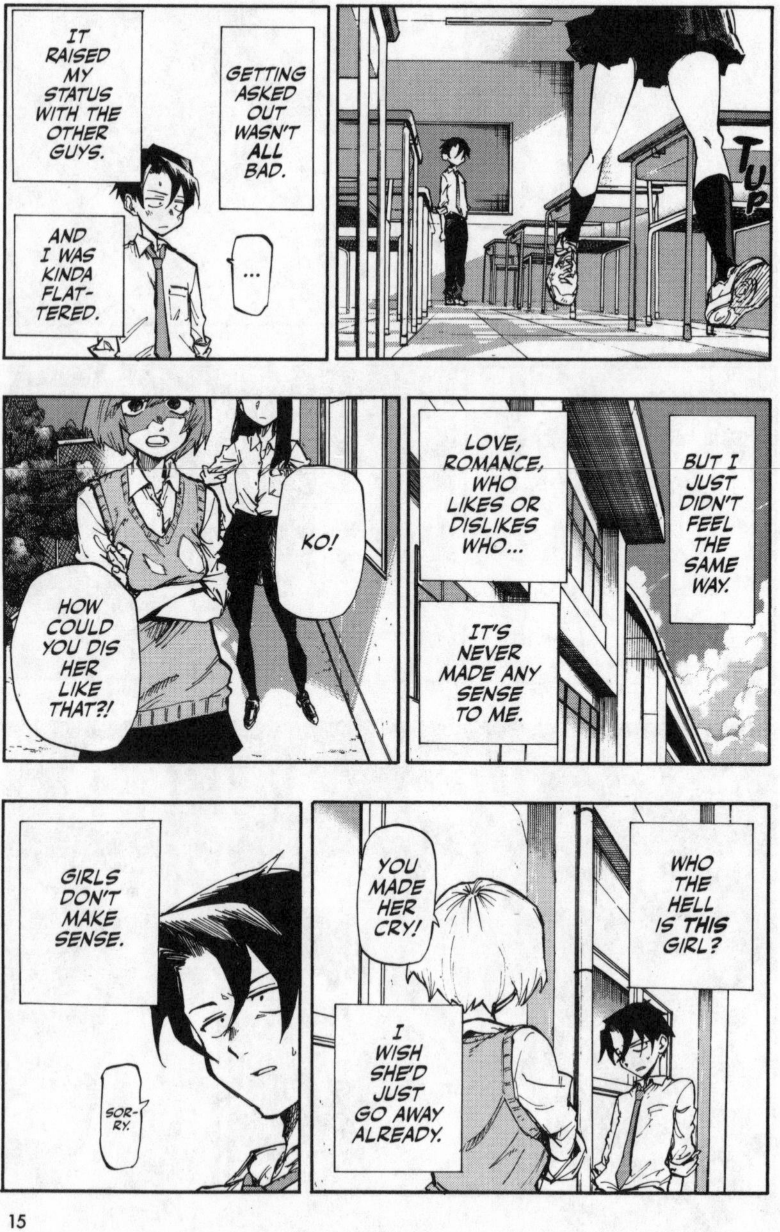
TUP
GETTING ASKED OUT WASN'T ALL BAD.
IT RAISED MY STATUS WITH THE OTHER GUYS.
...
AND I WAS KINDA FLAT-TERED.
BUT I JUST DIDN'T FEEL THE SAME WAY.
LOVE, ROMANCE, WHO LIKES OR DISLIKES WHO...
IT'S NEVER MADE ANY SENSE TO ME.
KO!
HOW COULD YOU DIS HER LIKE THAT?!
WHO THE HELL IS THIS GIRL?
YOU MADE HER CRY!
I WISH SHE'D JUST GO AWAY ALREADY.
GIRLS DON'T MAKE SENSE.
SOR-RY.

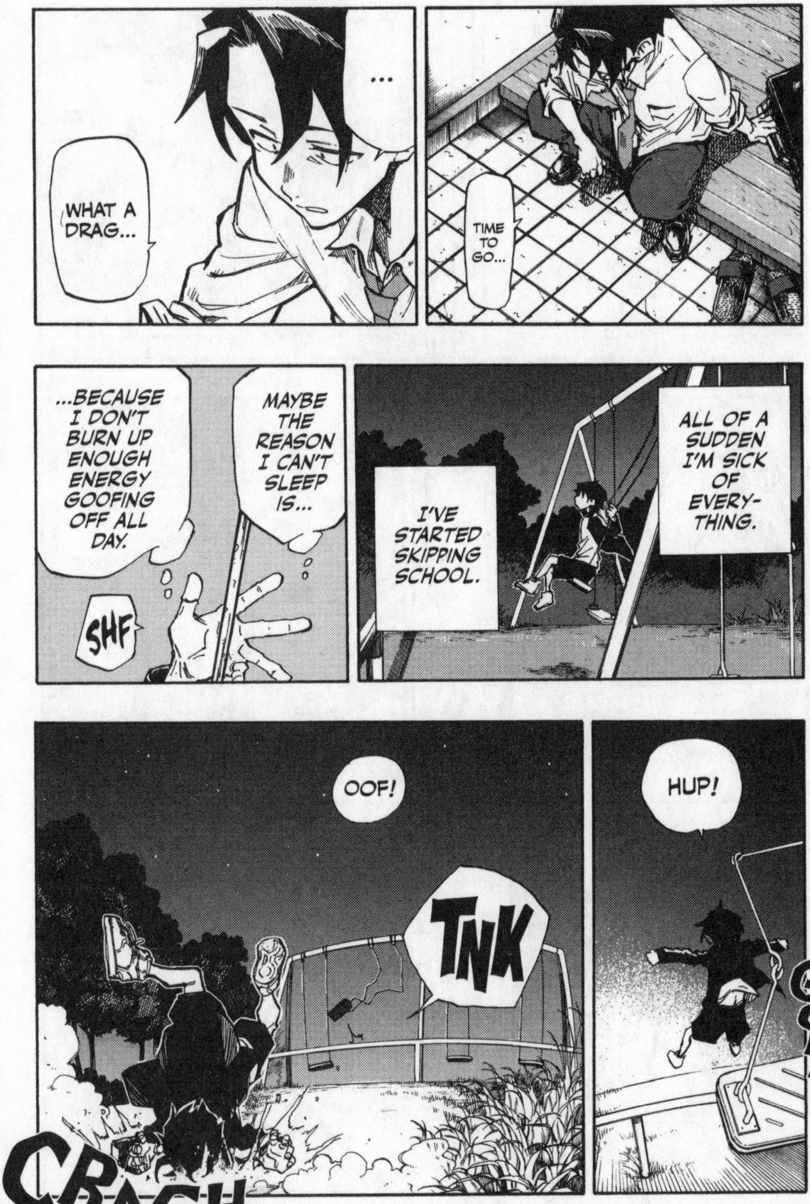
TIME TO GO...
...
WHAT A DRAG...
ALL OF A SUDDEN I'M SICK OF EVERY-THING.
I'VE STARTED SKIPPING SCHOOL.
MAYBE THE REASON I CAN'T SLEEP IS...
...BECAUSE I DON'T BURN UP ENOUGH ENERGY GOOFING OFF ALL DAY.
SHF
HUP!
GCHK
OOF!
TNK
CRASH

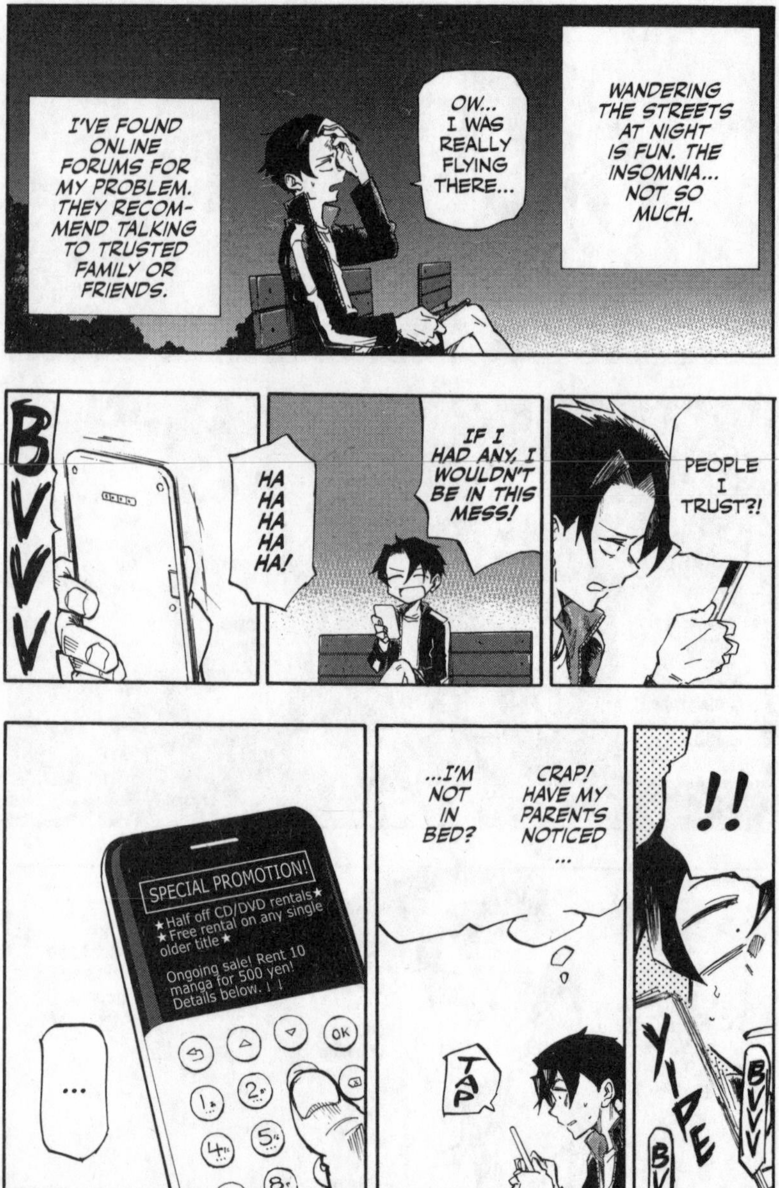
WANDERING THE STREETS AT NIGHT IS FUN. THE INSOMNIA... NOT SO MUCH.
OW... I WAS REALLY FLYING THERE...
I'VE FOUND ONLINE FORUMS FOR MY PROBLEM. THEY RECOMMEND TALKING TO TRUSTED FAMILY OR FRIENDS.
PEOPLE I TRUST?!
IF I HAD ANY, I WOULDN'T BE IN THIS MESS!
HA HA HA HA HA!
BVVVV
!!
YIPE
BVVV
BVVV
CRAP! HAVE MY PARENTS NOTICED...
...I'M NOT IN BED?
TAP
SPECIAL PROMOTION!
★Half off CD/DVD rentals★
★Free rental on any single older title★
Ongoing sale! Rent 10 manga for 500 yen! Details below. ↓↓
OK
...

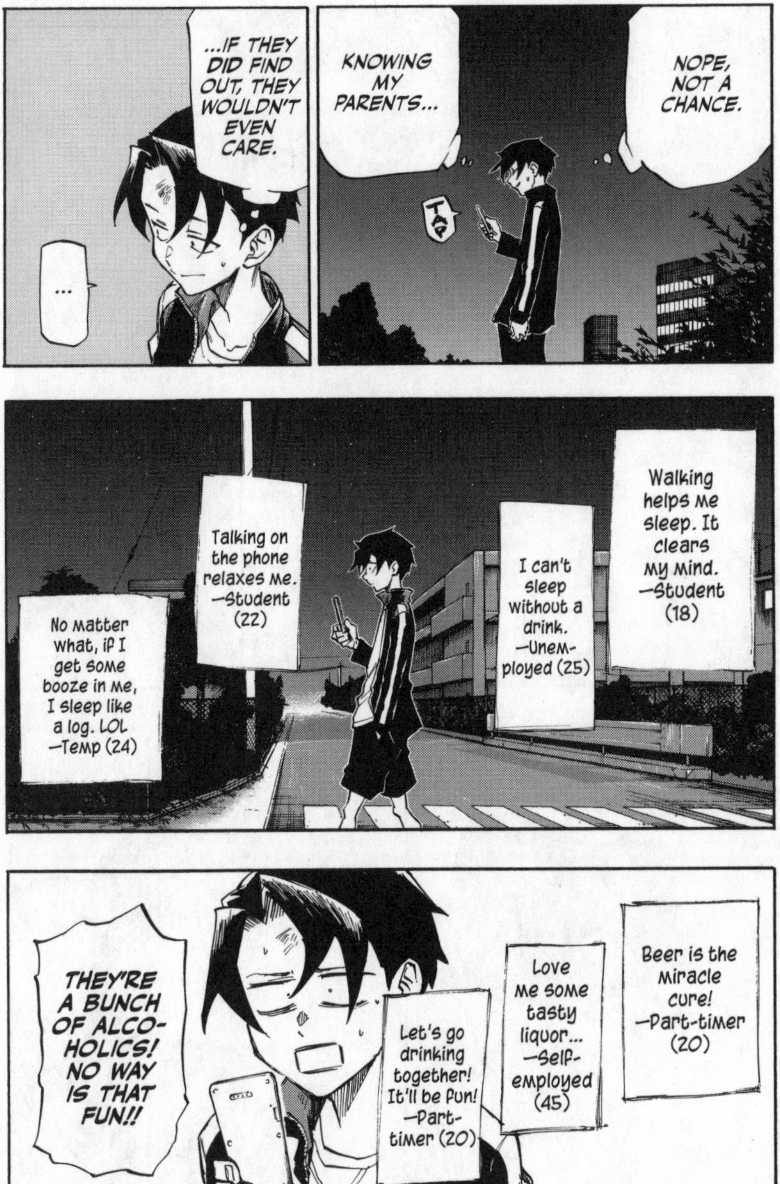
NOPE, NOT A CHANCE.
KNOWING MY PARENTS...
TAP
...IF THEY DID FIND OUT, THEY WOULDN'T EVEN CARE.
...
Walking helps me sleep. It clears my mind. —Student (18)
I can't sleep without a drink. —Unemployed (25)
Talking on the phone relaxes me. —Student (22)
No matter what, if I get some booze in me, I sleep like a log. LOL —Temp (24)
Beer is the miracle cure! —Part-timer (20)
Love me some tasty liquor... —Self-employed (45)
Let's go drinking together! It'll be fun! —Part-timer (20)
THEY'RE A BUNCH OF ALCOHOLICS! NO WAY IS THAT FUN!!

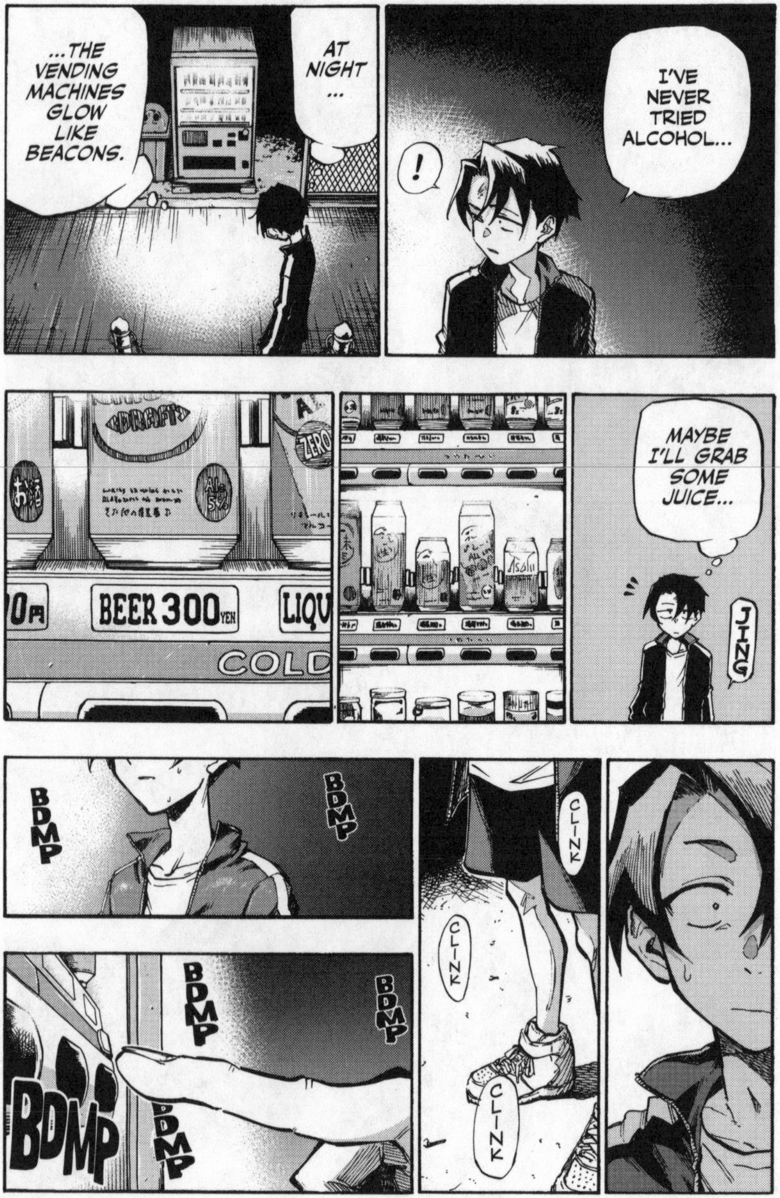

!
I'VE NEVER TRIED ALCOHOL...
AT NIGHT ...
...THE VENDING MACHINES GLOW LIKE BEACONS.
MAYBE I'LL GRAB SOME JUICE...
JING
BEER 300YEN
COLD
CLINK
CLINK
CLINK
BDMP
BDMP
BDMP
BDMP
BDMP
BDMP

YOU GETTING A BEER?
BIP
YUM!
TNK
HOW OLD ARE YOU?
NO *WAY* ARE YOU LEGAL.

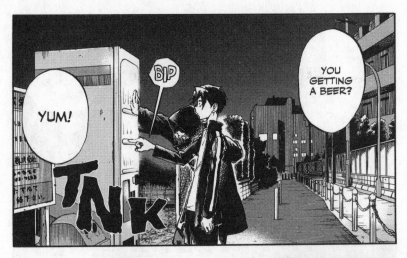

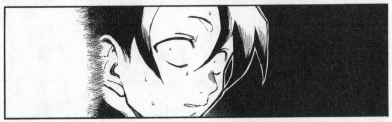

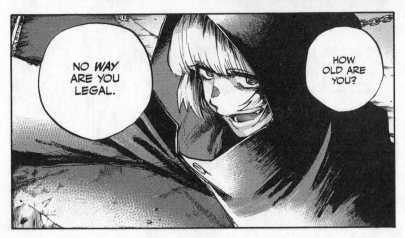

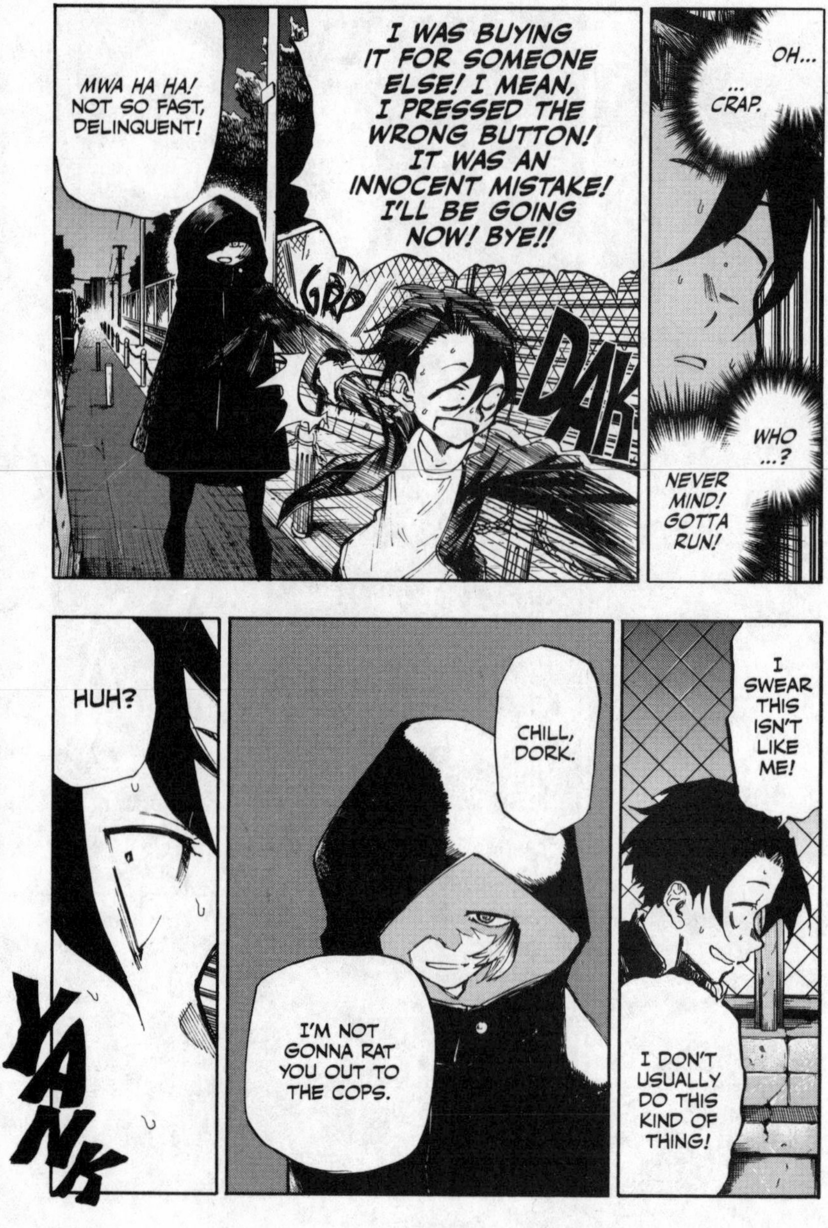
OH...
... CRAP.
WHO ...?
NEVER MIND! GOTTA RUN!
I WAS BUYING IT FOR SOMEONE ELSE! I MEAN, I PRESSED THE WRONG BUTTON! IT WAS AN INNOCENT MISTAKE! I'LL BE GOING NOW! BYE!!
MWA HA HA! NOT SO FAST, DELINQUENT!
GRP
DAK
I SWEAR THIS ISN'T LIKE ME!
I DON'T USUALLY DO THIS KIND OF THING!
CHILL, DORK.
I'M NOT GONNA RAT YOU OUT TO THE COPS.
HUH?
YANK

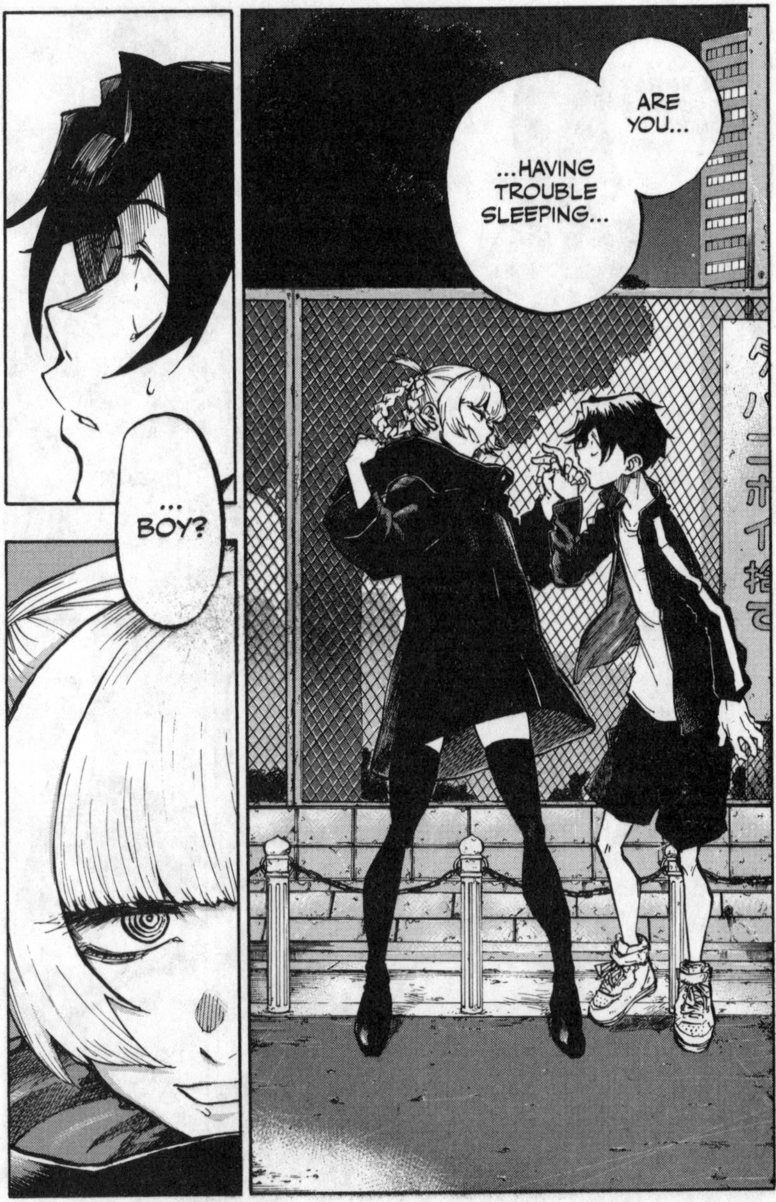
ARE YOU...
...HAVING TROUBLE SLEEPING...
...BOY?

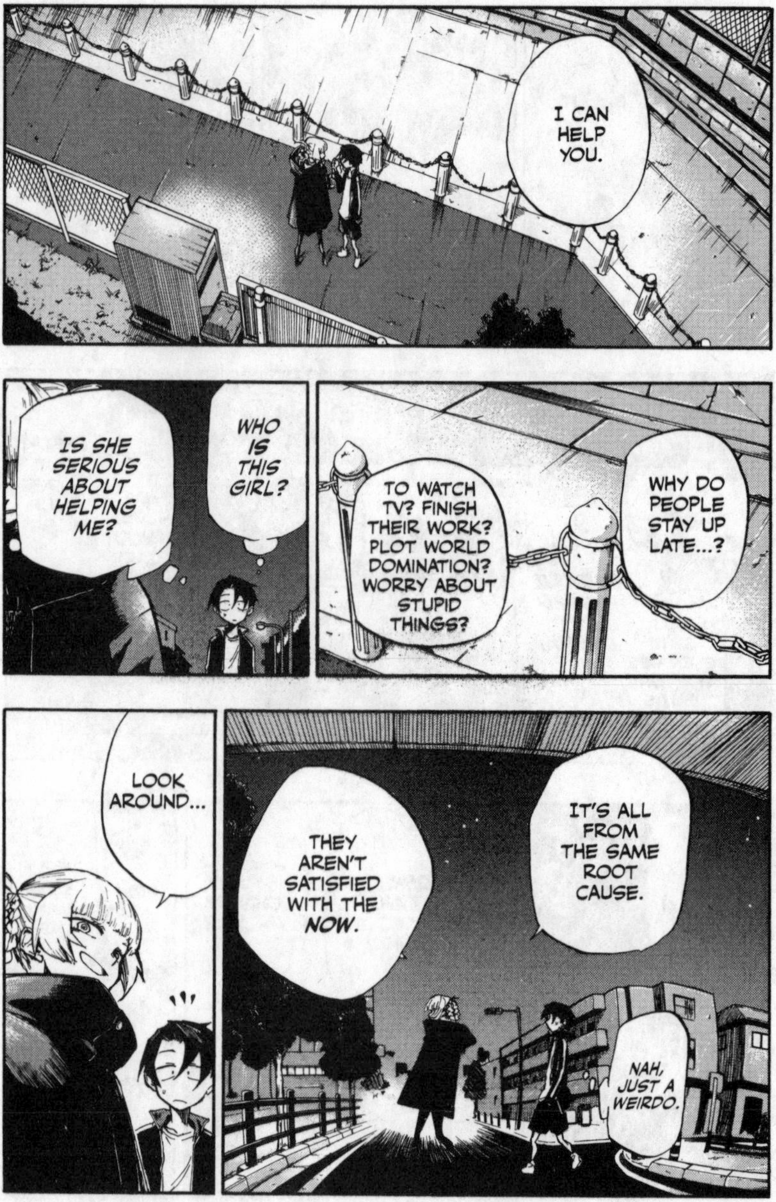
I CAN HELP YOU.
WHY DO PEOPLE STAY UP LATE...?
TO WATCH TV? FINISH THEIR WORK? PLOT WORLD DOMINATION? WORRY ABOUT STUPID THINGS?
WHO IS THIS GIRL?
IS SHE SERIOUS ABOUT HELPING ME?
IT'S ALL FROM THE SAME ROOT CAUSE.
THEY AREN'T SATISFIED WITH THE *NOW*.
NAH, JUST A WEIRDO.
LOOK AROUND...

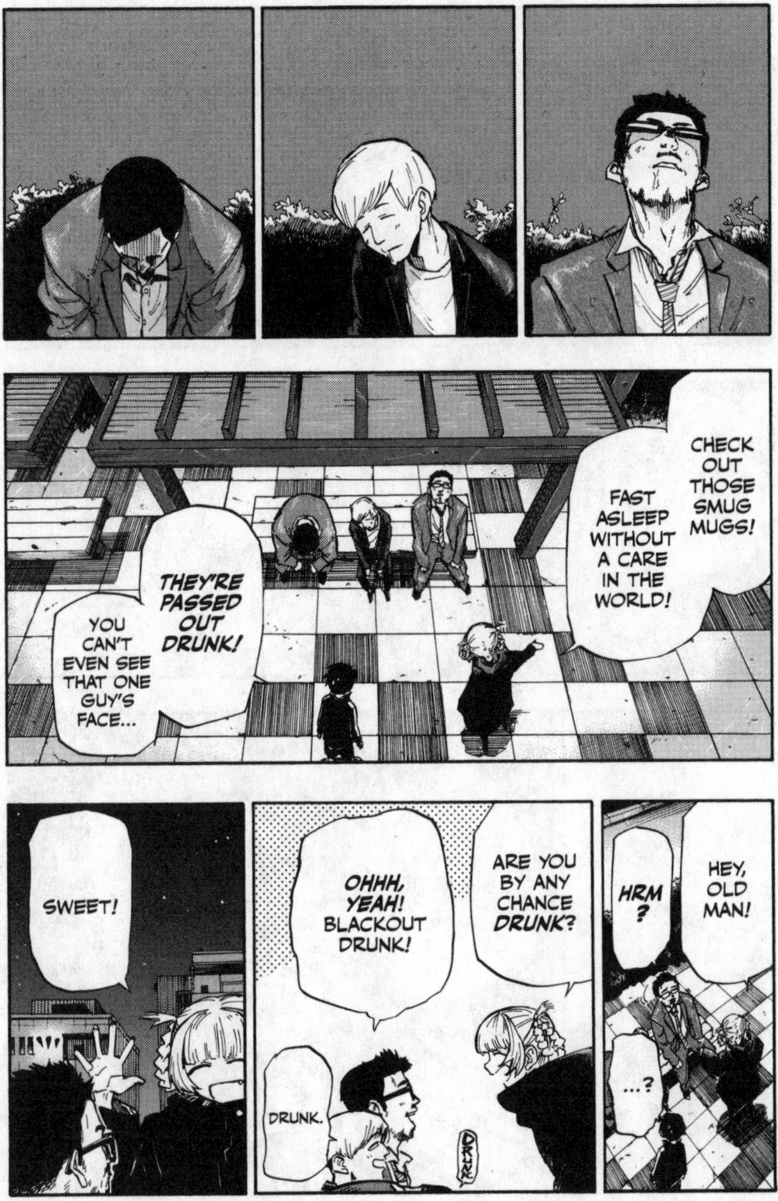
CHECK OUT THOSE SMUG MUGS!
FAST ASLEEP WITHOUT A CARE IN THE WORLD!
THEY'RE PASSED OUT DRUNK!
YOU CAN'T EVEN SEE THAT ONE GUY'S FACE...
HEY, OLD MAN!
HRM?
...?
ARE YOU BY ANY CHANCE DRUNK?
OHHH, YEAH! BLACKOUT DRUNK!
DRUNK
DRUNK.
SWEET!

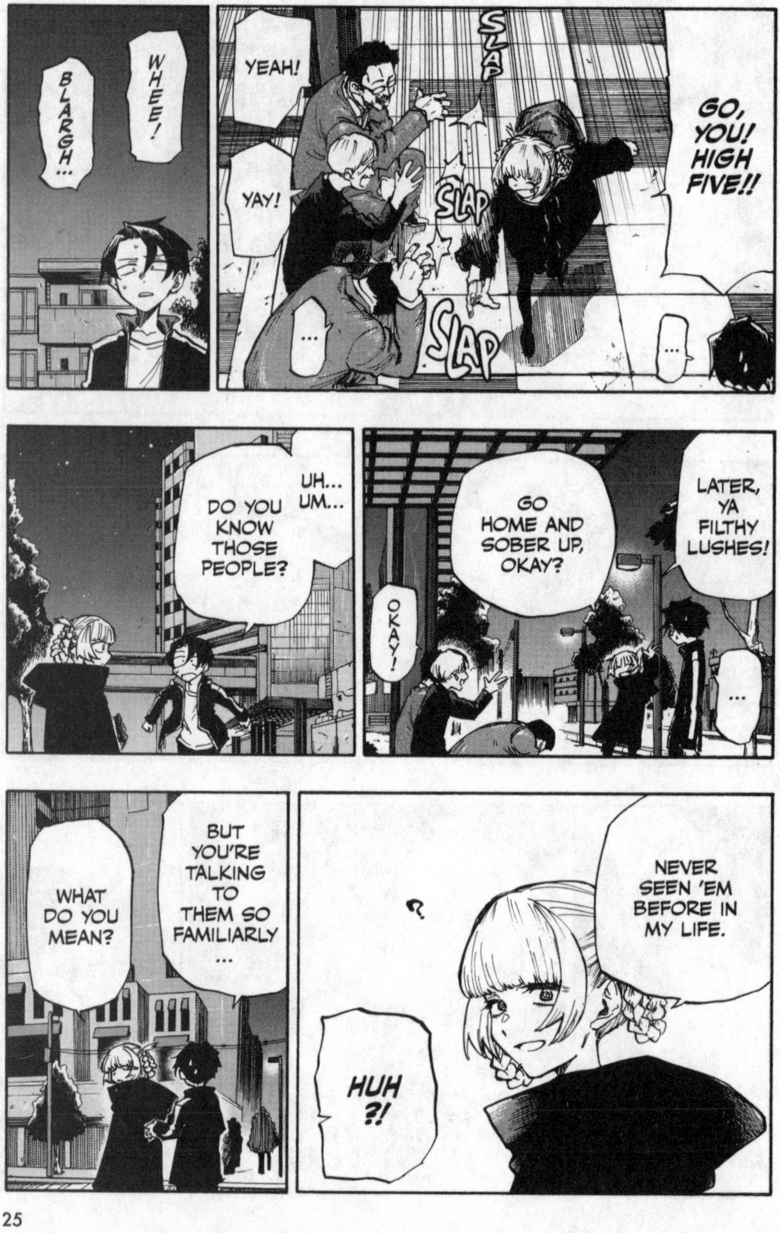
GO, YOU! HIGH FIVE!!
...
SLAP
SLAP
SLAP
YEAH!
YAY!
...
WHEE!
BLARGH...
LATER, YA FILTHY LUSHES!
GO HOME AND SOBER UP, OKAY?
OKAY!
...
UH... UM...
DO YOU KNOW THOSE PEOPLE?
NEVER SEEN 'EM BEFORE IN MY LIFE.
?
HUH ?!
BUT YOU'RE TALKING TO THEM SO FAMILIARLY ...
WHAT DO YOU MEAN?

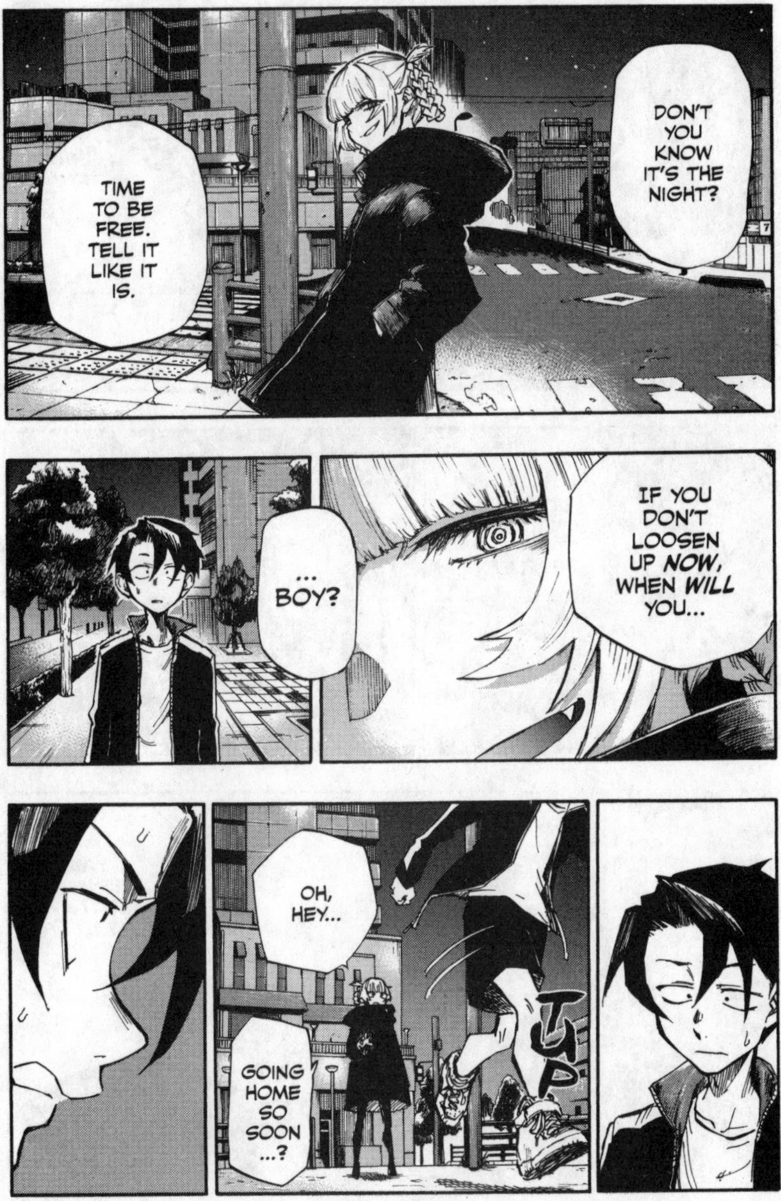
DON'T YOU KNOW IT'S THE NIGHT?
TIME TO BE FREE. TELL IT LIKE IT IS.
IF YOU DON'T LOOSEN UP *NOW*, WHEN *WILL* YOU...
... BOY?
OH, HEY...
TUP
GOING HOME SO SOON ...?

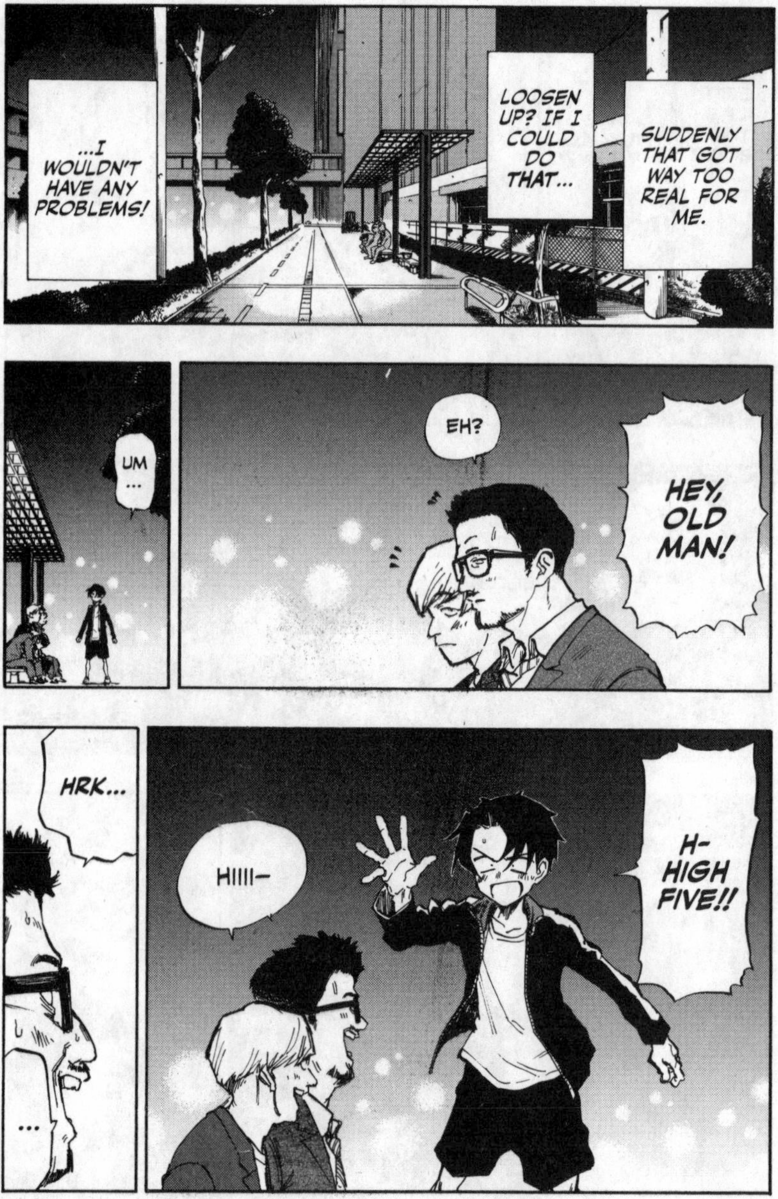
SUDDENLY THAT GOT WAY TOO REAL FOR ME.
LOOSEN UP? IF I COULD DO THAT...
...I WOULDN'T HAVE ANY PROBLEMS!
HEY, OLD MAN!
EH?
UM ...
H- HIGH FIVE!!
HIIII-
HRK...
...

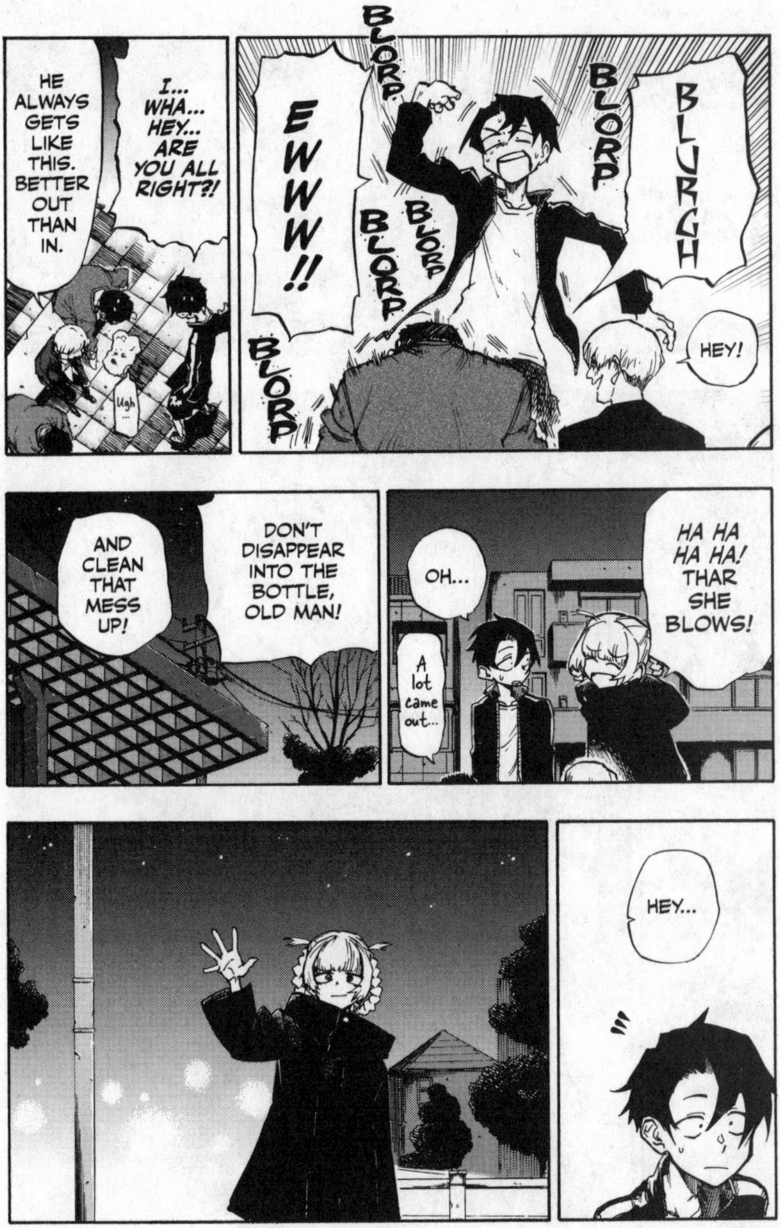
BLURGH
BLORP
HEY!
BLORP
EWWW!!
BLORP
BLORP
BLORP
I... WHA... HEY... ARE YOU ALL RIGHT?!
HE ALWAYS GETS LIKE THIS. BETTER OUT THAN IN.
Ugh...
HA HA HA HA! THAR SHE BLOWS!
OH...
A lot came out...
DON'T DISAPPEAR INTO THE BOTTLE, OLD MAN!
AND CLEAN THAT MESS UP!
HEY...

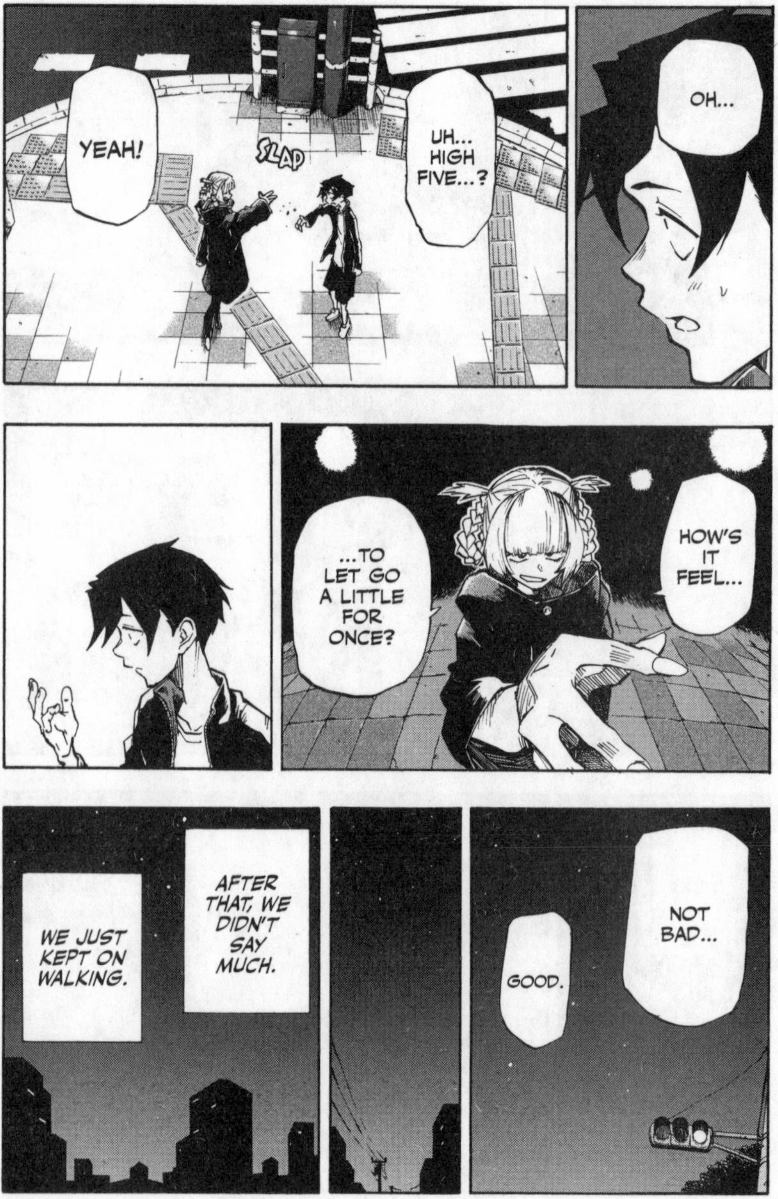
OH...
UH... HIGH FIVE...?
SLAP
YEAH!
HOW'S IT FEEL...
...TO LET GO A LITTLE FOR ONCE?
NOT BAD...
GOOD.
AFTER THAT, WE DIDN'T SAY MUCH.
WE JUST KEPT ON WALKING.

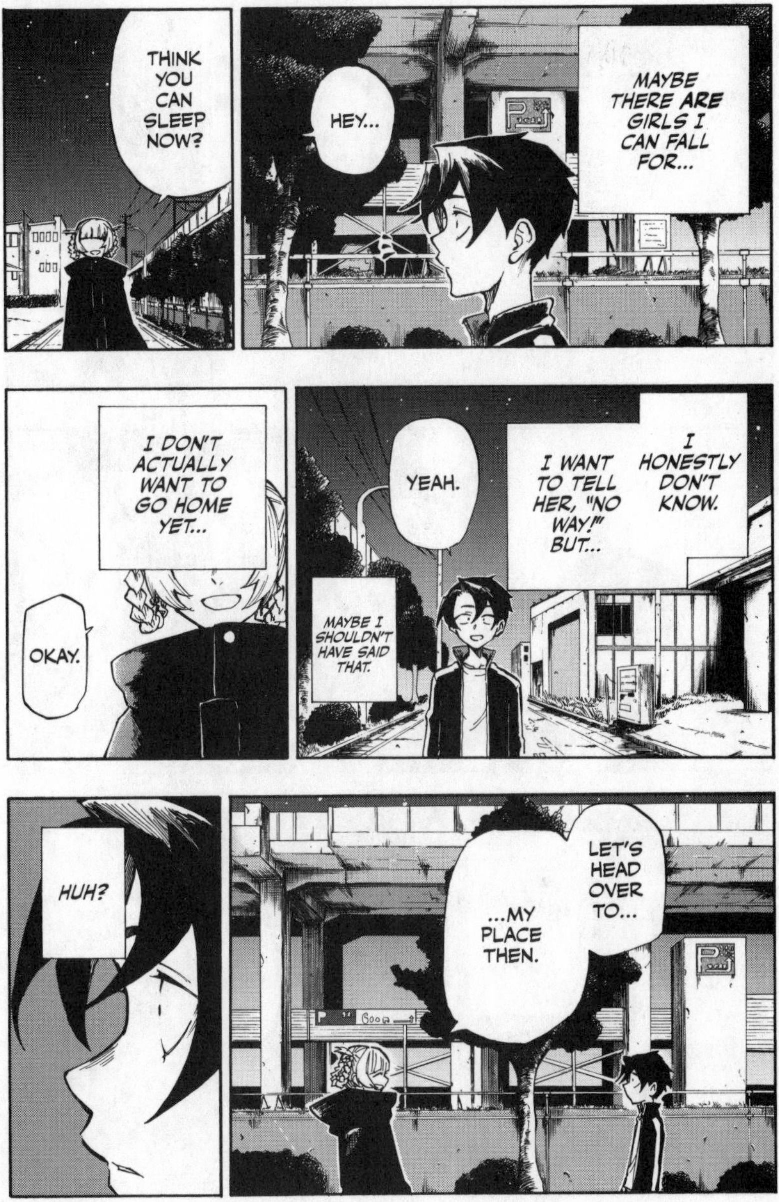
MAYBE THERE ARE GIRLS I CAN FALL FOR...
HEY...
THINK YOU CAN SLEEP NOW?
I HONESTLY DON'T KNOW.
I WANT TO TELL HER, "NO WAY!" BUT...
YEAH.
MAYBE I SHOULDN'T HAVE SAID THAT.
I DON'T ACTUALLY WANT TO GO HOME YET...
OKAY.
LET'S HEAD OVER TO...
...MY PLACE THEN.
HUH?

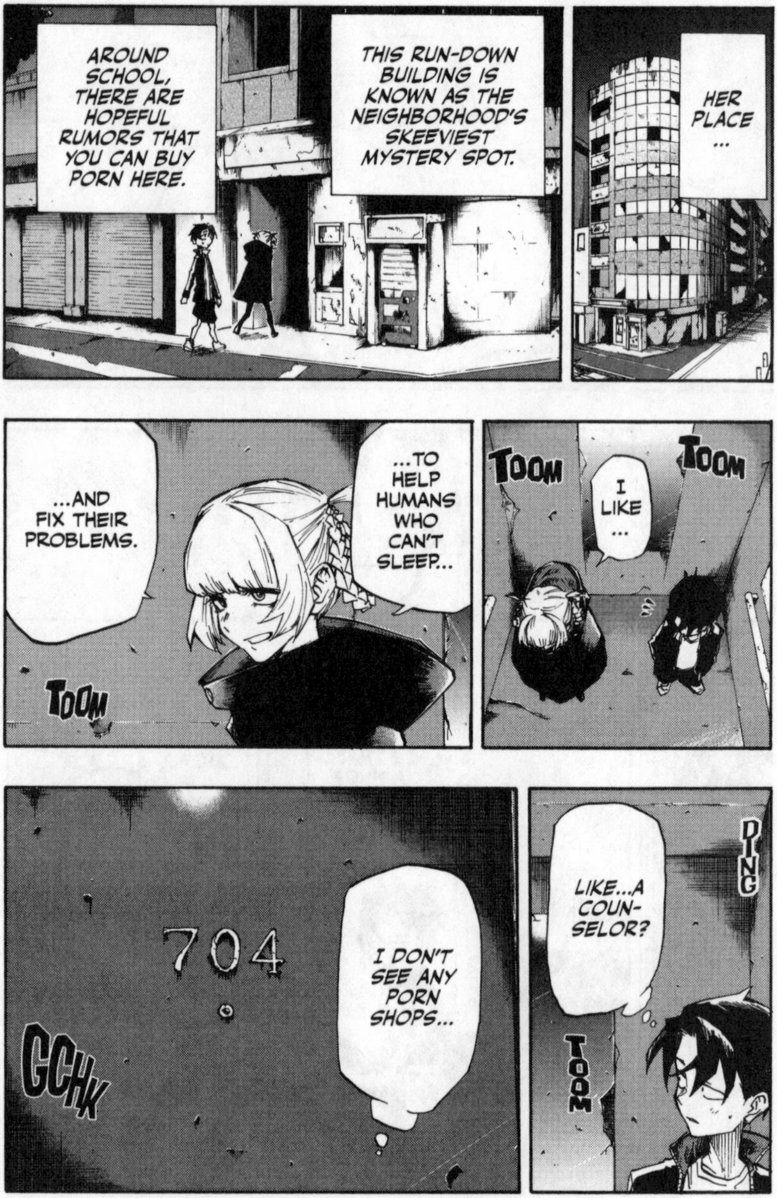
HER PLACE ...
THIS RUN-DOWN BUILDING IS KNOWN AS THE NEIGHBORHOOD'S SKEEVIEST MYSTERY SPOT.
AROUND SCHOOL, THERE ARE HOPEFUL RUMORS THAT YOU CAN BUY PORN HERE.
TOOM
I LIKE ...
TOOM
...TO HELP HUMANS WHO CAN'T SLEEP...
...AND FIX THEIR PROBLEMS.
TOOM
DING
LIKE...A COUN-SELOR?
TOOM
I DON'T SEE ANY PORN SHOPS...
704
GCHK

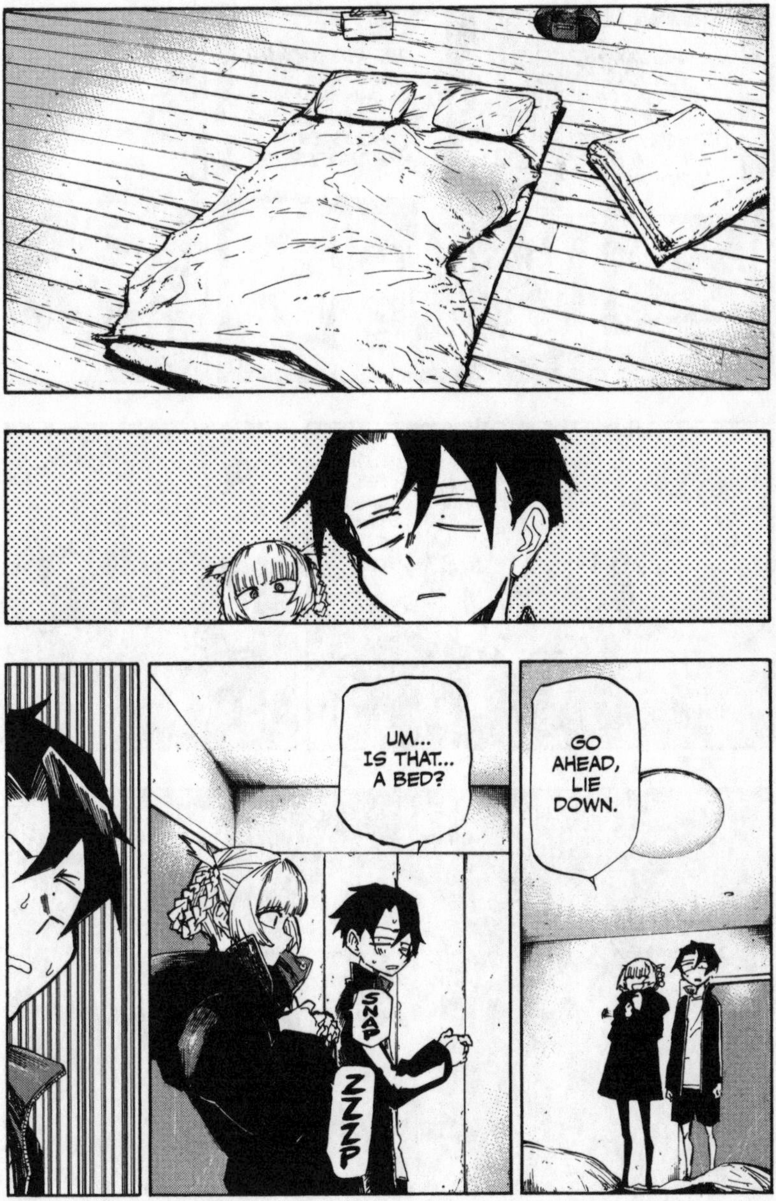
GO AHEAD, LIE DOWN.
UM... IS THAT... A BED?
SNAP
ZZZP

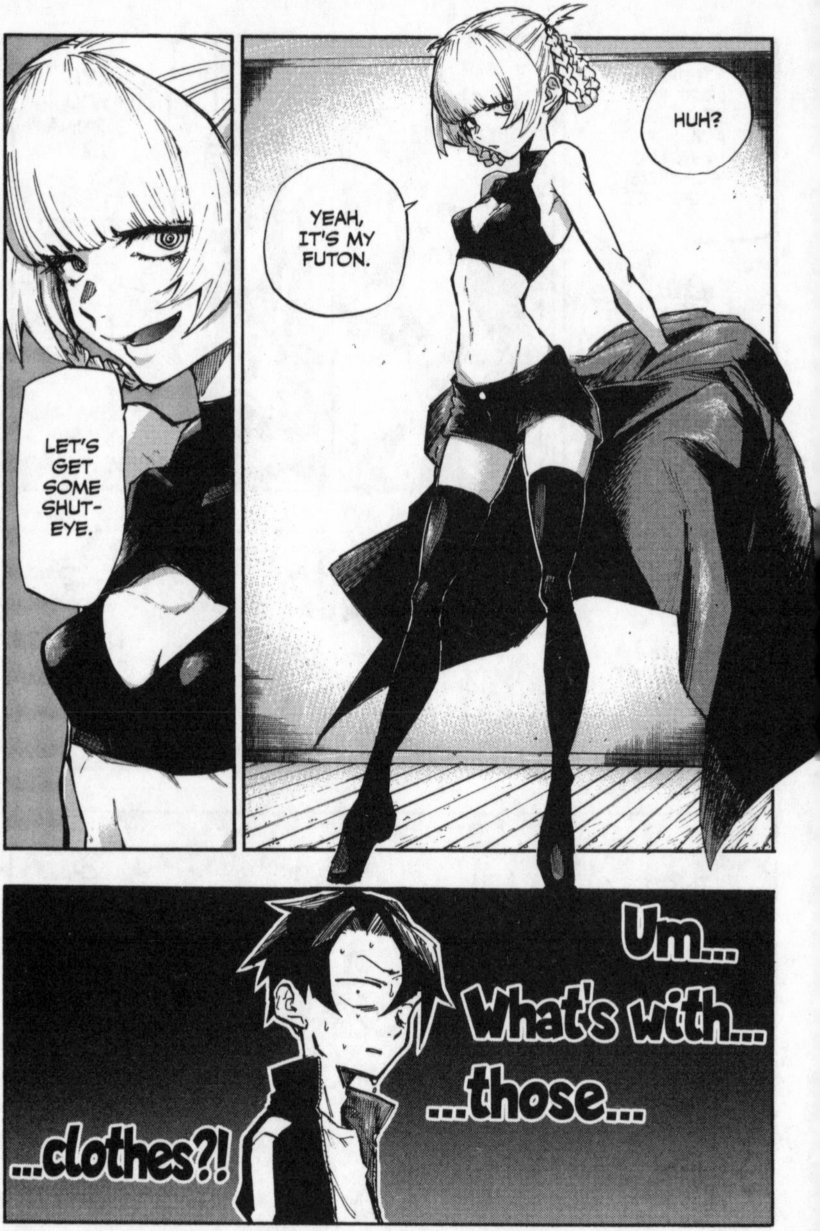
HUH?
YEAH, IT'S MY FUTON.
LET'S GET SOME SHUT-EYE.
Um... What's with... ...those... ...clothes?!

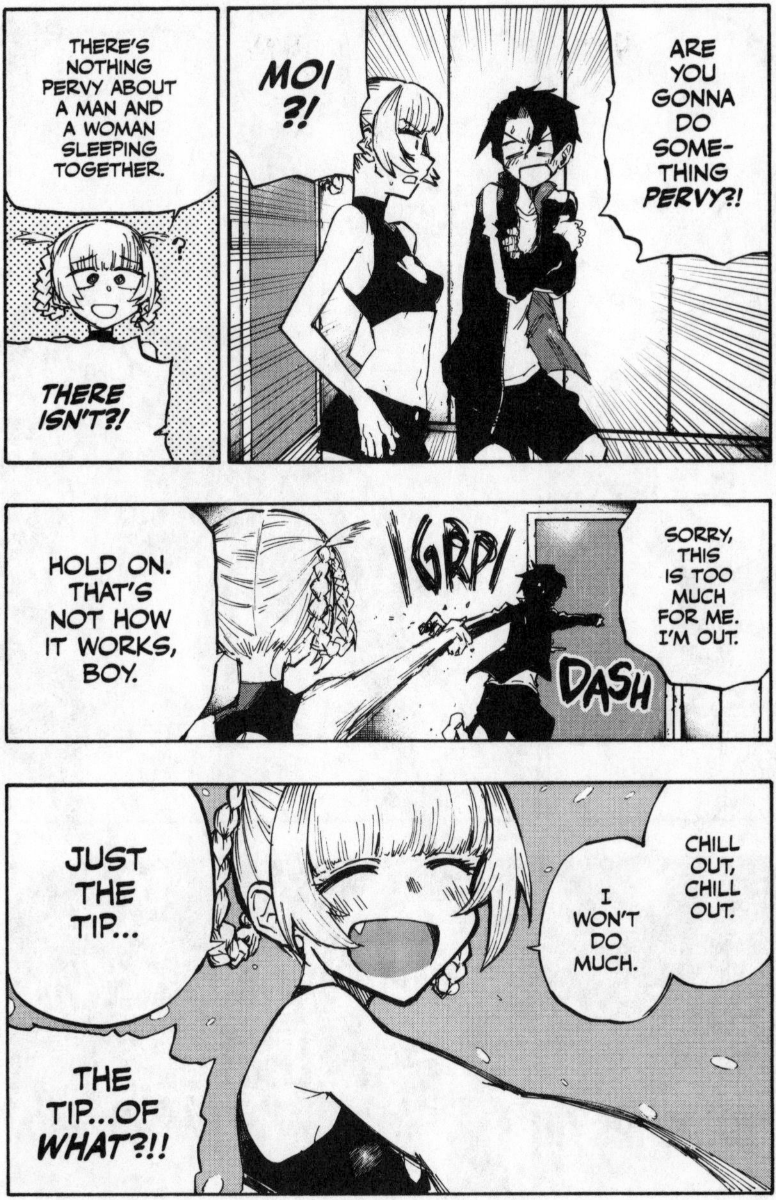
ARE YOU GONNA DO SOMETHING PERVY?!
MOI ?!
THERE'S NOTHING PERVY ABOUT A MAN AND A WOMAN SLEEPING TOGETHER.
?
THERE ISN'T?!
SORRY, THIS IS TOO MUCH FOR ME. I'M OUT.
DASH
GRP
HOLD ON. THAT'S NOT HOW IT WORKS, BOY.
CHILL OUT, CHILL OUT.
I WON'T DO MUCH.
JUST THE TIP...
THE TIP...OF WHAT?!!

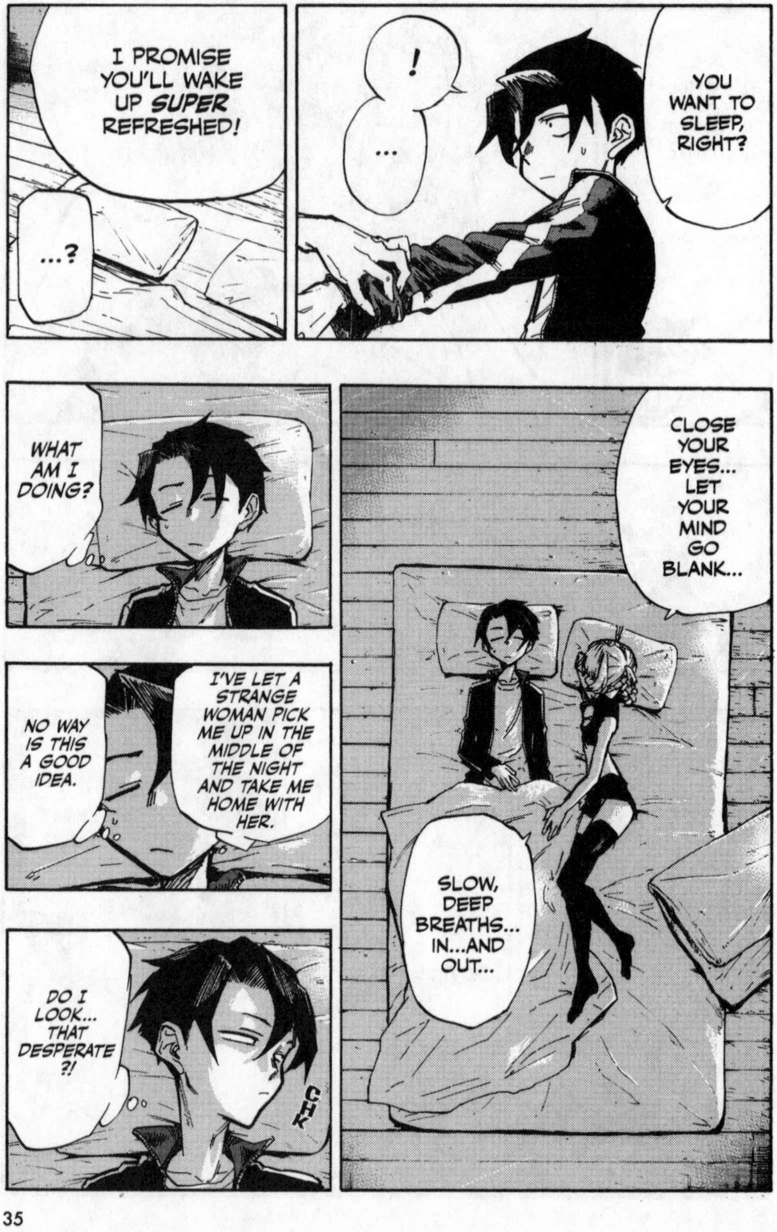
YOU WANT TO SLEEP, RIGHT?
!
...
I PROMISE YOU'LL WAKE UP SUPER REFRESHED!
...?
CLOSE YOUR EYES... LET YOUR MIND GO BLANK...
SLOW, DEEP BREATHS... IN...AND OUT...
WHAT AM I DOING?
I'VE LET A STRANGE WOMAN PICK ME UP IN THE MIDDLE OF THE NIGHT AND TAKE ME HOME WITH HER.
NO WAY IS THIS A GOOD IDEA.
DO I LOOK... THAT DESPERATE?!
CHK

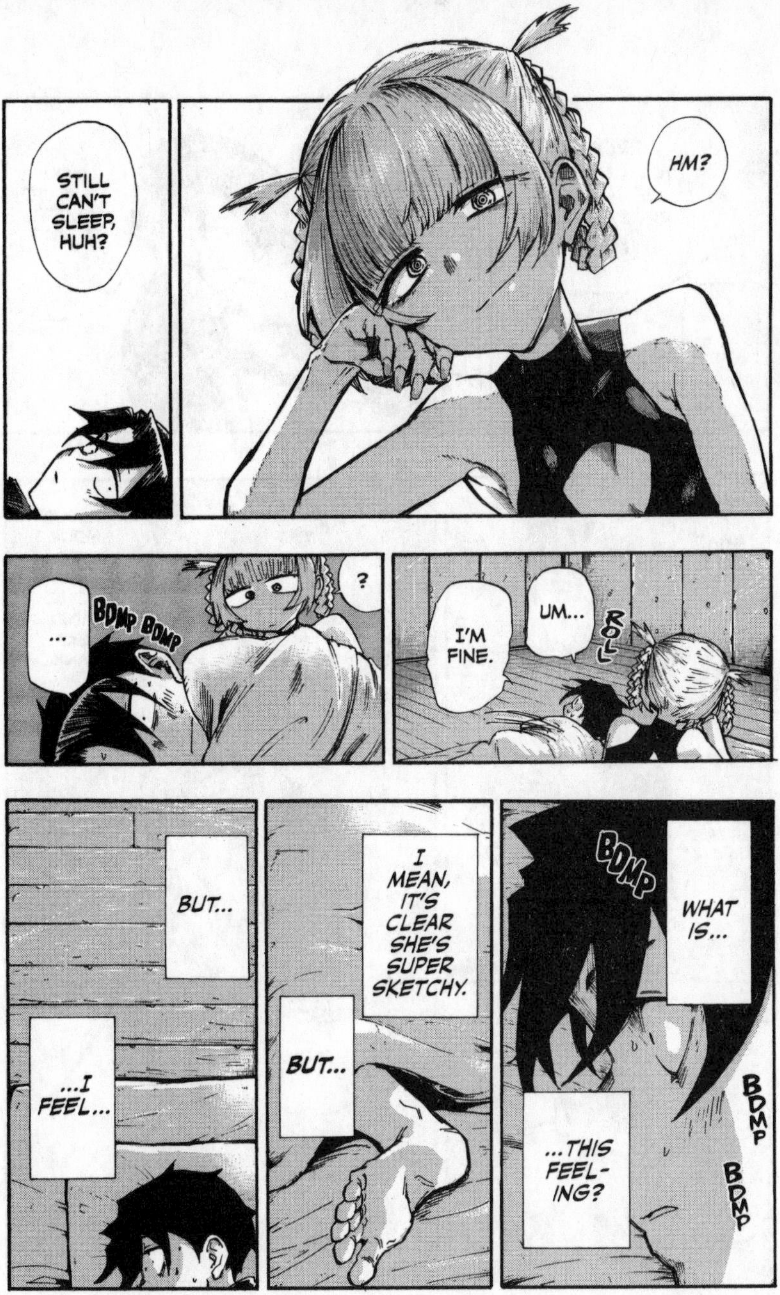
HM?
STILL CAN'T SLEEP, HUH?
ROLL
UM...
I'M FINE.
?
BDMP BDMP
...
WHAT IS...
BDMP
BDMP
BDMP
...THIS FEEL-ING?
I MEAN, IT'S CLEAR SHE'S SUPER SKETCHY.
BUT...
BUT...
...I FEEL...

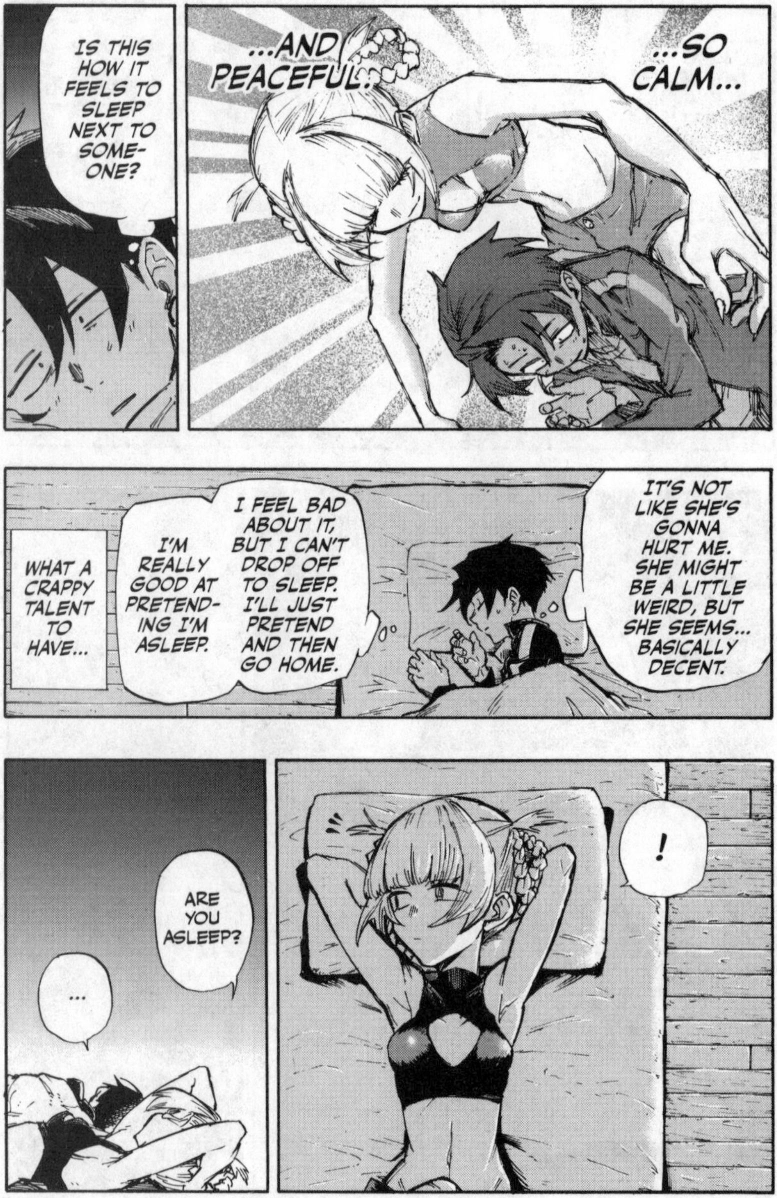
...SO CALM...
...AND PEACEFUL.
IS THIS HOW IT FEELS TO SLEEP NEXT TO SOME-ONE?
IT'S NOT LIKE SHE'S GONNA HURT ME. SHE MIGHT BE A LITTLE WEIRD, BUT SHE SEEMS... BASICALLY DECENT.
I FEEL BAD ABOUT IT, BUT I CAN'T DROP OFF TO SLEEP. I'LL JUST PRETEND AND THEN GO HOME.
I'M REALLY GOOD AT PRETEND-ING I'M ASLEEP.
WHAT A CRAPPY TALENT TO HAVE...
!
ARE YOU ASLEEP?
...

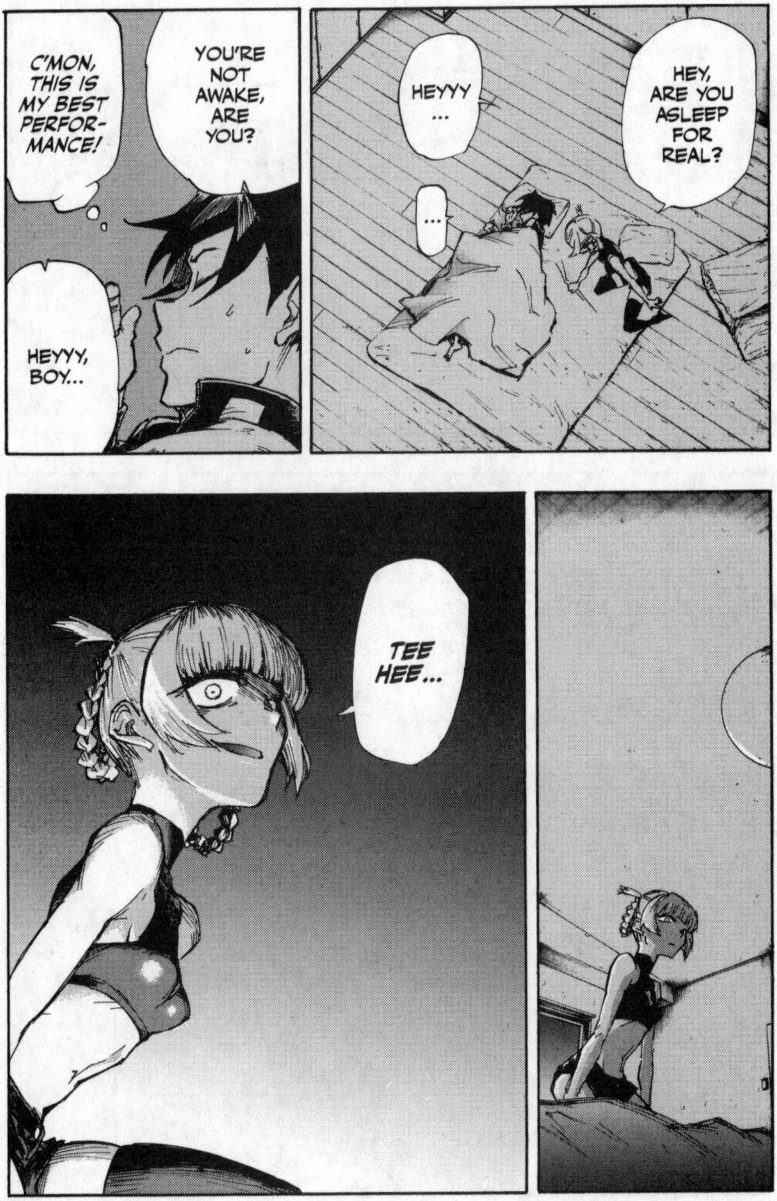
HEY, ARE YOU ASLEEP FOR REAL?
HEYYY ...
...
YOU'RE NOT AWAKE, ARE YOU?
C'MON, THIS IS MY BEST PERFORMANCE!
HEYYY, BOY...
TEE HEE...

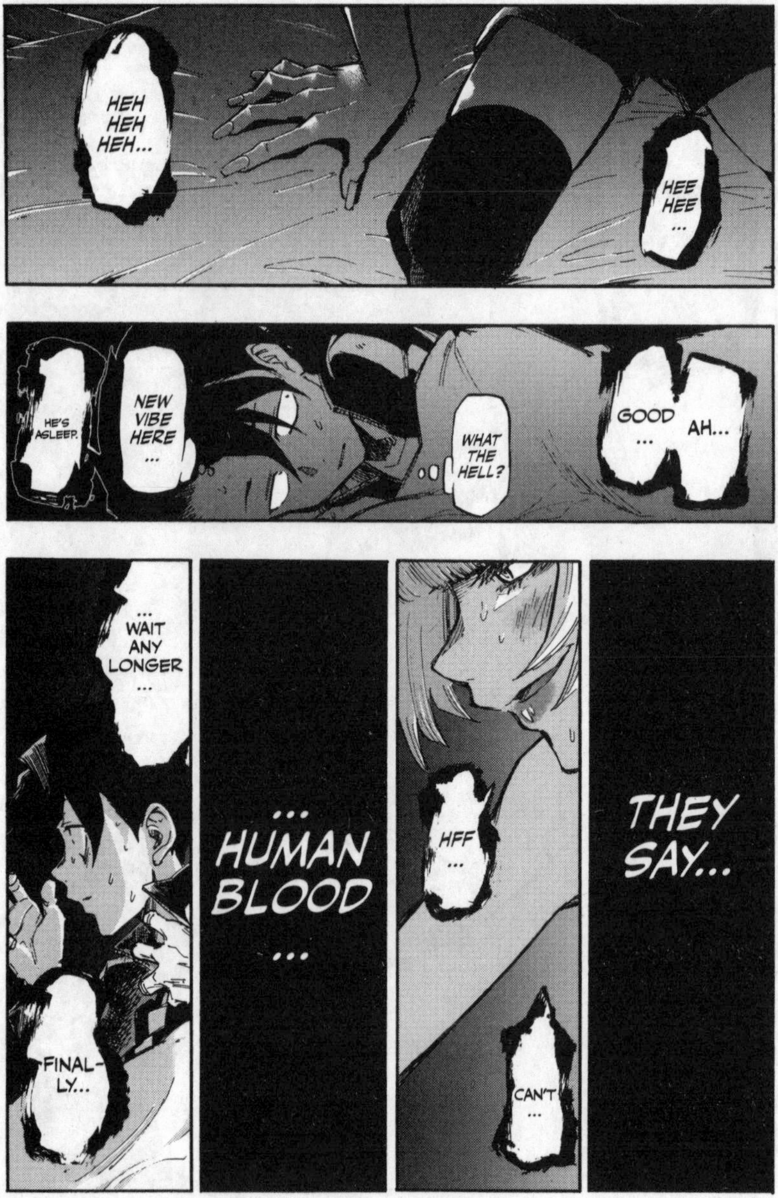
HEE HEE ...
HEH HEH HEH...
AH...
GOOD ...
WHAT THE HELL?
NEW VIBE HERE ...
HE'S ASLEEP.
THEY SAY...
HFF ...
CAN'T ...
... HUMAN BLOOD ...
... WAIT ANY LONGER ...
FINAL-LY...

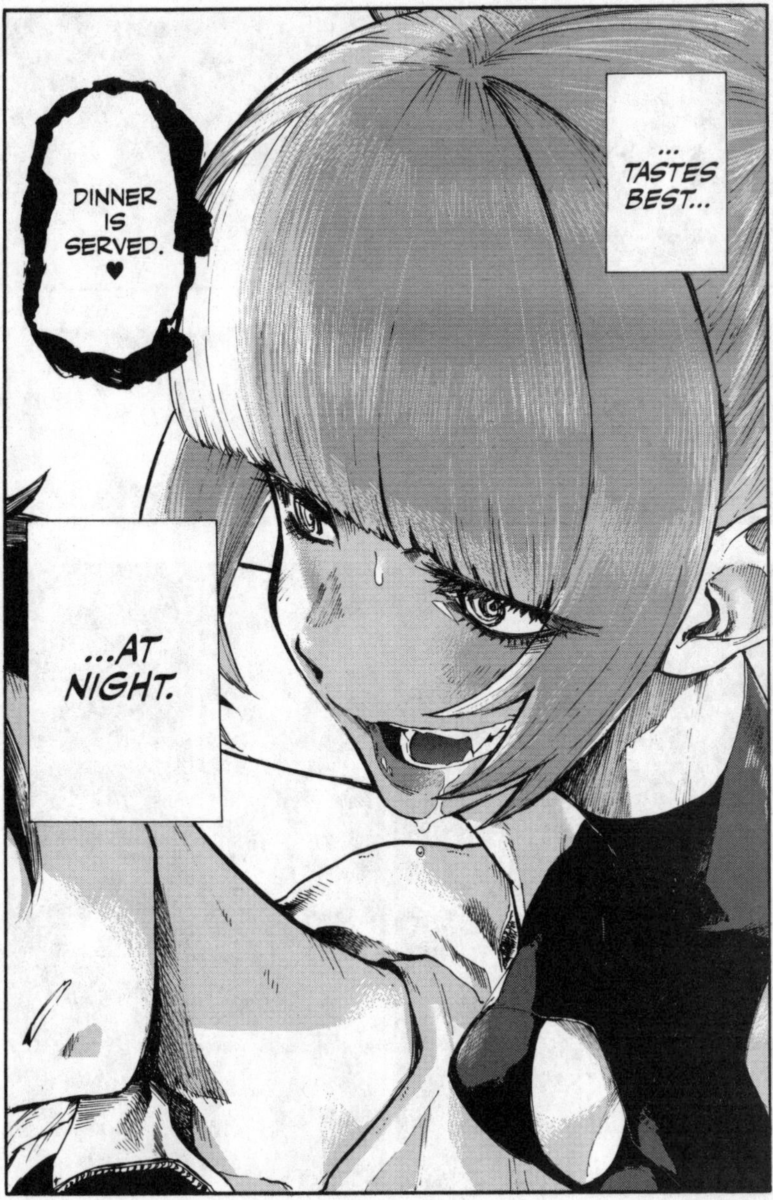
...
TASTES
BEST...
DINNER
IS
SERVED. ♥
...AT
NIGHT.

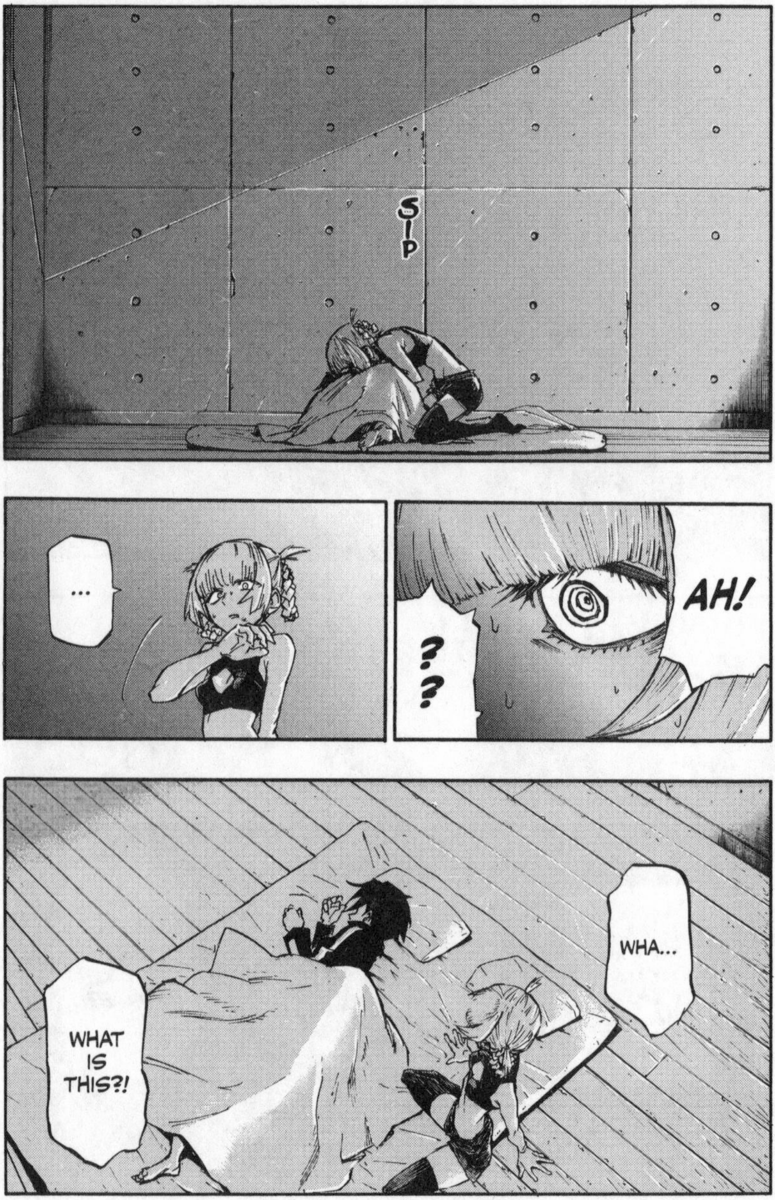
SIP
AH!
??
...
WHA...
WHAT IS THIS?!

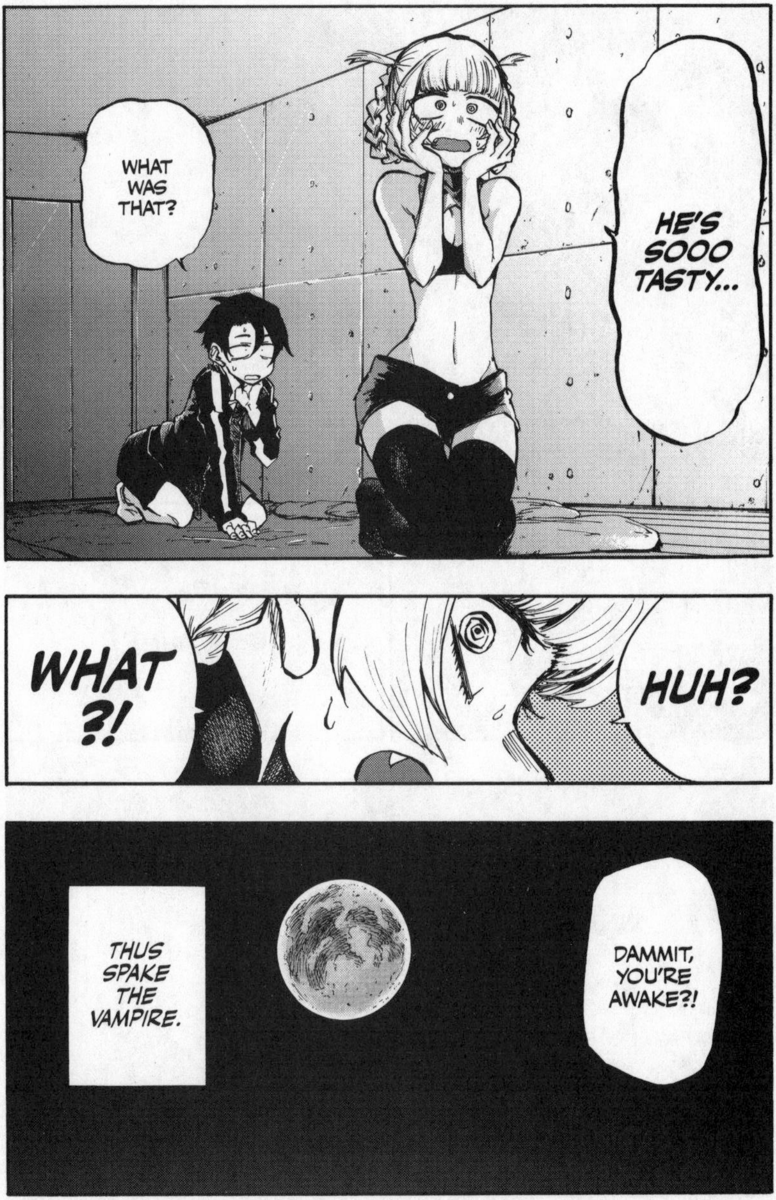
HE'S SOOO TASTY...
WHAT WAS THAT?
HUH?
WHAT?!
DAMMIT, YOU'RE AWAKE?!
THUS SPAKE THE VAMPIRE.

NIGHT 2: A PRETTY BIG MOSQUITO

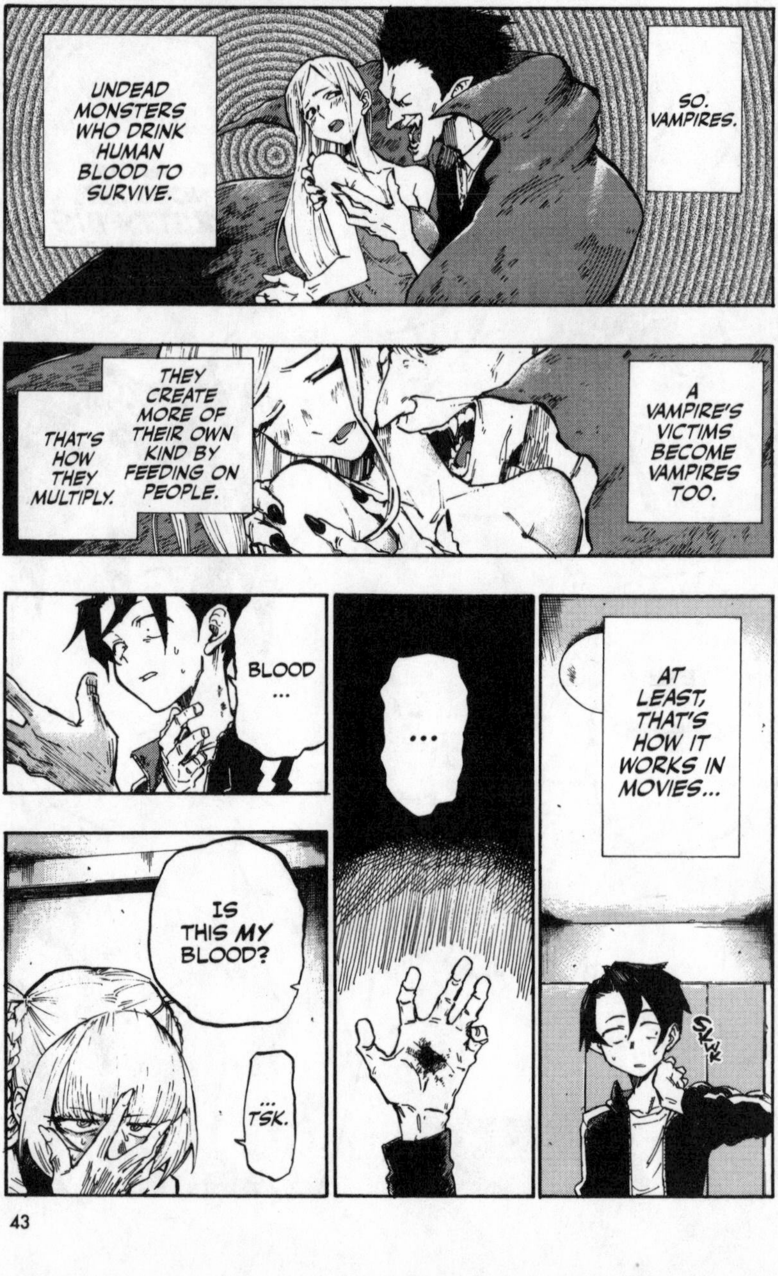
SO. VAMPIRES.
UNDEAD MONSTERS WHO DRINK HUMAN BLOOD TO SURVIVE.
A VAMPIRE'S VICTIMS BECOME VAMPIRES TOO.
THEY CREATE MORE OF THEIR OWN KIND BY FEEDING ON PEOPLE.
THAT'S HOW THEY MULTIPLY.
AT LEAST, THAT'S HOW IT WORKS IN MOVIES...
SKWK
...
BLOOD ...
IS THIS MY BLOOD?
... TSK.

NIGHT 2: A PRETTY BIG MOSQUITO

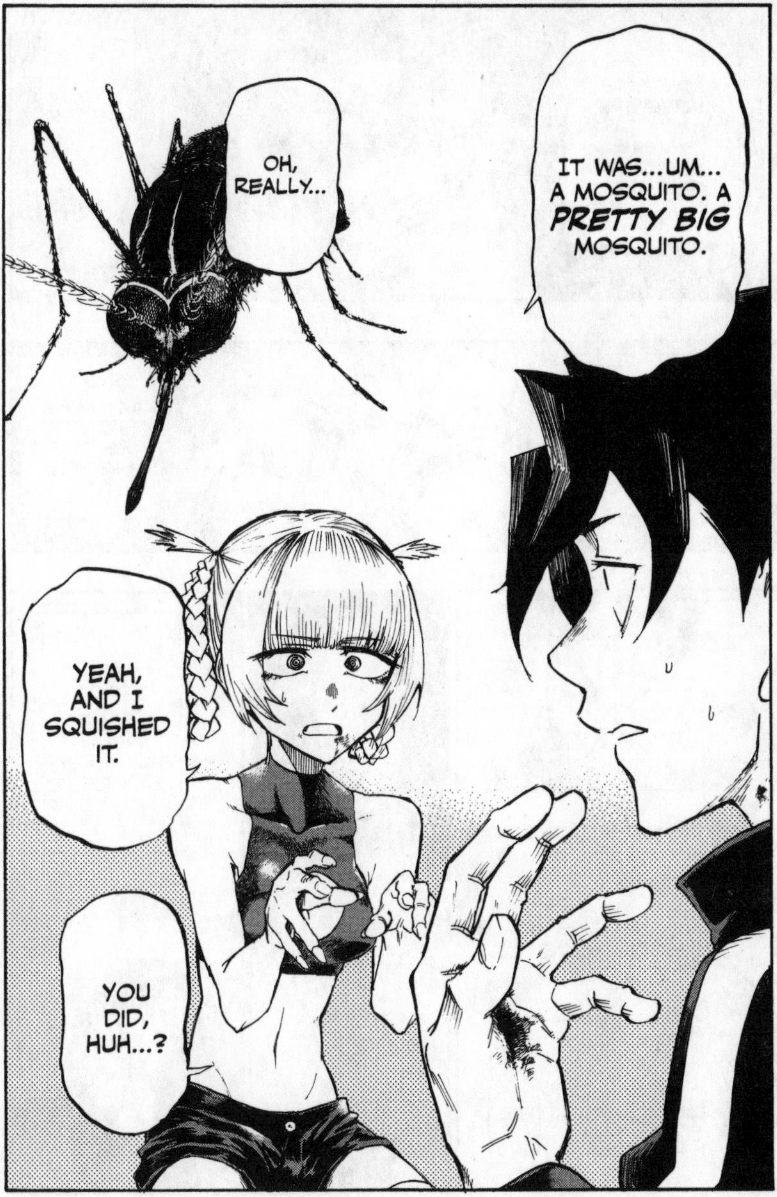
IT WAS...UM... A MOSQUITO. A *PRETTY BIG* MOSQUITO.
OH, REALLY...
YEAH, AND I SQUISHED IT.
YOU DID, HUH...?

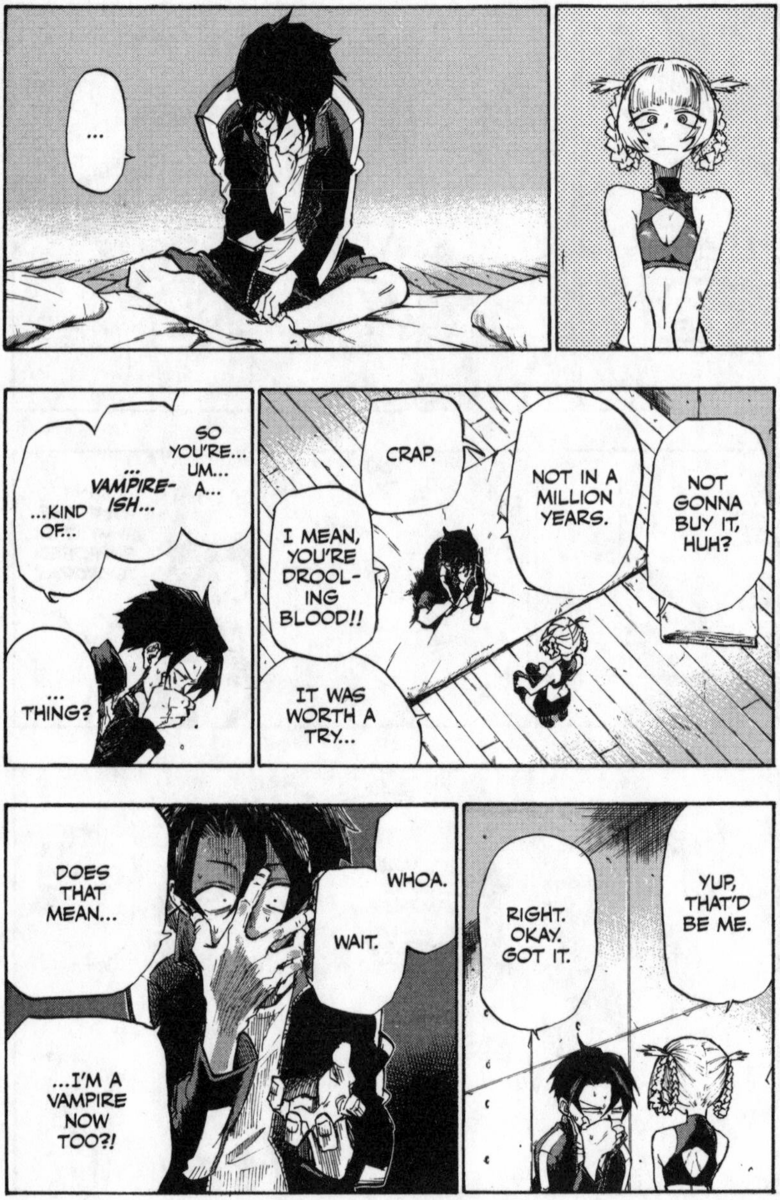
...
NOT GONNA BUY IT, HUH?
NOT IN A MILLION YEARS.
CRAP.
I MEAN, YOU'RE DROOLING BLOOD!!
IT WAS WORTH A TRY...
SO YOU'RE... UM... A...
...VAMPIRE-ISH...
...KIND OF...
...THING?
YUP, THAT'D BE ME.
RIGHT. OKAY. GOT IT.
WHOA.
WAIT.
DOES THAT MEAN...
...I'M A VAMPIRE NOW TOO?!

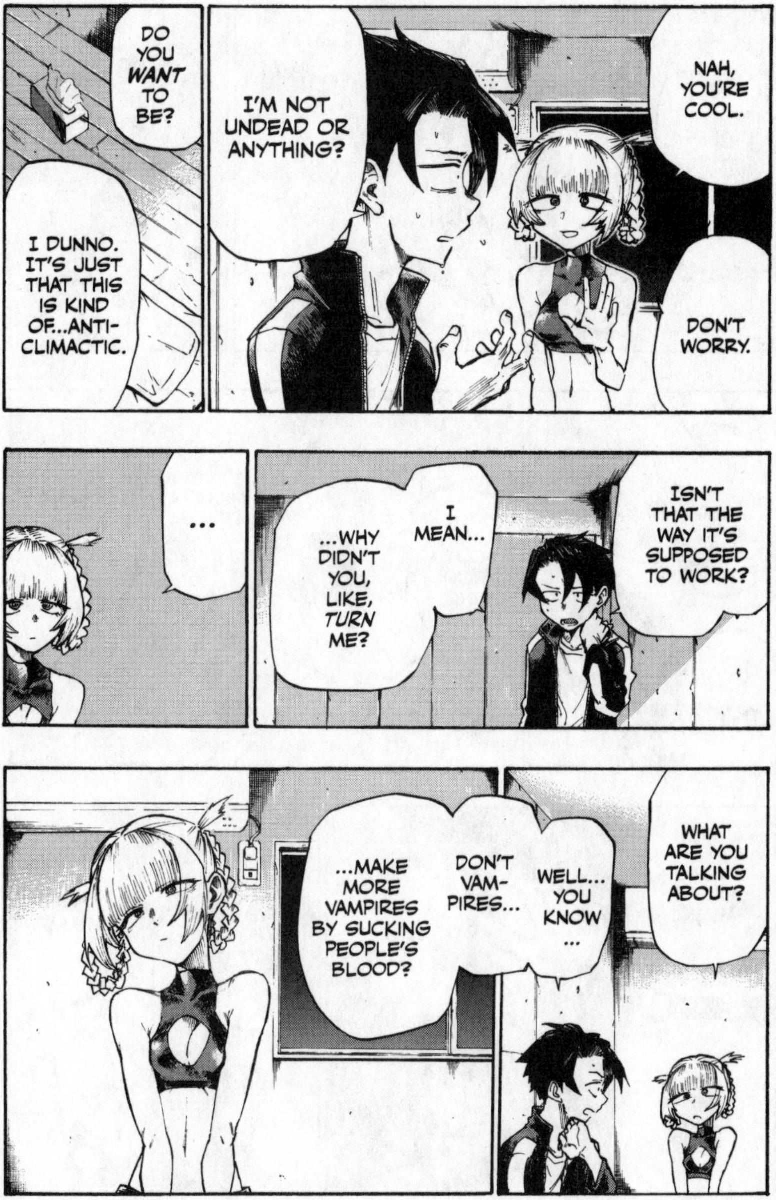
I'M NOT UNDEAD OR ANYTHING?
NAH, YOU'RE COOL.
DON'T WORRY.
DO YOU WANT TO BE?
I DUNNO. IT'S JUST THAT THIS IS KIND OF...ANTI-CLIMACTIC.
I MEAN...
...WHY DIDN'T YOU, LIKE, TURN ME?
ISN'T THAT THE WAY IT'S SUPPOSED TO WORK?
...
WHAT ARE YOU TALKING ABOUT?
WELL... YOU KNOW...
DON'T VAMPIRES...
...MAKE MORE VAMPIRES BY SUCKING PEOPLE'S BLOOD?

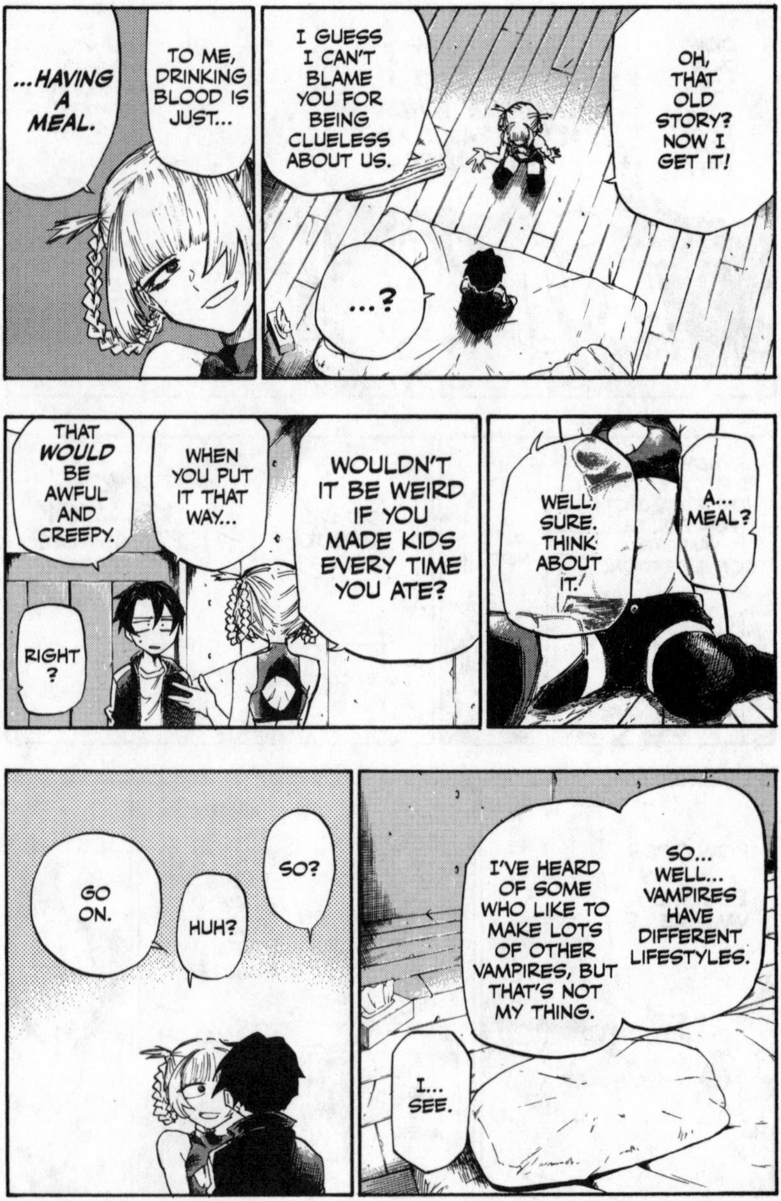
OH, THAT OLD STORY? NOW I GET IT!
I GUESS I CAN'T BLAME YOU FOR BEING CLUELESS ABOUT US.
...?
TO ME, DRINKING BLOOD IS JUST...
...HAVING A MEAL.
A... MEAL?
WELL, SURE. THINK ABOUT IT.
WOULDN'T IT BE WEIRD IF YOU MADE KIDS EVERY TIME YOU ATE?
RIGHT?
WHEN YOU PUT IT THAT WAY...
THAT WOULD BE AWFUL AND CREEPY.
SO... WELL... VAMPIRES HAVE DIFFERENT LIFESTYLES.
I'VE HEARD OF SOME WHO LIKE TO MAKE LOTS OF OTHER VAMPIRES, BUT THAT'S NOT MY THING.
I... SEE.
SO?
HUH?
GO ON.

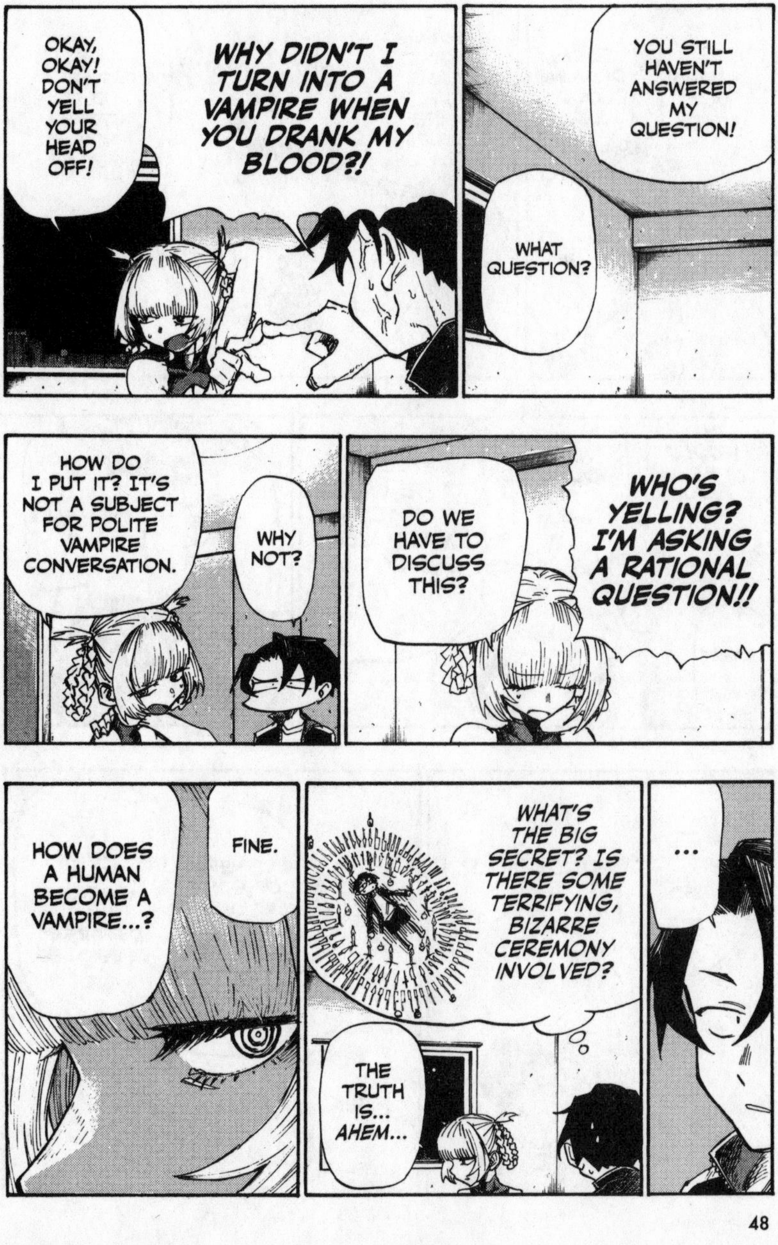
YOU STILL HAVEN'T ANSWERED MY QUESTION!
WHAT QUESTION?
WHY DIDN'T I TURN INTO A VAMPIRE WHEN YOU DRANK MY BLOOD?!
OKAY, OKAY! DON'T YELL YOUR HEAD OFF!
WHO'S YELLING? I'M ASKING A RATIONAL QUESTION!!
DO WE HAVE TO DISCUSS THIS?
WHY NOT?
HOW DO I PUT IT? IT'S NOT A SUBJECT FOR POLITE VAMPIRE CONVERSATION.
...
WHAT'S THE BIG SECRET? IS THERE SOME TERRIFYING, BIZARRE CEREMONY INVOLVED?
THE TRUTH IS... AHEM...
FINE.
HOW DOES A HUMAN BECOME A VAMPIRE...?

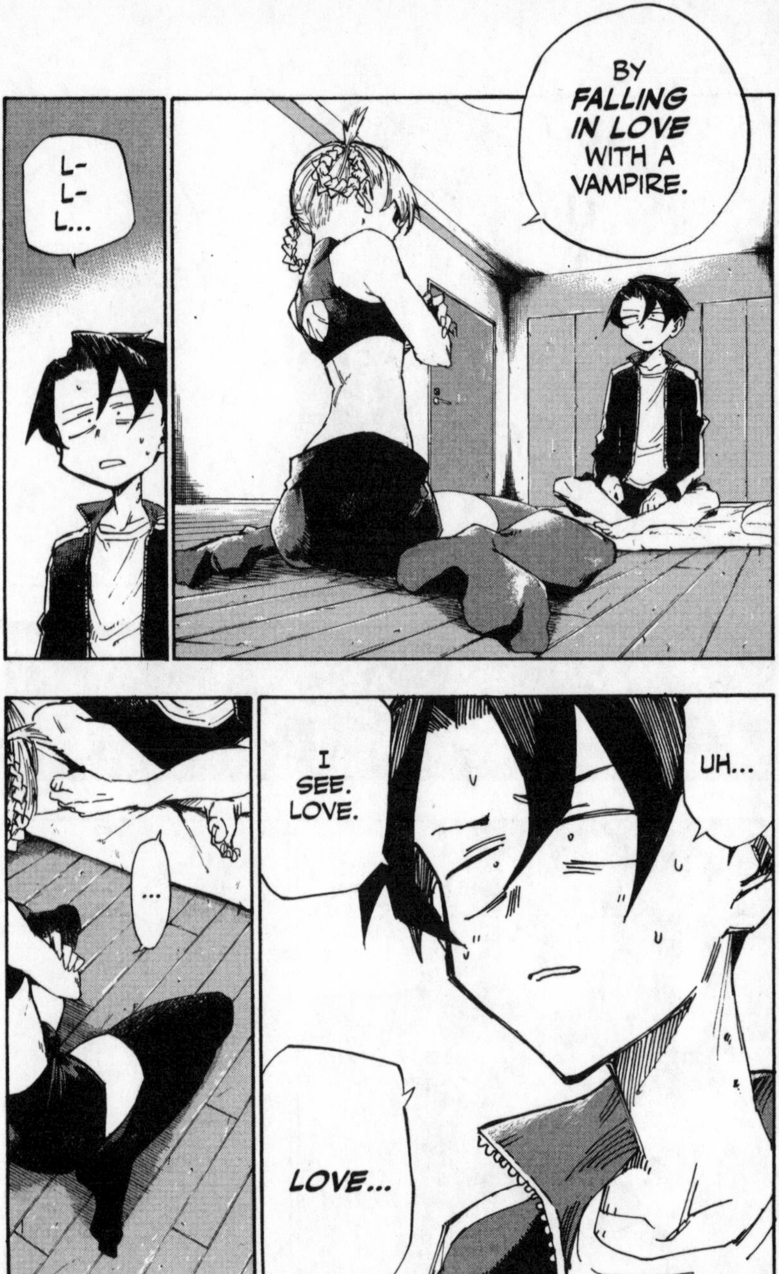
BY FALLING IN LOVE WITH A VAMPIRE.
L- L- L...
UH...
I SEE. LOVE.
LOVE...
...

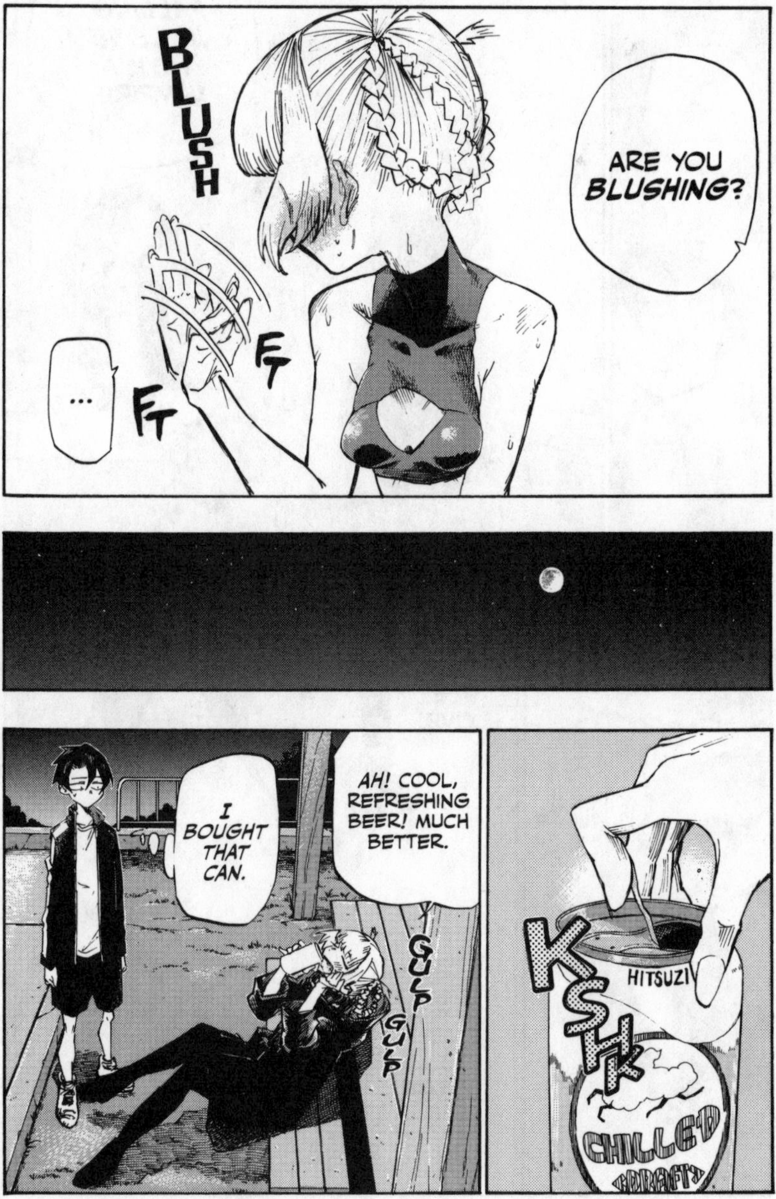
ARE YOU BLUSHING?
BLUSH
FT
FT
...
KSHK
HITSUZI
CHILLED DRAFT
AH! COOL, REFRESHING BEER! MUCH BETTER.
I BOUGHT THAT CAN.
GULP
GULP

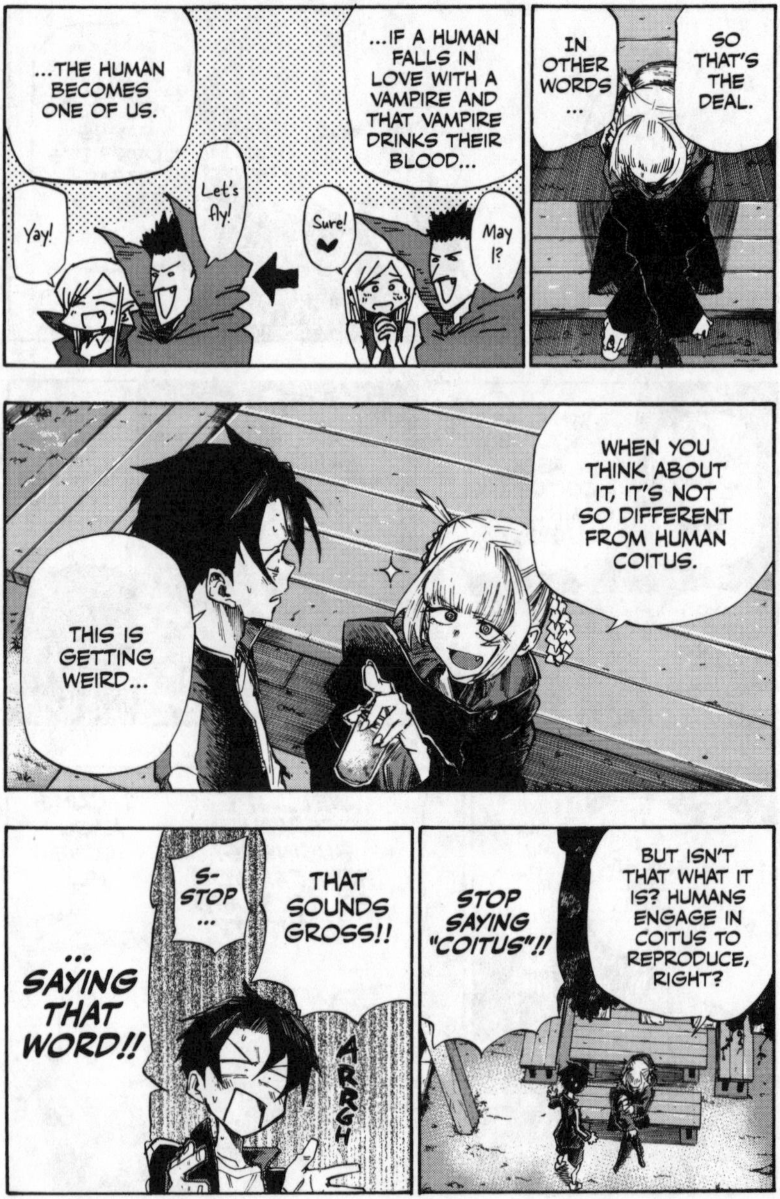
SO THAT'S THE DEAL.
IN OTHER WORDS...
...IF A HUMAN FALLS IN LOVE WITH A VAMPIRE AND THAT VAMPIRE DRINKS THEIR BLOOD...
May I?
Sure!
...THE HUMAN BECOMES ONE OF US.
Let's fly!
Yay!
WHEN YOU THINK ABOUT IT, IT'S NOT SO DIFFERENT FROM HUMAN COITUS.
THIS IS GETTING WEIRD...
BUT ISN'T THAT WHAT IT IS? HUMANS ENGAGE IN COITUS TO REPRODUCE, RIGHT?
STOP SAYING "COITUS"!!
THAT SOUNDS GROSS!!
S-STOP...
...SAYING THAT WORD!!
ARRGH

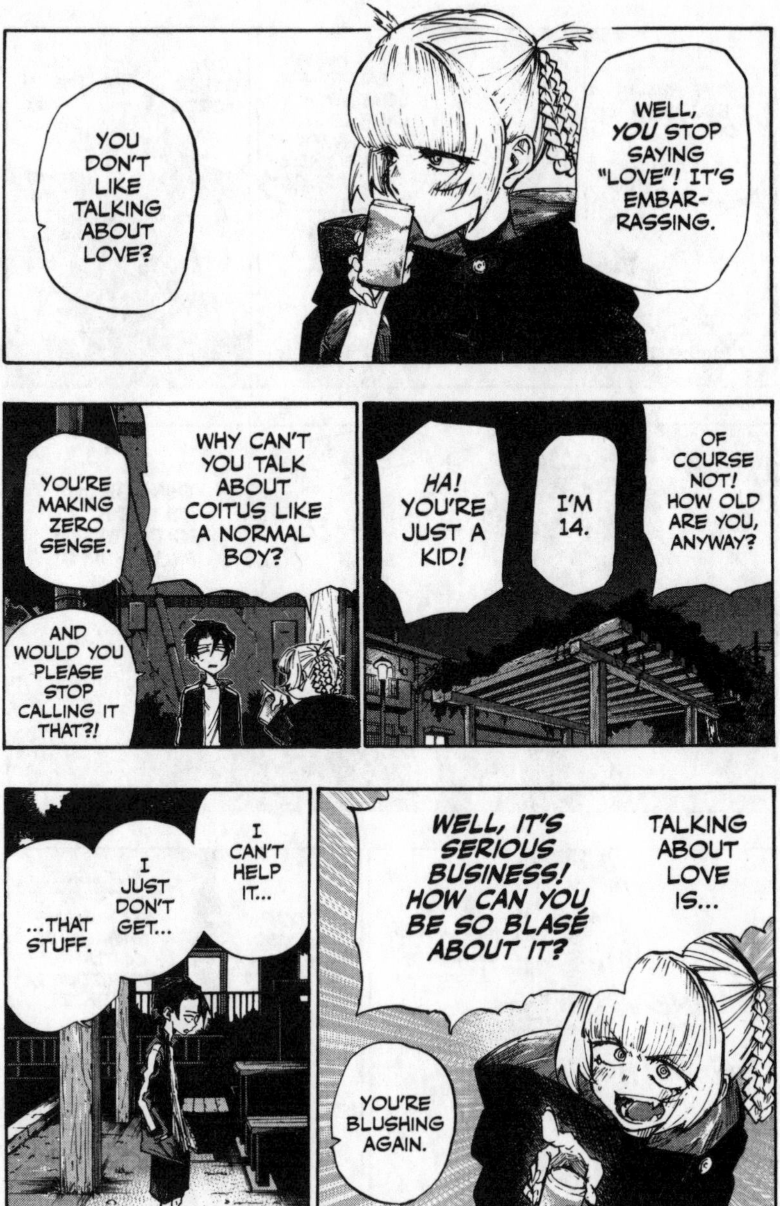
WELL, YOU STOP SAYING "LOVE"! IT'S EMBAR-RASSING.
YOU DON'T LIKE TALKING ABOUT LOVE?
OF COURSE NOT! HOW OLD ARE YOU, ANYWAY?
I'M 14.
HA! YOU'RE JUST A KID!
WHY CAN'T YOU TALK ABOUT COITUS LIKE A NORMAL BOY?
YOU'RE MAKING ZERO SENSE.
AND WOULD YOU PLEASE STOP CALLING IT THAT?!
TALKING ABOUT LOVE IS...
WELL, IT'S SERIOUS BUSINESS! HOW CAN YOU BE SO BLASÉ ABOUT IT?
YOU'RE BLUSHING AGAIN.
I CAN'T HELP IT...
I JUST DON'T GET...
...THAT STUFF.

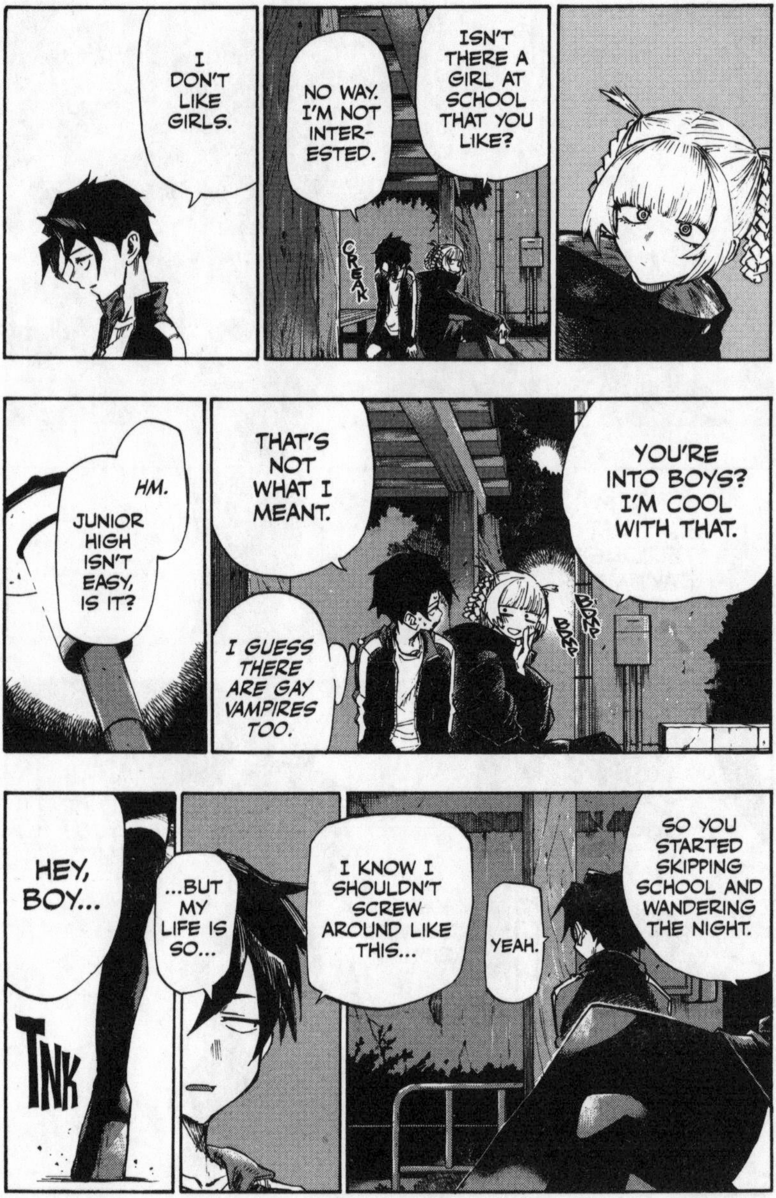
ISN'T THERE A GIRL AT SCHOOL THAT YOU LIKE?
NO WAY. I'M NOT INTER-ESTED.
CREAK
I DON'T LIKE GIRLS.
YOU'RE INTO BOYS? I'M COOL WITH THAT.
BDMP BDMP
THAT'S NOT WHAT I MEANT.
I GUESS THERE ARE GAY VAMPIRES TOO.
HM.
JUNIOR HIGH ISN'T EASY, IS IT?
SO YOU STARTED SKIPPING SCHOOL AND WANDERING THE NIGHT.
YEAH.
I KNOW I SHOULDN'T SCREW AROUND LIKE THIS...
...BUT MY LIFE IS SO...
HEY, BOY...
TNK

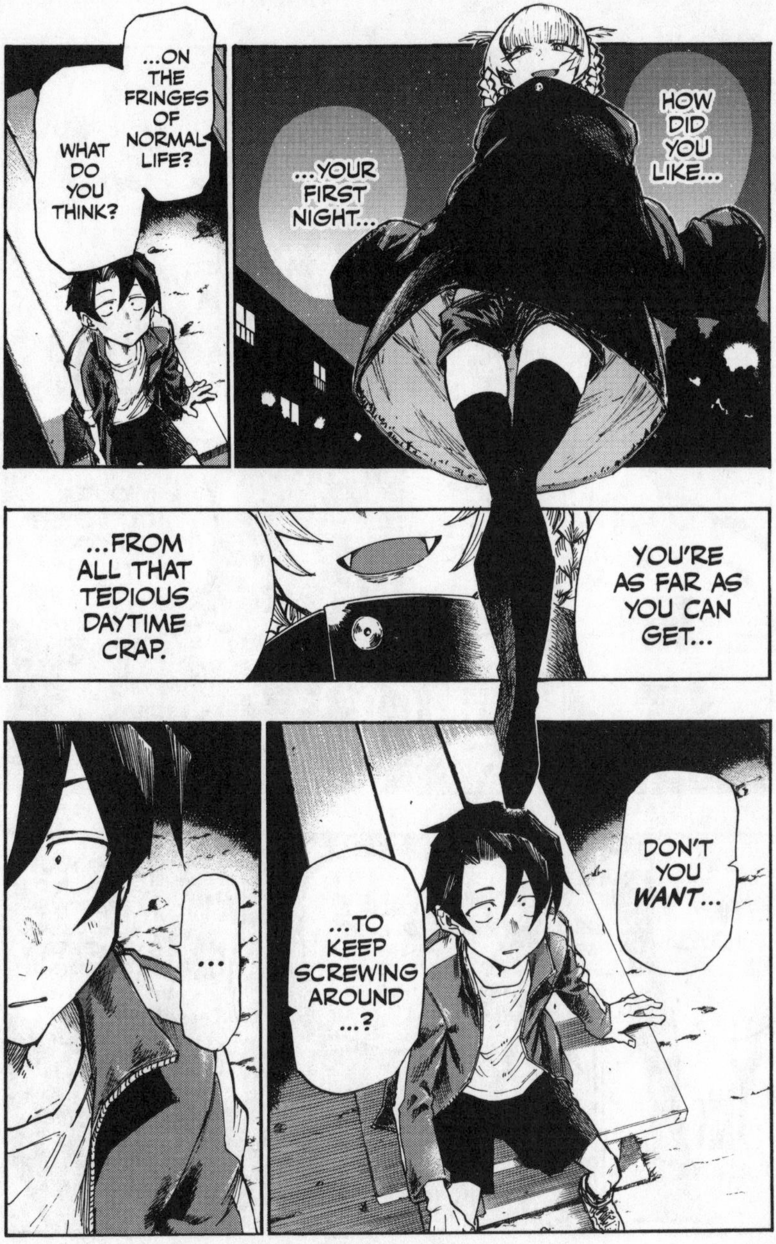
HOW DID YOU LIKE...
...YOUR FIRST NIGHT...
...ON THE FRINGES OF NORMAL LIFE?
WHAT DO YOU THINK?
YOU'RE AS FAR AS YOU CAN GET...
...FROM ALL THAT TEDIOUS DAYTIME CRAP.
DON'T YOU *WANT*...
...TO KEEP SCREWING AROUND ...?
...

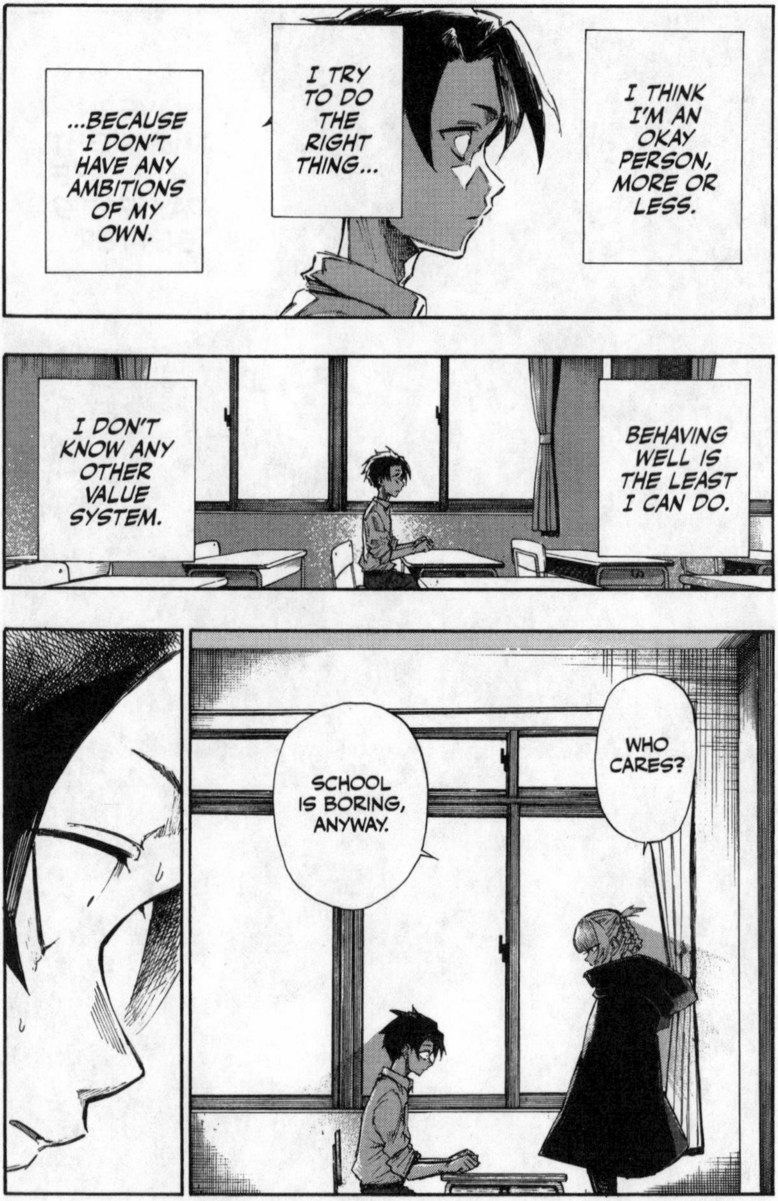
I THINK I'M AN OKAY PERSON, MORE OR LESS.
I TRY TO DO THE RIGHT THING...
...BECAUSE I DON'T HAVE ANY AMBITIONS OF MY OWN.
BEHAVING WELL IS THE LEAST I CAN DO.
I DON'T KNOW ANY OTHER VALUE SYSTEM.
WHO CARES?
SCHOOL IS BORING, ANYWAY.

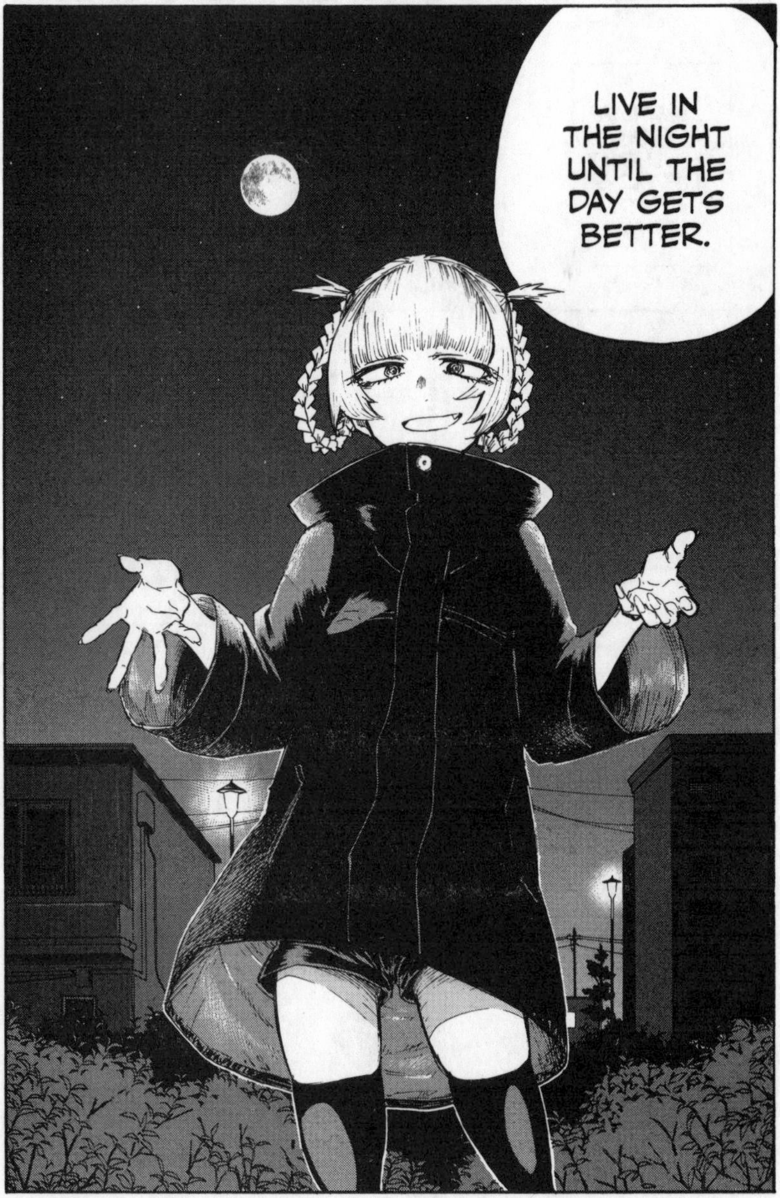
LIVE IN THE NIGHT UNTIL THE DAY GETS BETTER.

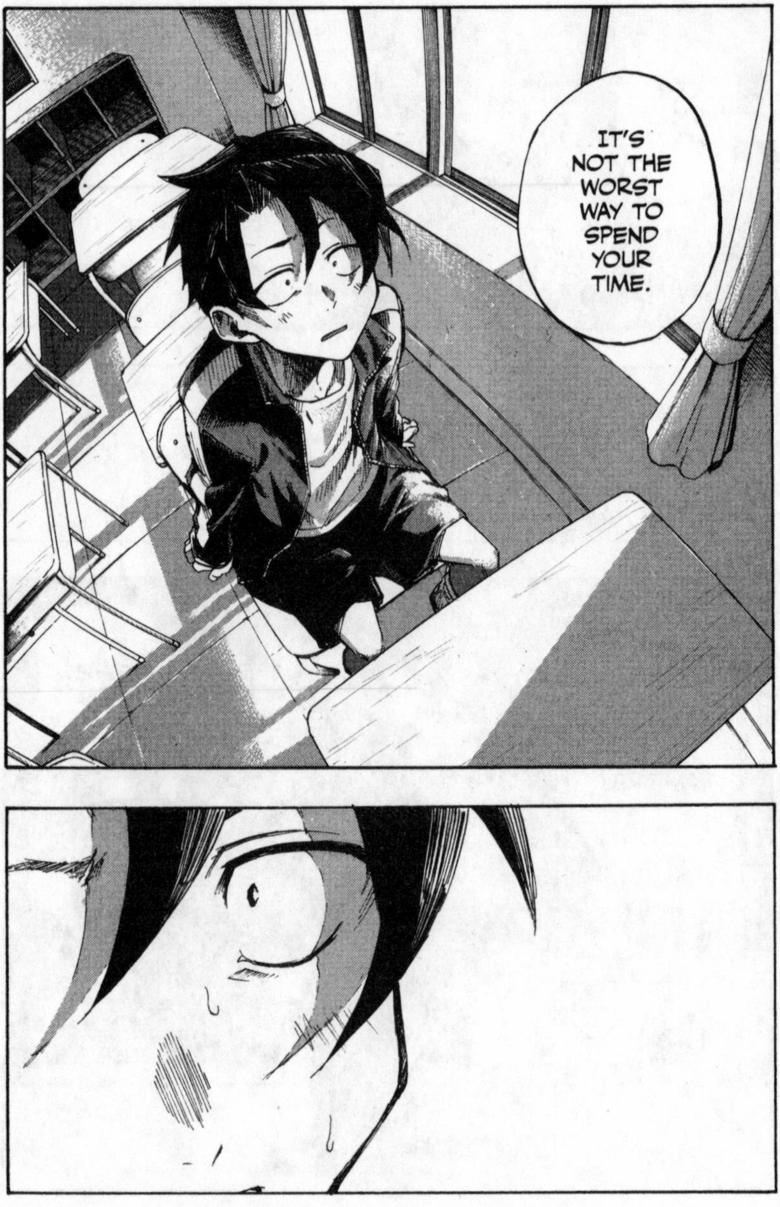
IT'S NOT THE WORST WAY TO SPEND YOUR TIME.

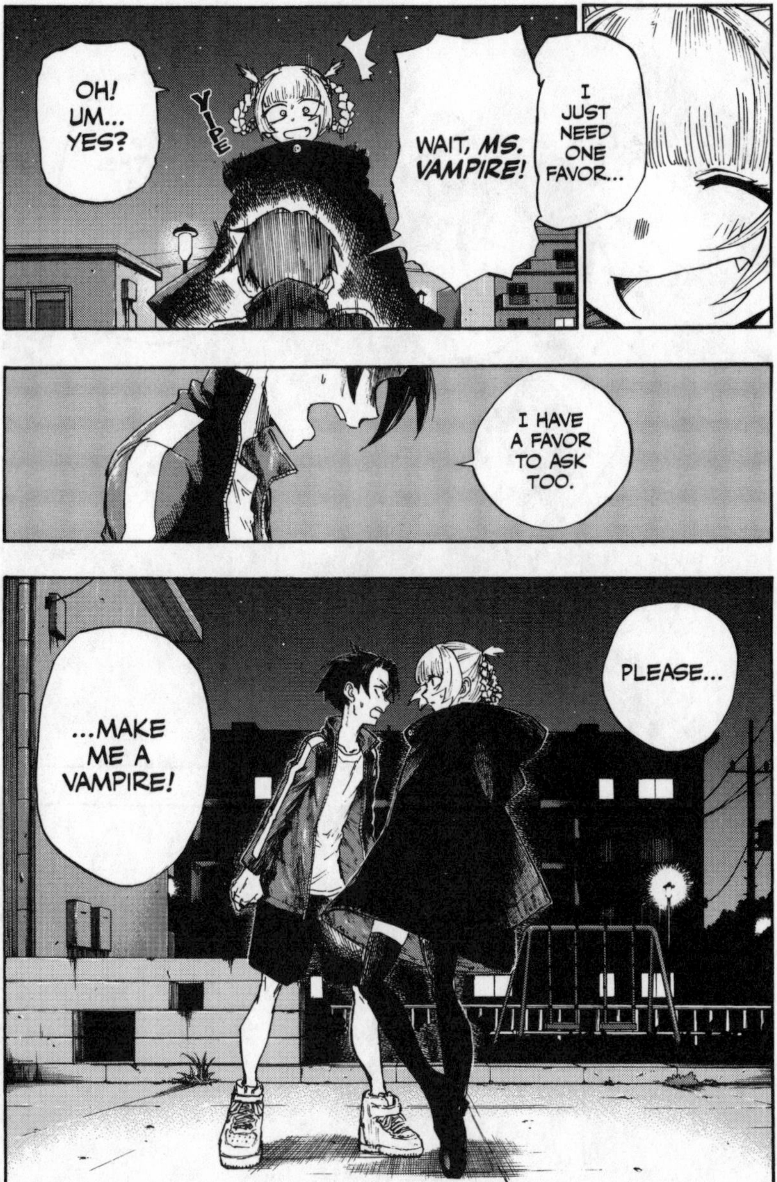
I JUST NEED ONE FAVOR...
WAIT, MS. VAMPIRE!
YIPE
OH! UM... YES?
I HAVE A FAVOR TO ASK TOO.
PLEASE...
...MAKE ME A VAMPIRE!

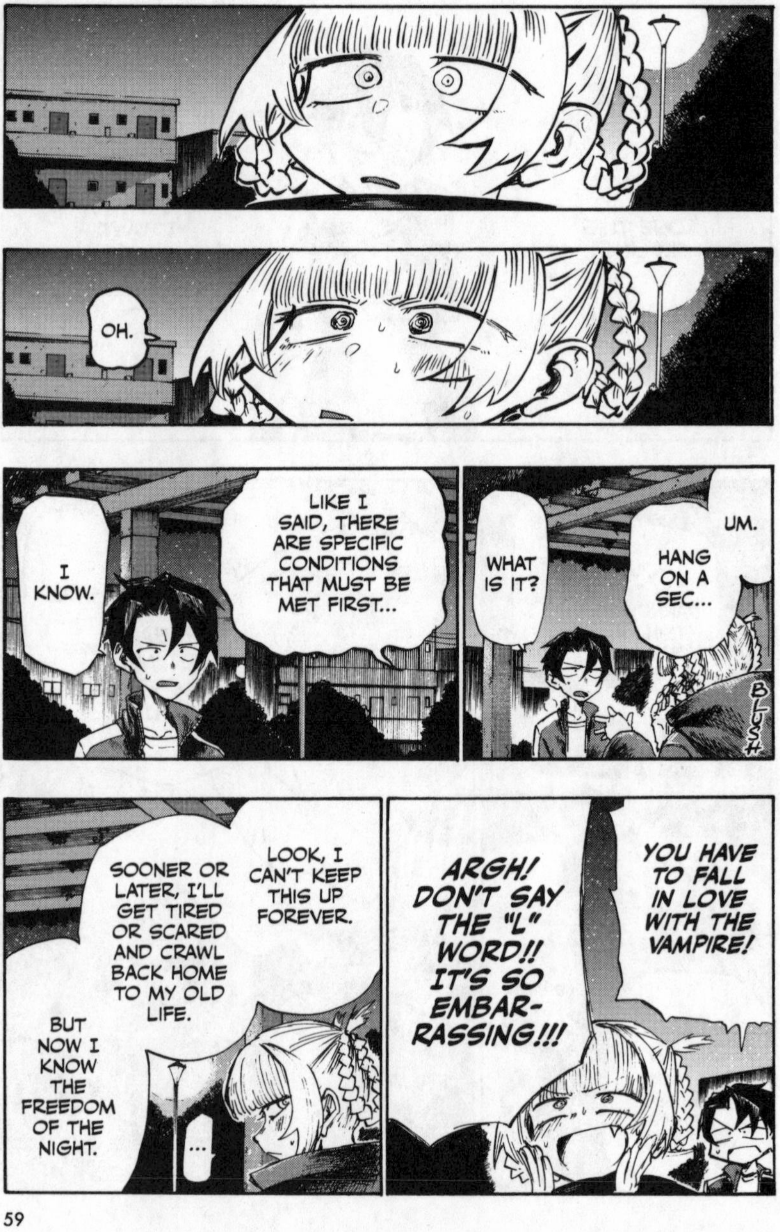

OH.
UM.
HANG ON A SEC...
WHAT IS IT?
BLUSH
LIKE I SAID, THERE ARE SPECIFIC CONDITIONS THAT MUST BE MET FIRST...
I KNOW.
YOU HAVE TO FALL IN LOVE WITH THE VAMPIRE!
ARGH! DON'T SAY THE "L" WORD!! IT'S SO EMBARRASSING!!!
LOOK, I CAN'T KEEP THIS UP FOREVER.
SOONER OR LATER, I'LL GET TIRED OR SCARED AND CRAWL BACK HOME TO MY OLD LIFE.
BUT NOW I KNOW THE FREEDOM OF THE NIGHT.
...

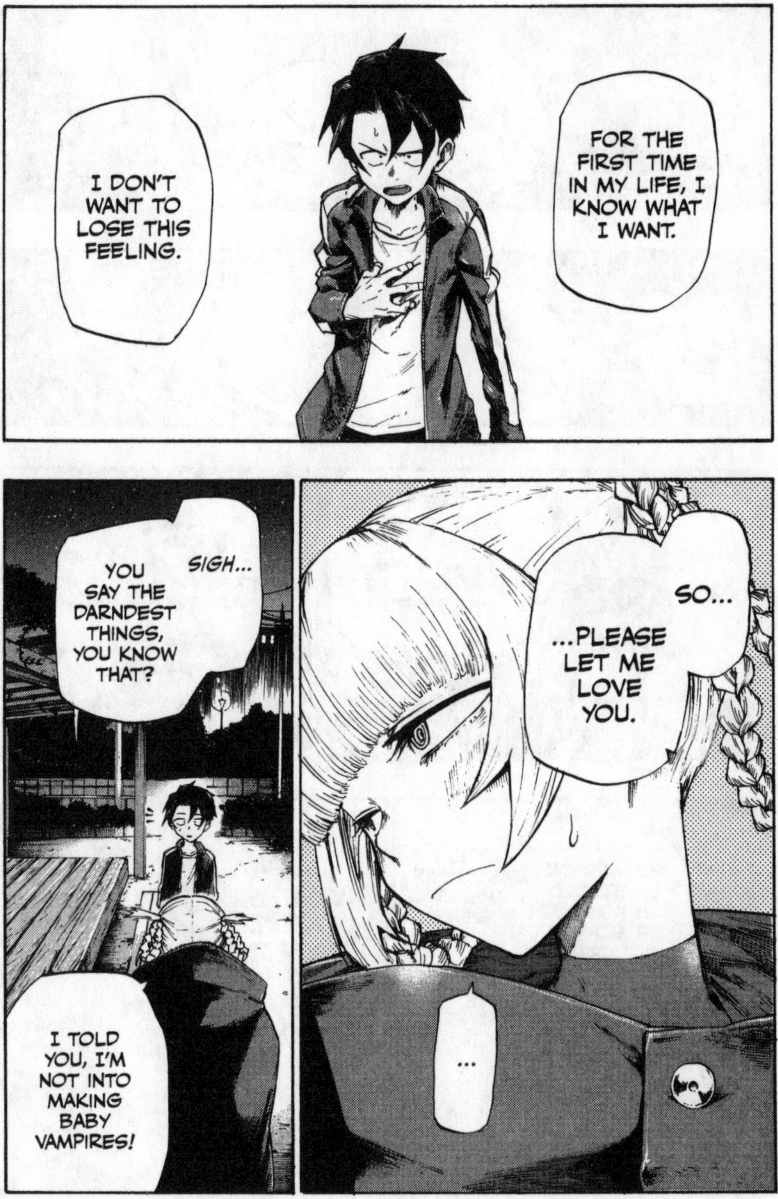
FOR THE FIRST TIME IN MY LIFE, I KNOW WHAT I WANT.
I DON'T WANT TO LOSE THIS FEELING.
SO...
...PLEASE LET ME LOVE YOU.
...
SIGH...
YOU SAY THE DARNDEST THINGS, YOU KNOW THAT?
I TOLD YOU, I'M NOT INTO MAKING BABY VAMPIRES!

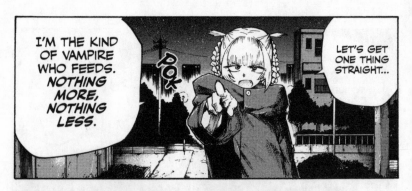

LET'S GET ONE THING STRAIGHT...
POK
I'M THE KIND OF VAMPIRE WHO FEEDS. NOTHING MORE, NOTHING LESS.
IF YOU WANNA FALL IN LOVE WITH ME, GO RIGHT AHEAD.
NOT MY PROB-LEM.
I'M NAZUNA NANAKUSA, BY THE WAY.
YOU?
KO YAMORI.

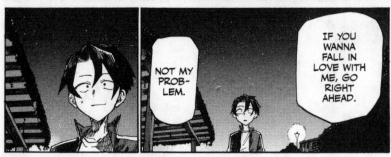

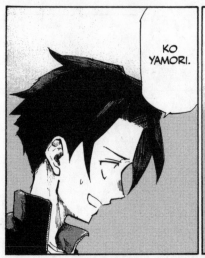

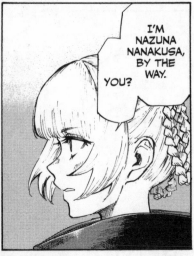

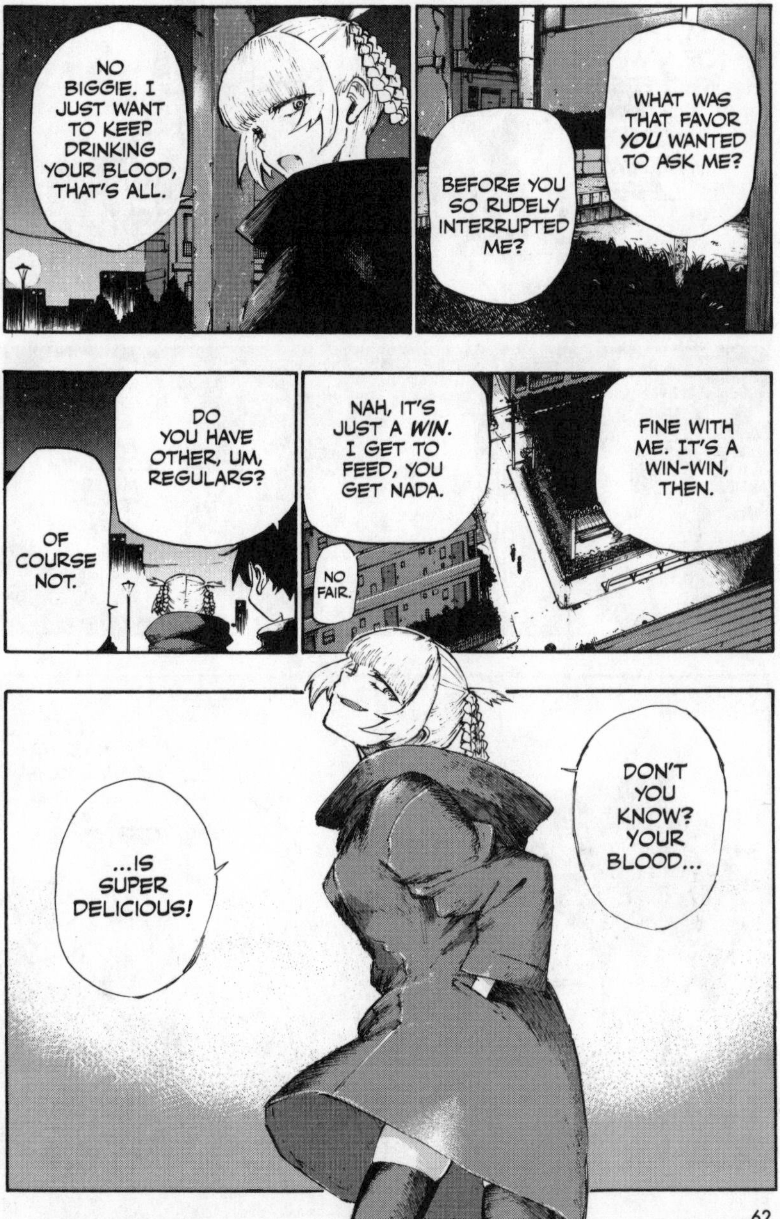
WHAT WAS THAT FAVOR *YOU* WANTED TO ASK ME?
BEFORE YOU SO RUDELY INTERRUPTED ME?
NO BIGGIE. I JUST WANT TO KEEP DRINKING YOUR BLOOD, THAT'S ALL.
FINE WITH ME. IT'S A WIN-WIN, THEN.
NAH, IT'S JUST A *WIN*. I GET TO FEED, YOU GET NADA.
NO FAIR.
DO YOU HAVE OTHER, UM, REGULARS?
OF COURSE NOT.
DON'T YOU KNOW? YOUR BLOOD...
...IS SUPER DELICIOUS!

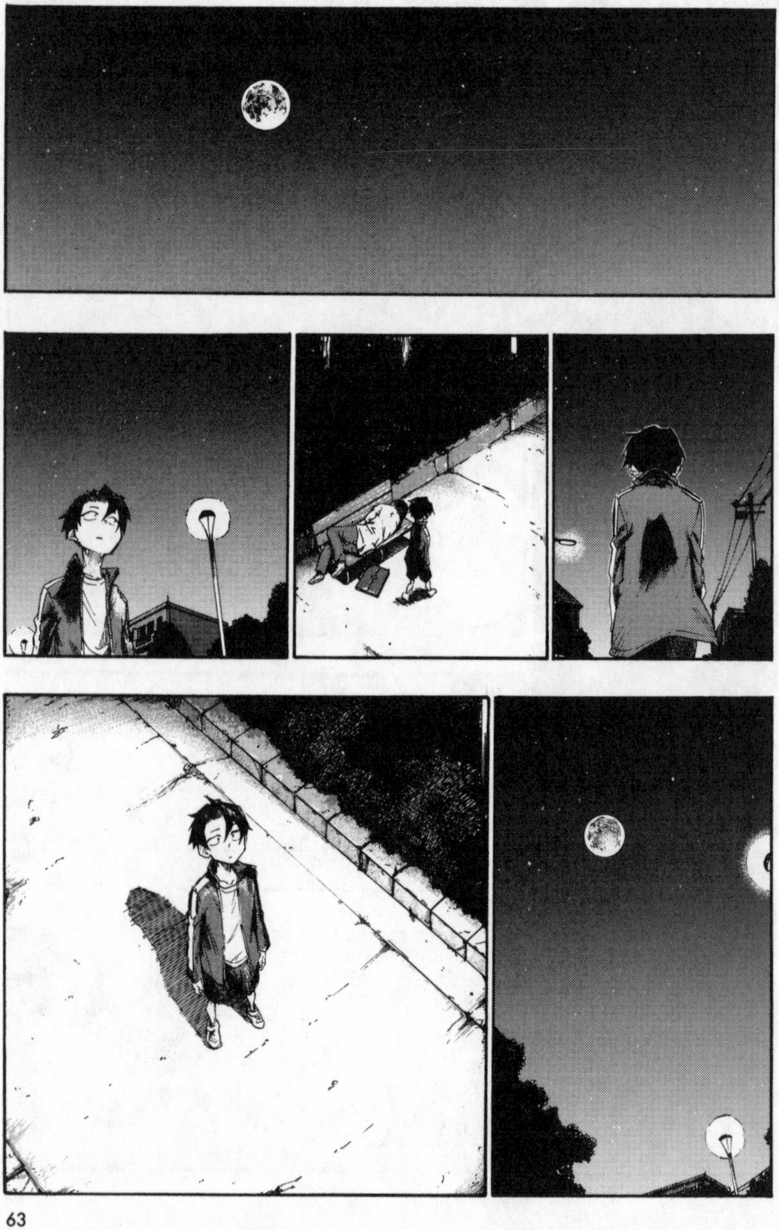

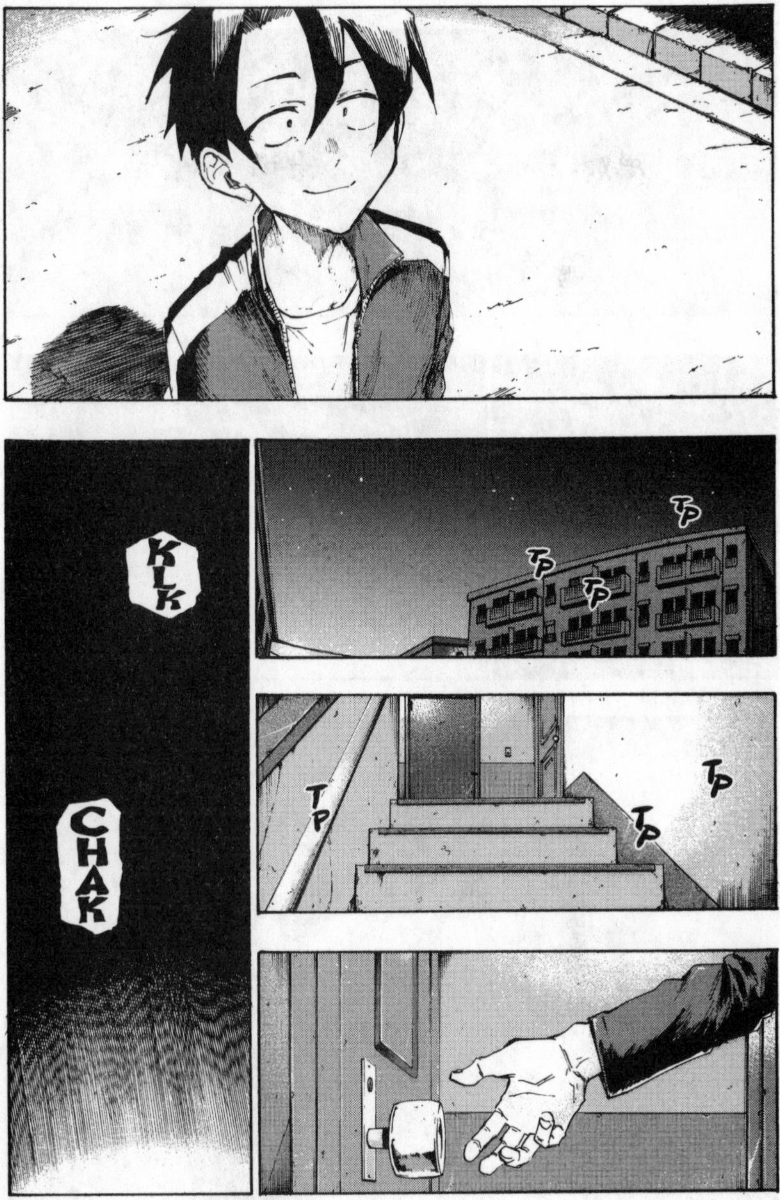
TP
TP
TP
TP
TP
TP
KLK
CHAK

Call of the Night

Call of the Night

NIGHT 3: NIGHT FLIGHT

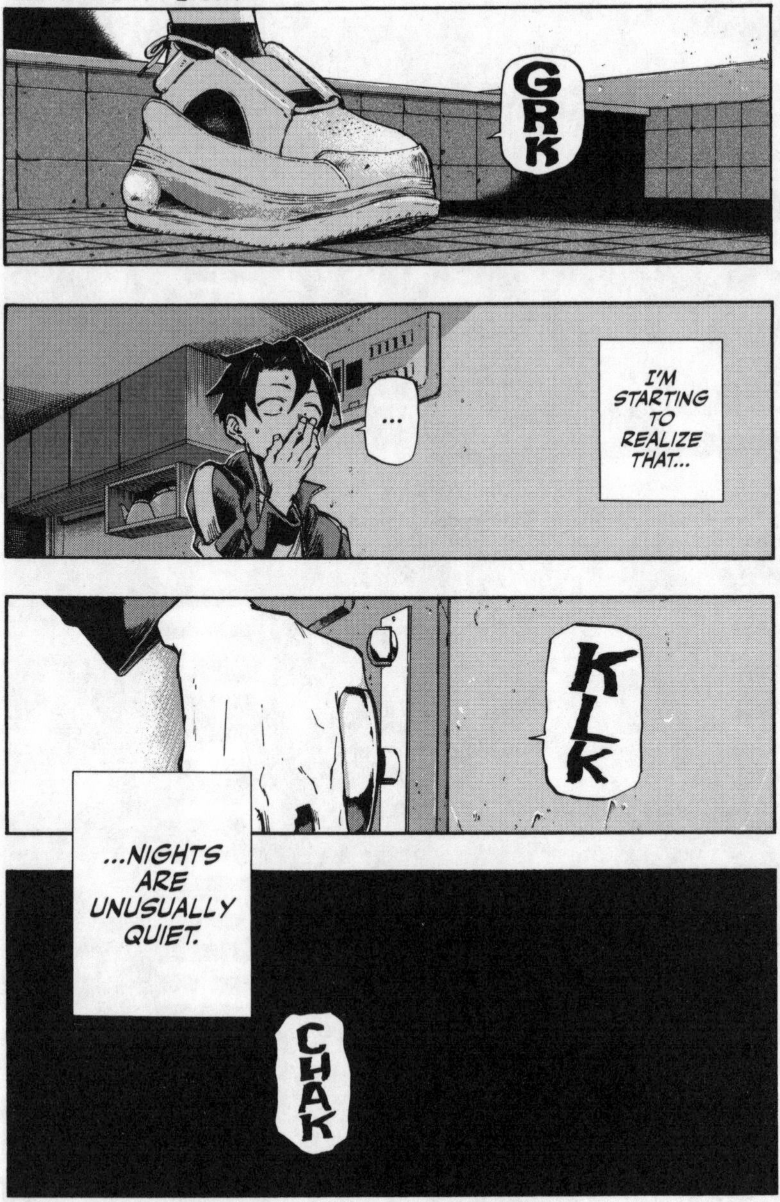
GRK
I'M STARTING TO REALIZE THAT...
...
KLK
...NIGHTS ARE UNUSUALLY QUIET.
CHAK

NIGHT 3: NIGHT FLIGHT

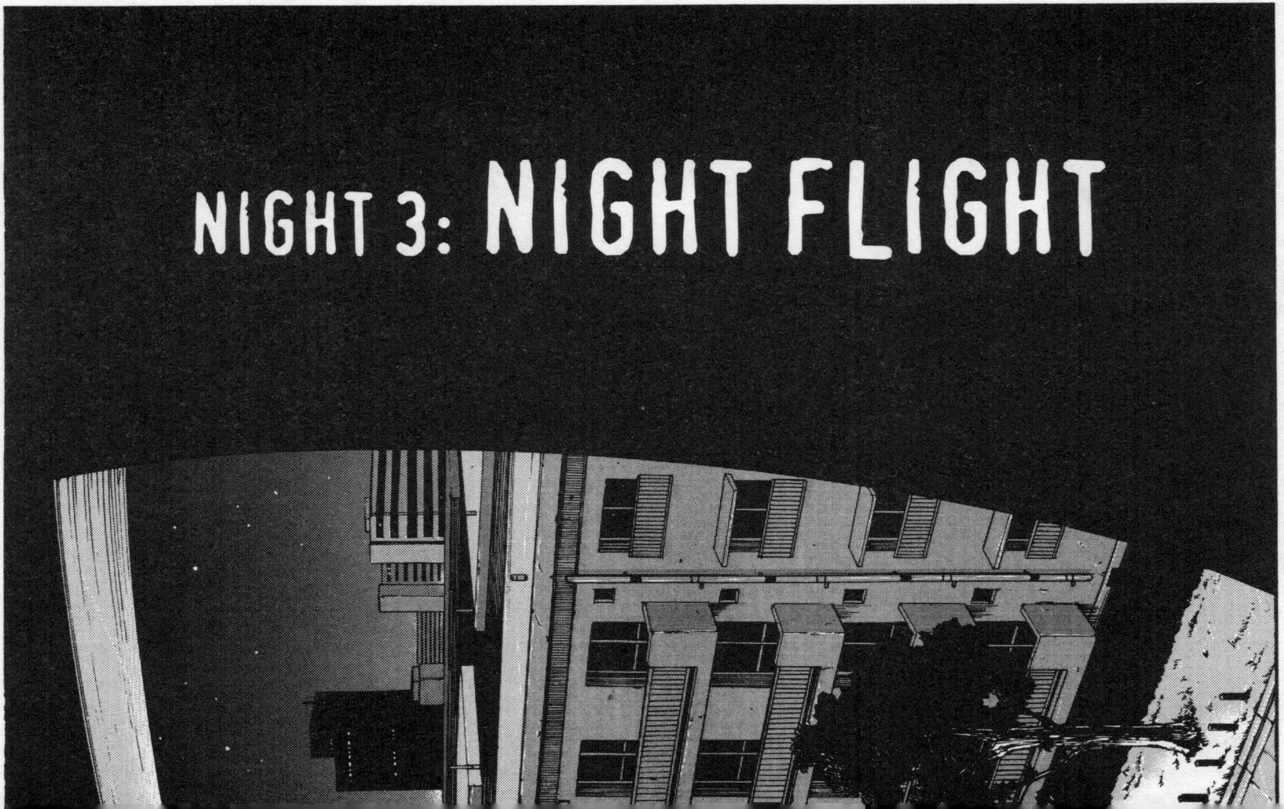

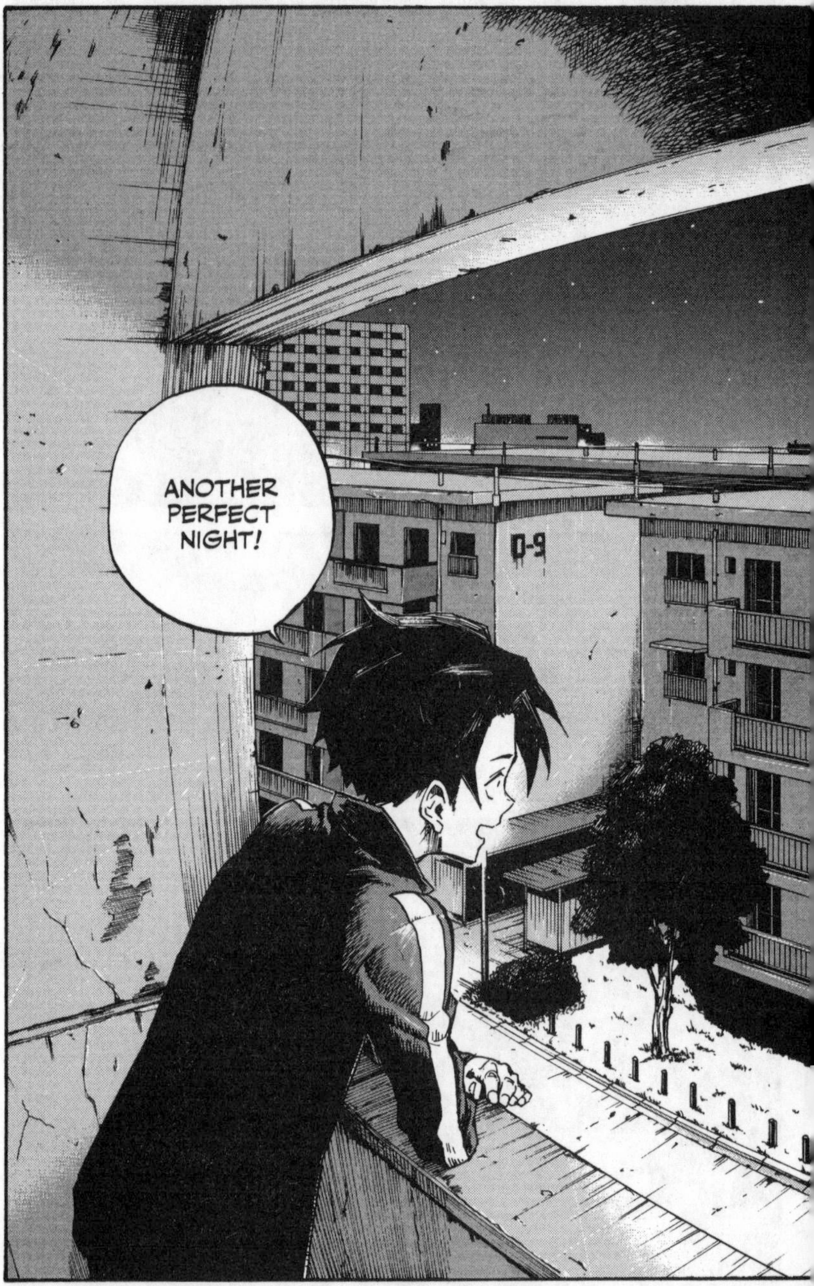
ANOTHER PERFECT NIGHT!

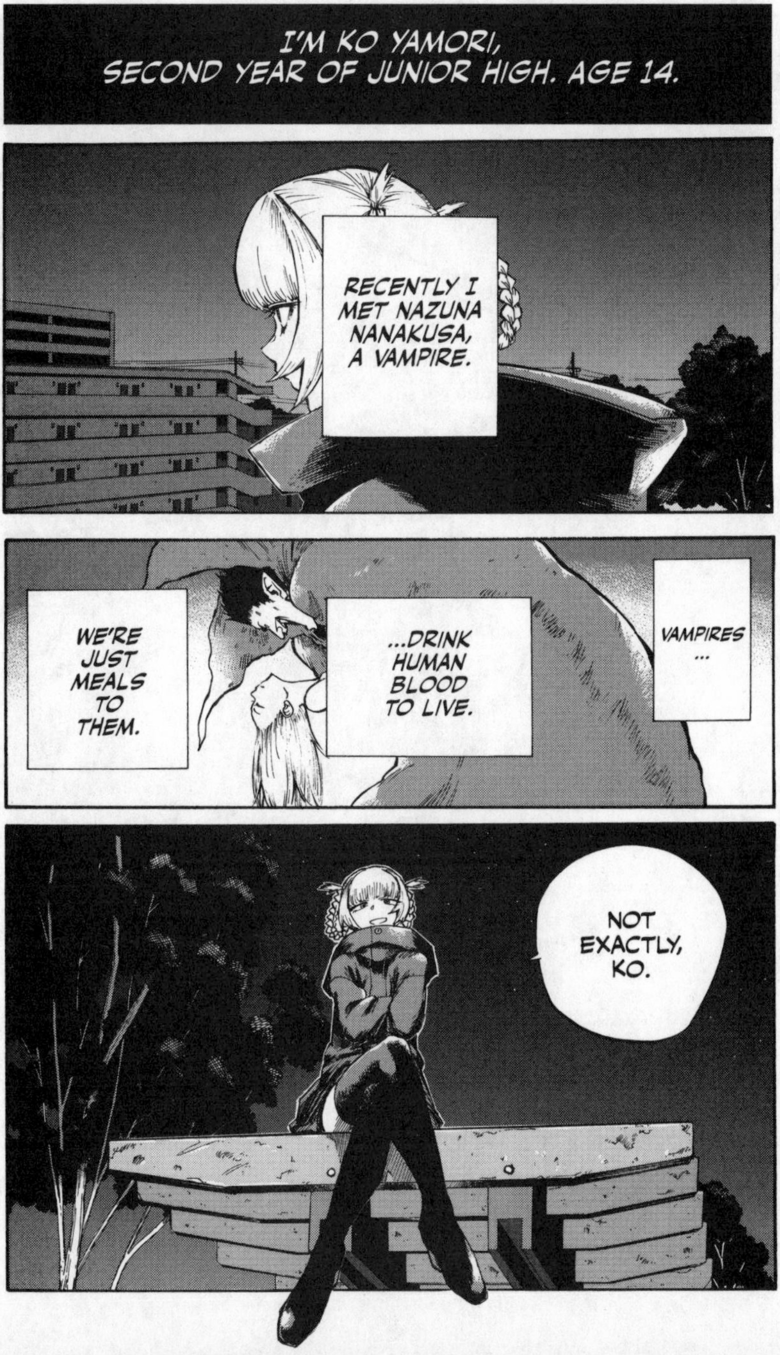
I'M KO YAMORI, SECOND YEAR OF JUNIOR HIGH. AGE 14.
RECENTLY I MET NAZUNA NANAKUSA, A VAMPIRE.
VAMPIRES...
...DRINK HUMAN BLOOD TO LIVE.
WE'RE JUST MEALS TO THEM.
NOT EXACTLY, KO.

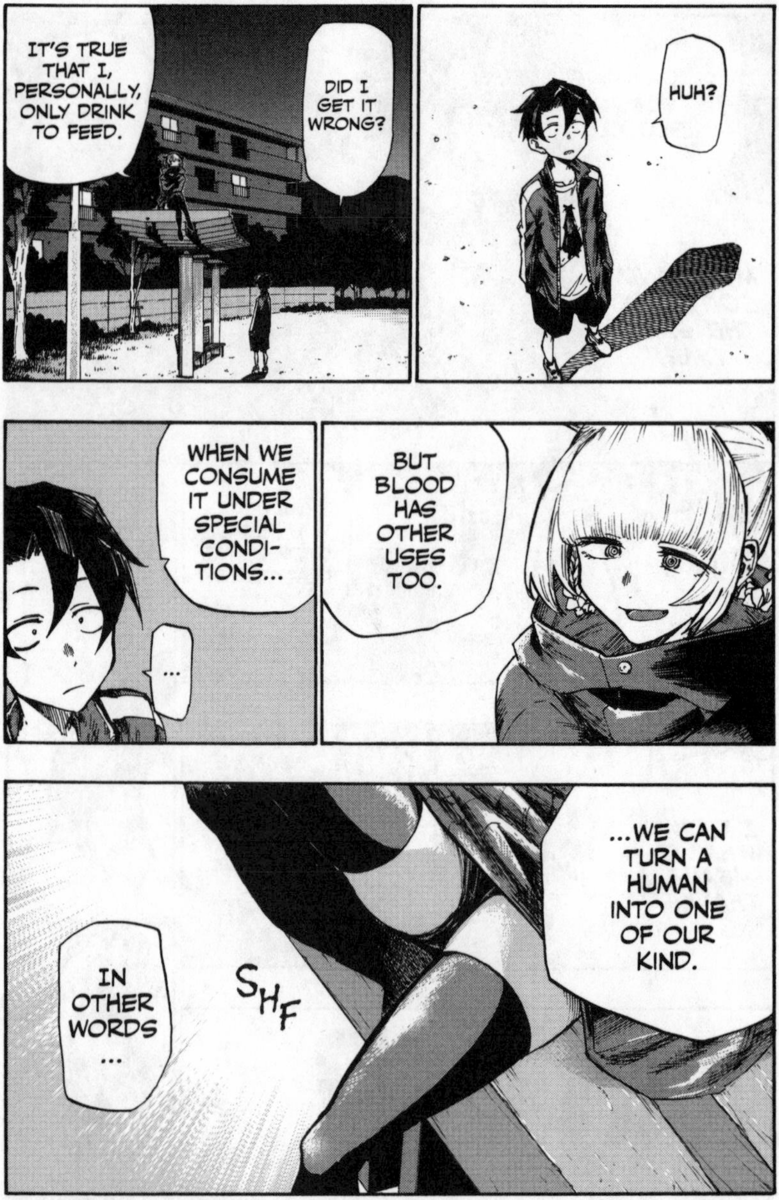
HUH?
DID I GET IT WRONG?
IT'S TRUE THAT I, PERSONALLY, ONLY DRINK TO FEED.
BUT BLOOD HAS OTHER USES TOO.
WHEN WE CONSUME IT UNDER SPECIAL CONDI-TIONS...
...
...WE CAN TURN A HUMAN INTO ONE OF OUR KIND.
SHF
IN OTHER WORDS ...

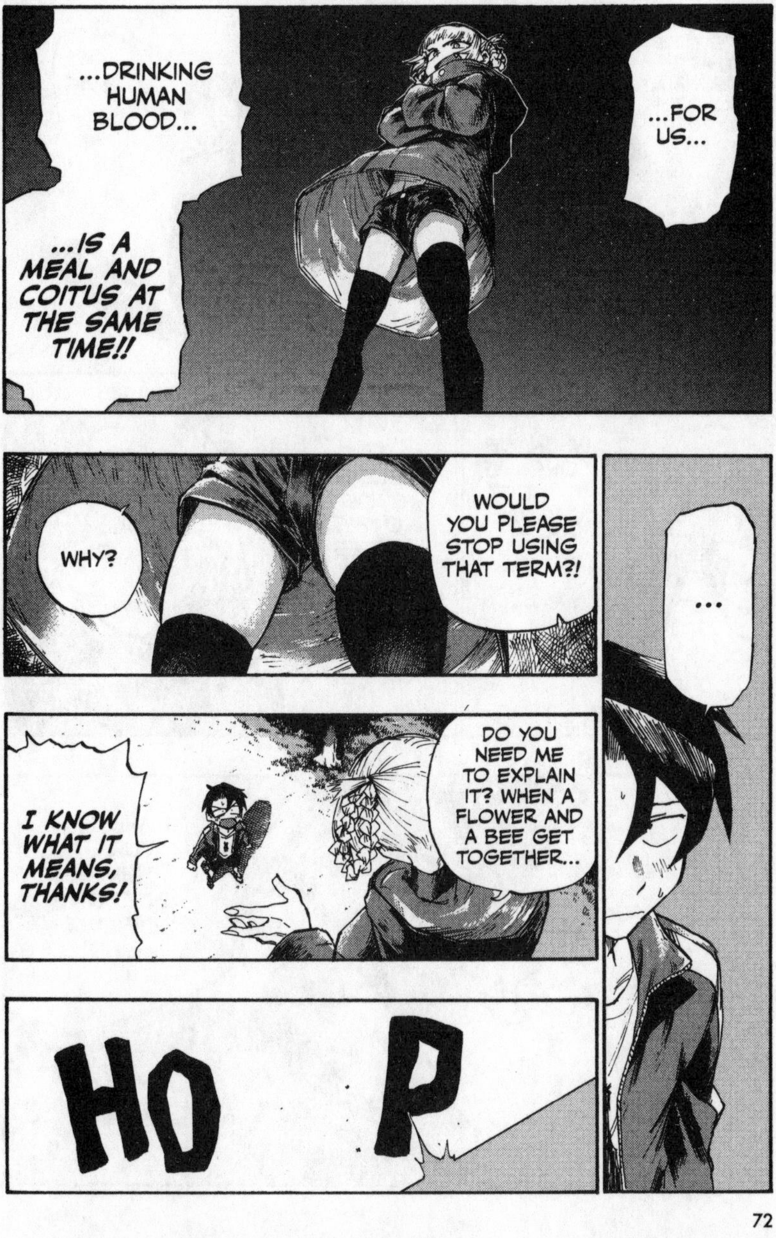
...FOR US...
...DRINKING HUMAN BLOOD...
...IS A MEAL AND COITUS AT THE SAME TIME!!
...
WOULD YOU PLEASE STOP USING THAT TERM?!
WHY?
DO YOU NEED ME TO EXPLAIN IT? WHEN A FLOWER AND A BEE GET TOGETHER...
I KNOW WHAT IT MEANS, THANKS!
HOP

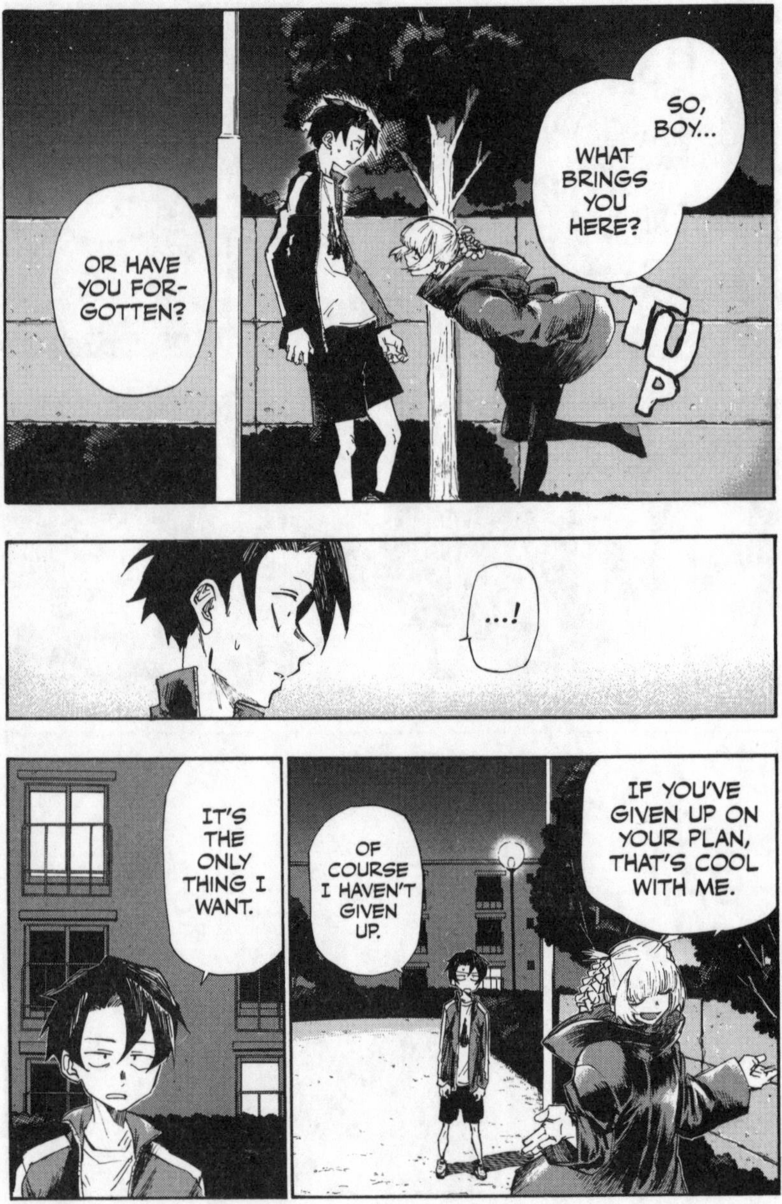
SO, BOY... WHAT BRINGS YOU HERE?
TUP
OR HAVE YOU FOR-GOTTEN?
...!
IF YOU'VE GIVEN UP ON YOUR PLAN, THAT'S COOL WITH ME.
OF COURSE I HAVEN'T GIVEN UP.
IT'S THE ONLY THING I WANT.

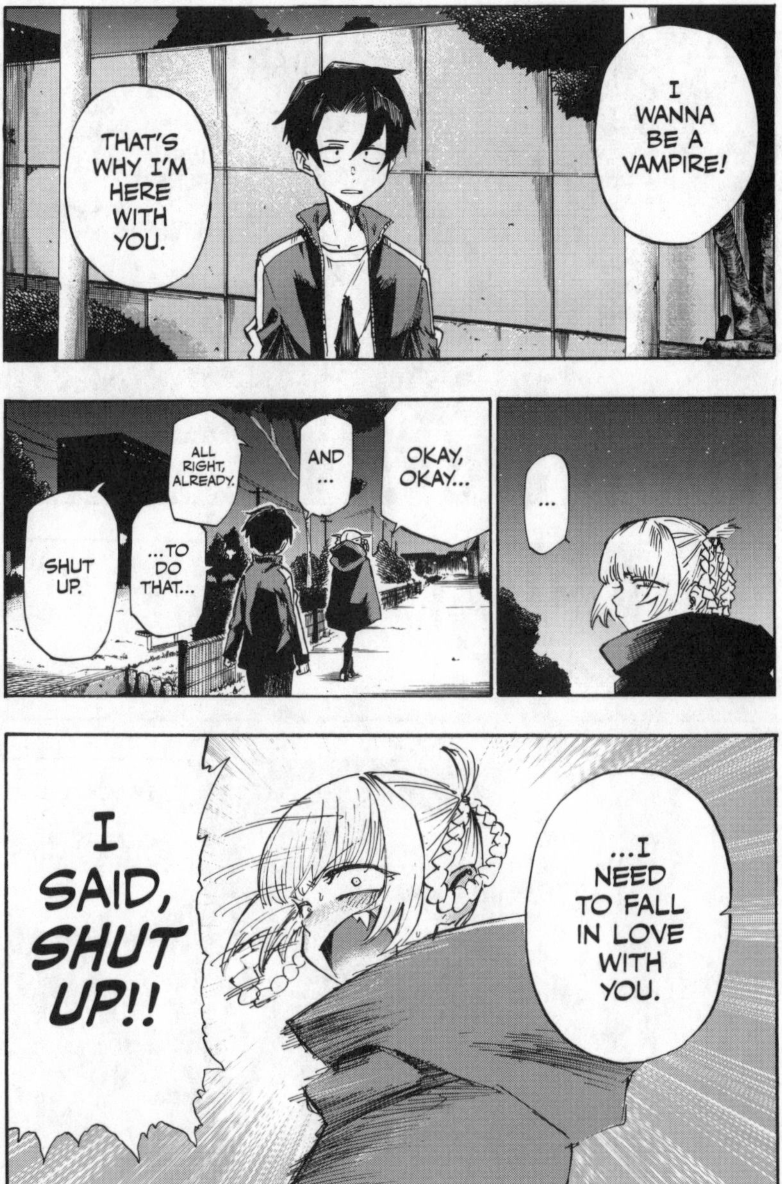
I WANNA BE A VAMPIRE!
THAT'S WHY I'M HERE WITH YOU.
...
OKAY, OKAY...
AND ...
ALL RIGHT, ALREADY.
...TO DO THAT...
SHUT UP.
...I NEED TO FALL IN LOVE WITH YOU.
I SAID, SHUT UP!!

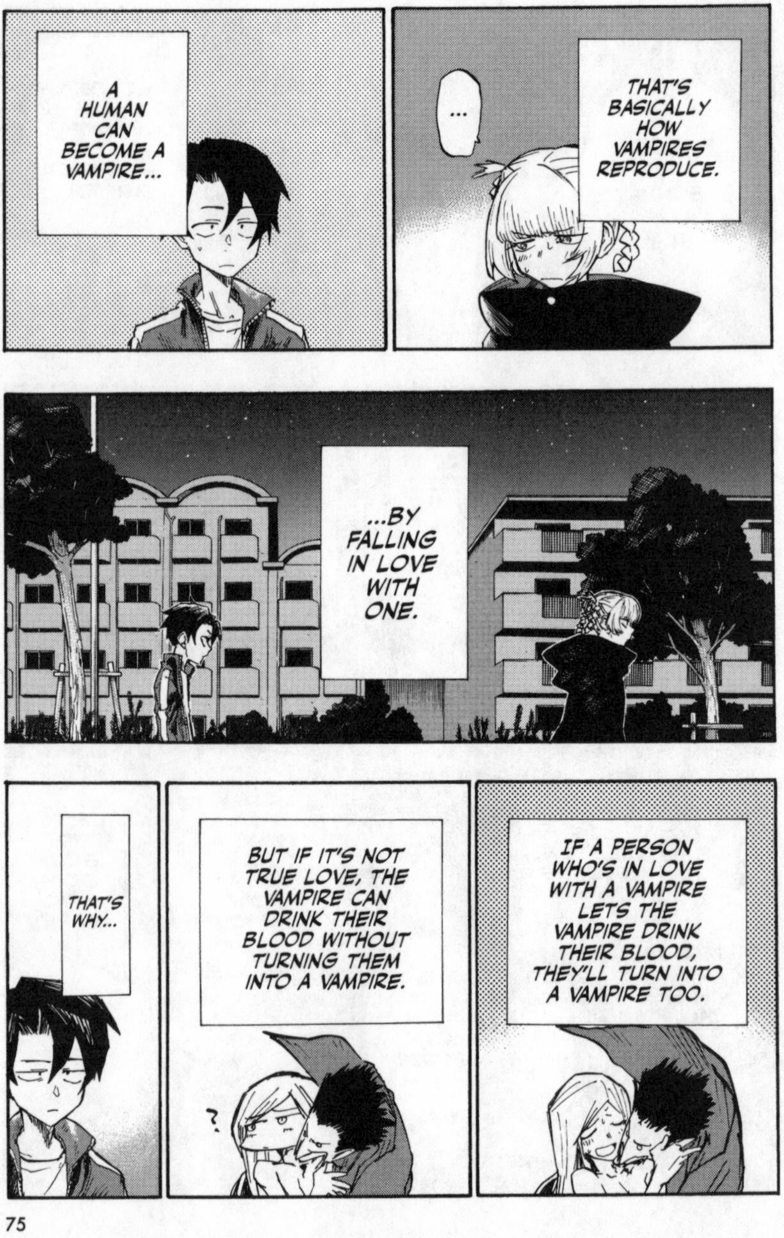
THAT'S BASICALLY HOW VAMPIRES REPRODUCE.
...
A HUMAN CAN BECOME A VAMPIRE...
...BY FALLING IN LOVE WITH ONE.
IF A PERSON WHO'S IN LOVE WITH A VAMPIRE LETS THE VAMPIRE DRINK THEIR BLOOD, THEY'LL TURN INTO A VAMPIRE TOO.
BUT IF IT'S NOT TRUE LOVE, THE VAMPIRE CAN DRINK THEIR BLOOD WITHOUT TURNING THEM INTO A VAMPIRE.
?
THAT'S WHY...

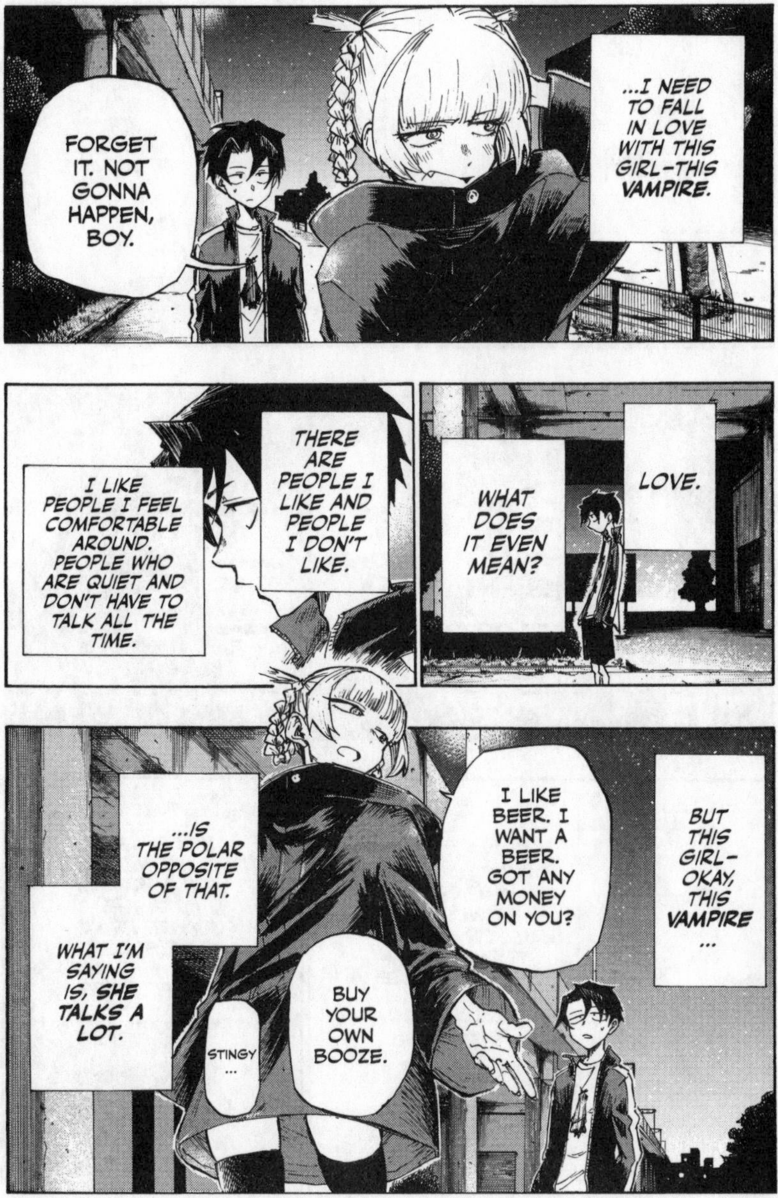
...I NEED TO FALL IN LOVE WITH THIS GIRL—THIS VAMPIRE.
FORGET IT. NOT GONNA HAPPEN, BOY.
LOVE.
WHAT DOES IT EVEN MEAN?
THERE ARE PEOPLE I LIKE AND PEOPLE I DON'T LIKE.
I LIKE PEOPLE I FEEL COMFORTABLE AROUND. PEOPLE WHO ARE QUIET AND DON'T HAVE TO TALK ALL THE TIME.
BUT THIS GIRL—OKAY, THIS VAMPIRE...
I LIKE BEER. I WANT A BEER. GOT ANY MONEY ON YOU?
...IS THE POLAR OPPOSITE OF THAT.
BUY YOUR OWN BOOZE.
WHAT I'M SAYING IS, SHE TALKS A LOT.
STINGY...

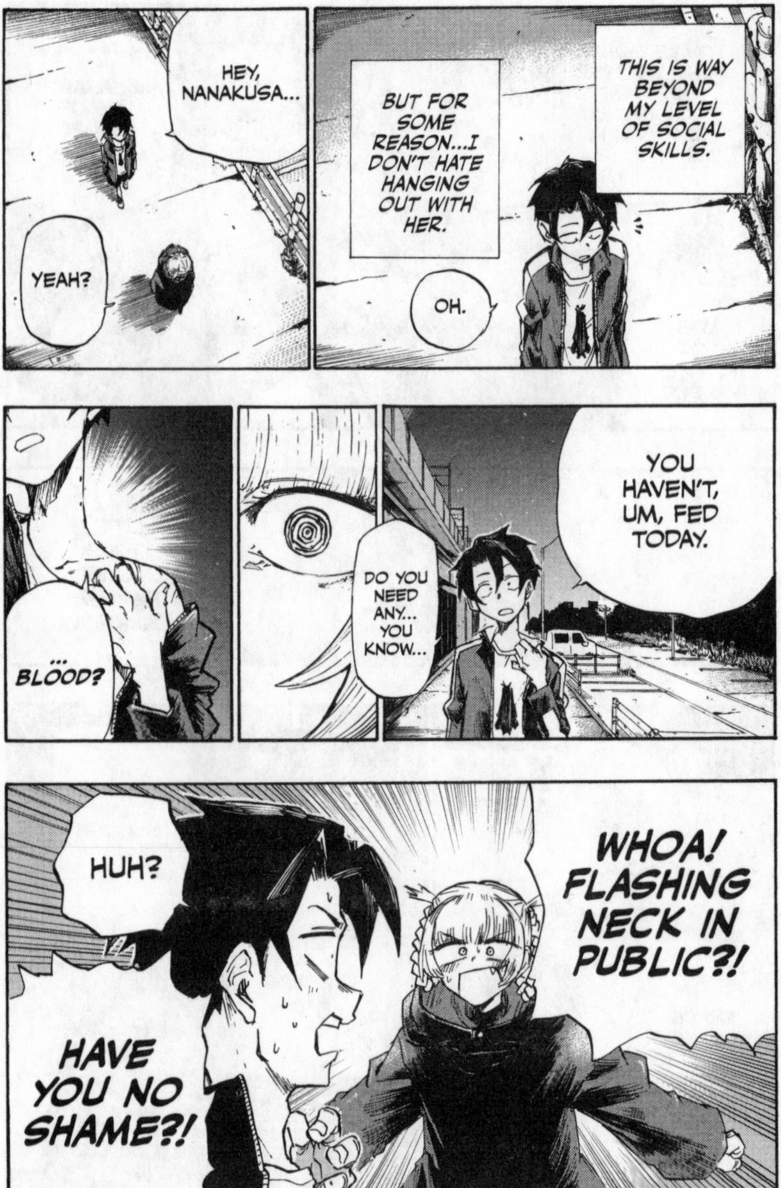
THIS IS WAY BEYOND MY LEVEL OF SOCIAL SKILLS.
BUT FOR SOME REASON...I DON'T HATE HANGING OUT WITH HER.
OH.
HEY, NANAKUSA...
YEAH?
YOU HAVEN'T, UM, FED TODAY.
DO YOU NEED ANY... YOU KNOW...
...BLOOD?
WHOA! FLASHING NECK IN PUBLIC?!
HUH?
HAVE YOU NO SHAME?!

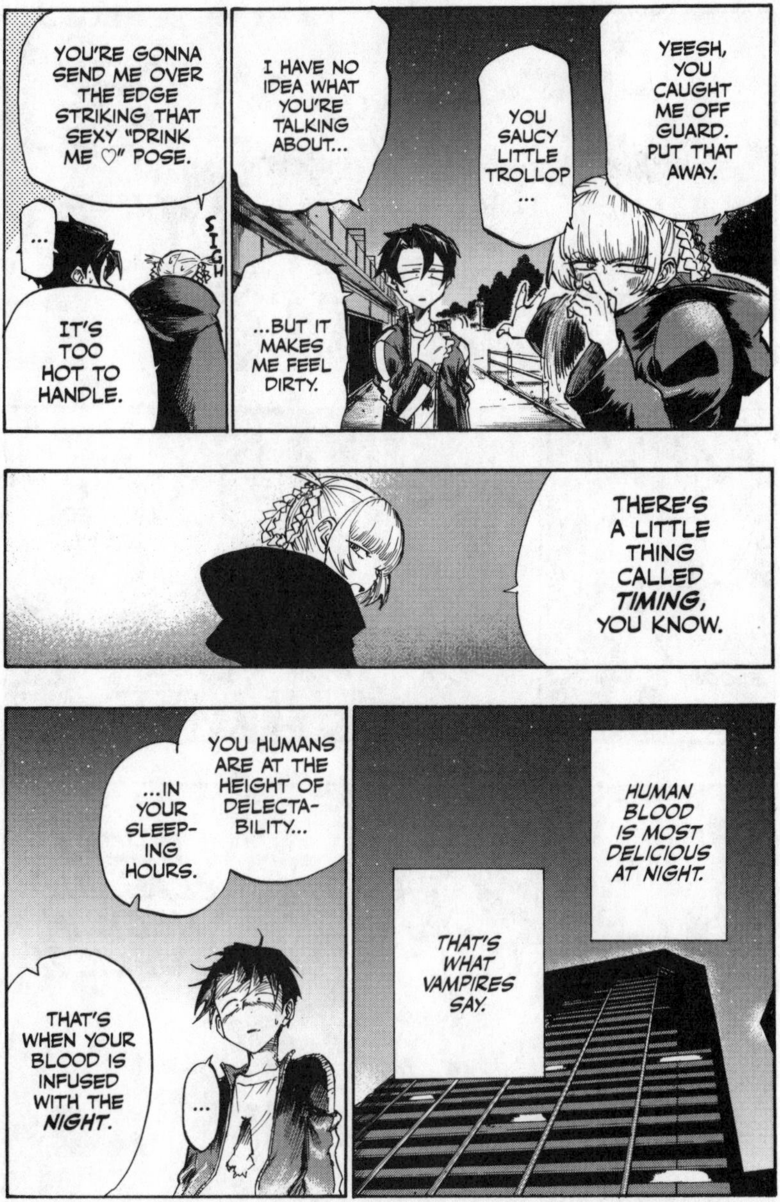
YEESH, YOU CAUGHT ME OFF GUARD. PUT THAT AWAY.
YOU SAUCY LITTLE TROLLOP ...
I HAVE NO IDEA WHAT YOU'RE TALKING ABOUT...
...BUT IT MAKES ME FEEL DIRTY.
YOU'RE GONNA SEND ME OVER THE EDGE STRIKING THAT SEXY "DRINK ME ♡" POSE.
SIGH
...
IT'S TOO HOT TO HANDLE.
THERE'S A LITTLE THING CALLED *TIMING*, YOU KNOW.
HUMAN BLOOD IS MOST DELICIOUS AT NIGHT.
THAT'S WHAT VAMPIRES SAY.
YOU HUMANS ARE AT THE HEIGHT OF DELECTA-BILITY...
...IN YOUR SLEEP-ING HOURS.
THAT'S WHEN YOUR BLOOD IS INFUSED WITH THE ***NIGHT***.
...

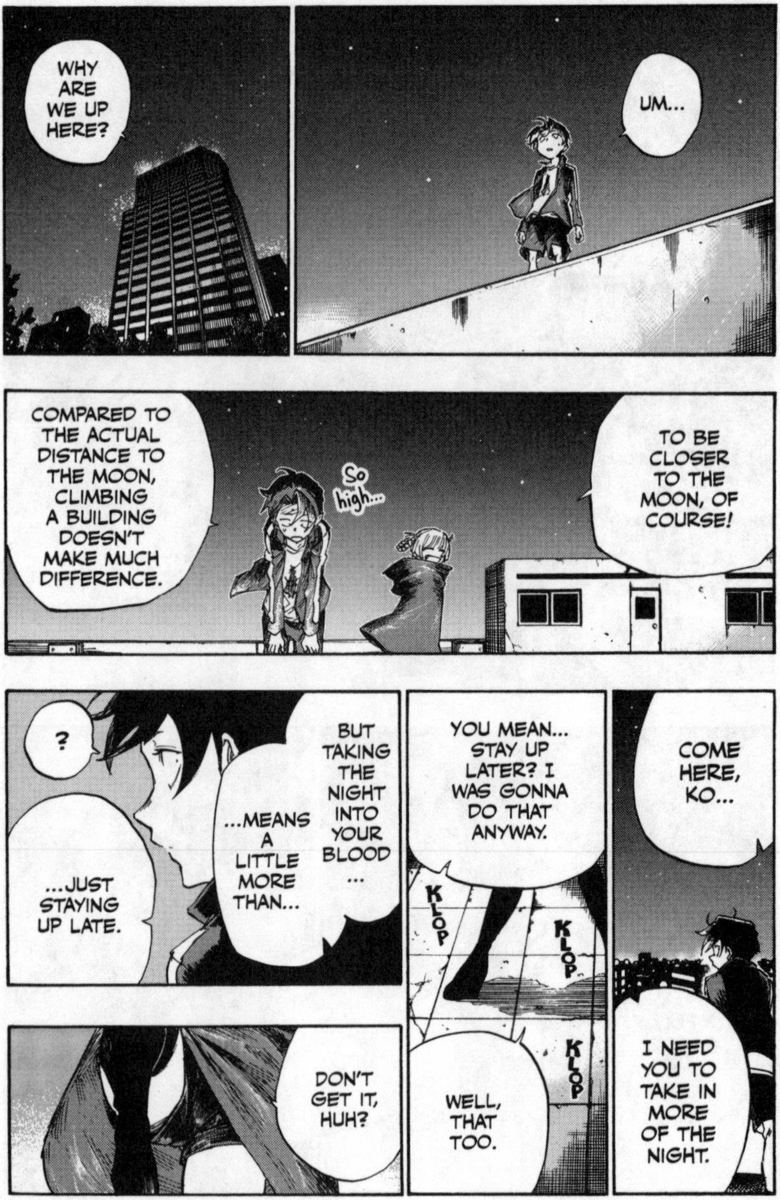
UM...
WHY ARE WE UP HERE?
TO BE CLOSER TO THE MOON, OF COURSE!
So high...
COMPARED TO THE ACTUAL DISTANCE TO THE MOON, CLIMBING A BUILDING DOESN'T MAKE MUCH DIFFERENCE.
COME HERE, KO...
I NEED YOU TO TAKE IN MORE OF THE NIGHT.
YOU MEAN... STAY UP LATER? I WAS GONNA DO THAT ANYWAY.
KLOP
KLOP
KLOP
WELL, THAT TOO.
BUT TAKING THE NIGHT INTO YOUR BLOOD...
...MEANS A LITTLE MORE THAN...
?
...JUST STAYING UP LATE.
DON'T GET IT, HUH?

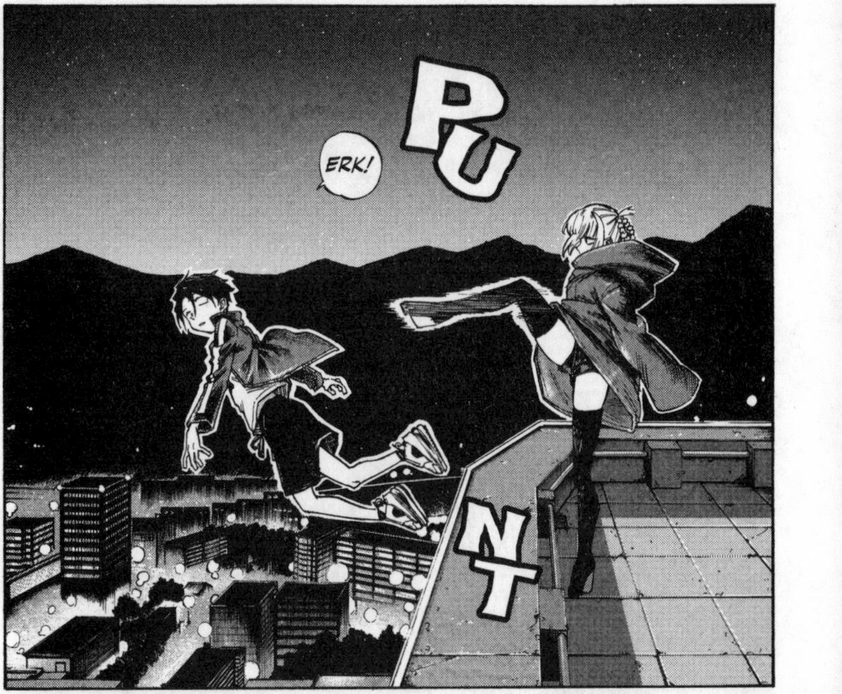
ERK!
PUNT

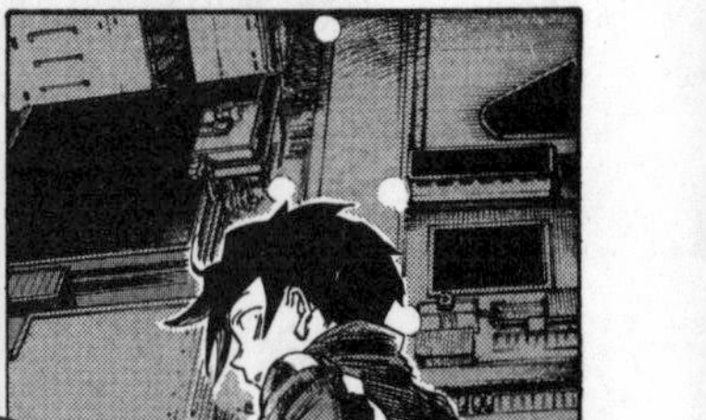

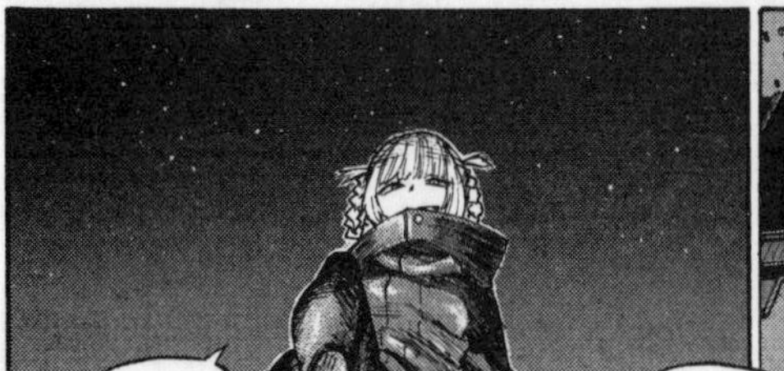
I'LL SHOW YOU...
...WHAT IT MEANS TO FULLY SAVOR THE NIGHT!

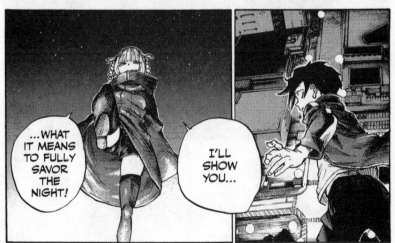

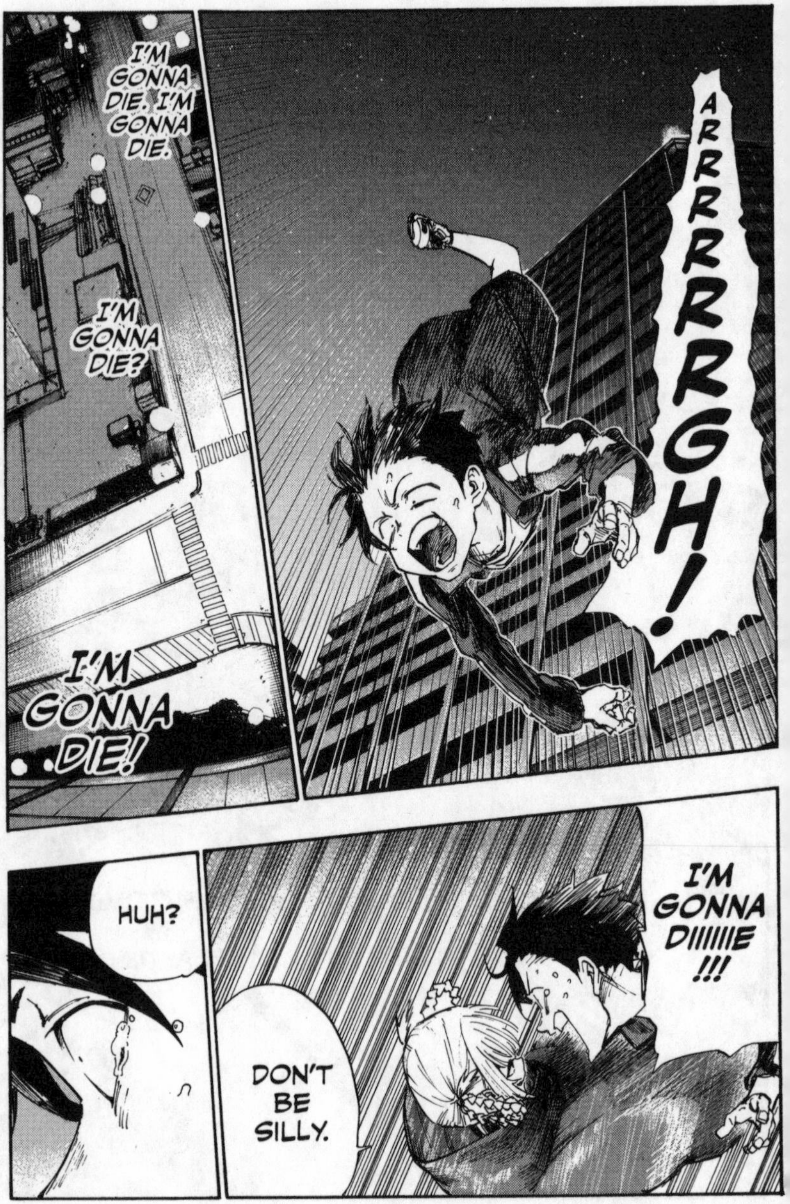
ARRRRRRGH!
I'M GONNA DIE. I'M GONNA DIE.
I'M GONNA DIE?
I'M GONNA DIE!
I'M GONNA DIIIIIIE !!!
DON'T BE SILLY.
HUH?

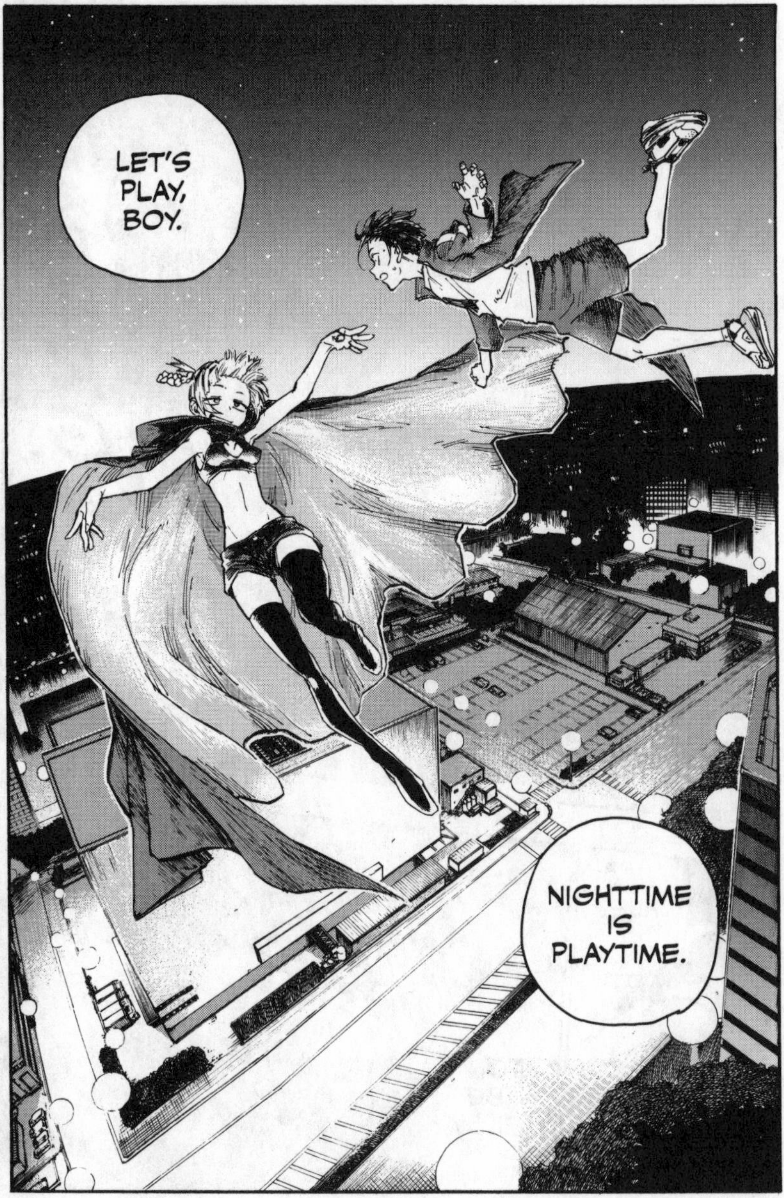
NIGHTTIME IS PLAYTIME.
LET'S PLAY, BOY.

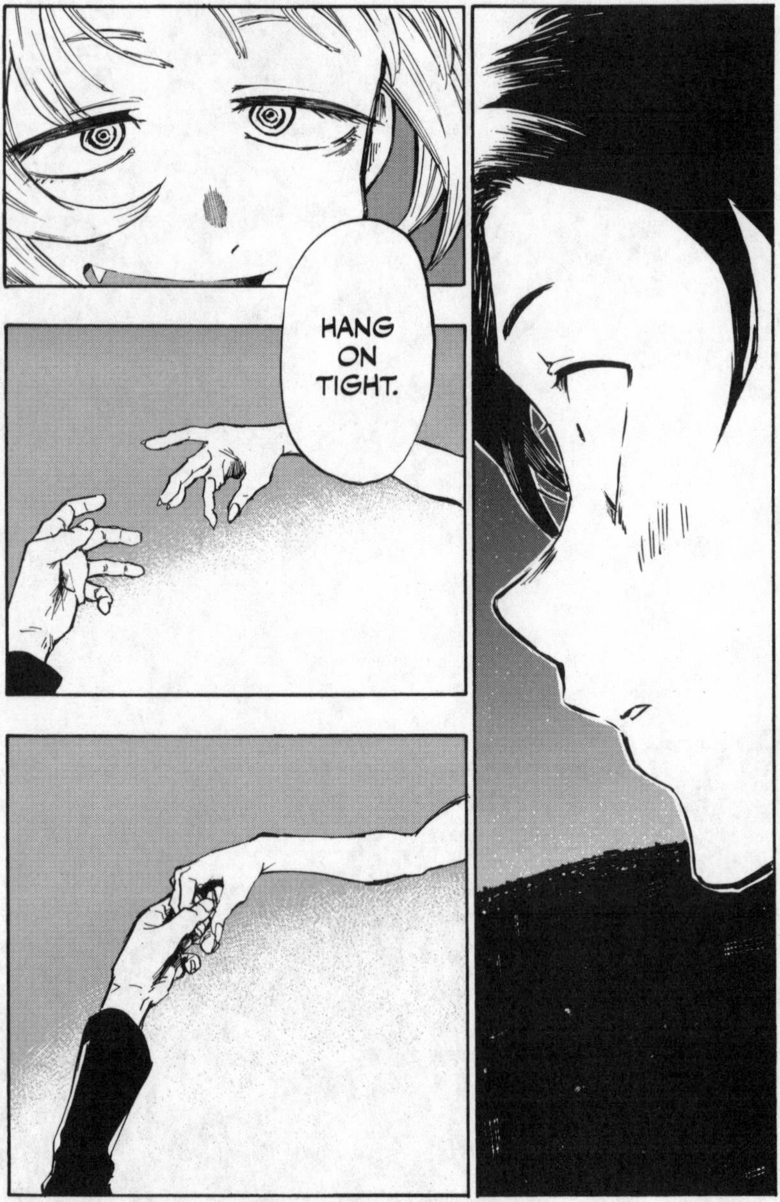
HANG ON TIGHT.

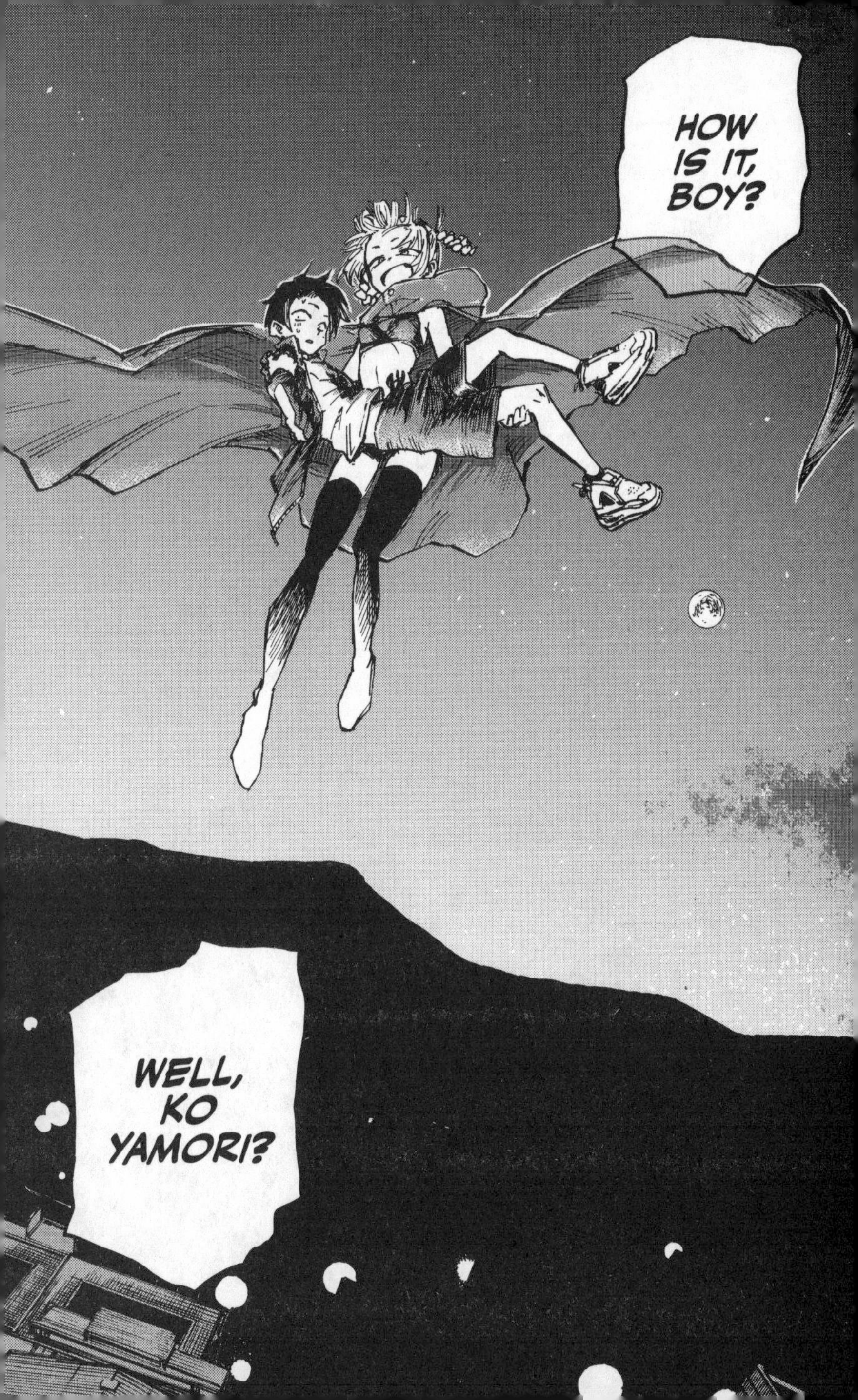
HOW IS IT, BOY?
WELL, KO YAMORI?

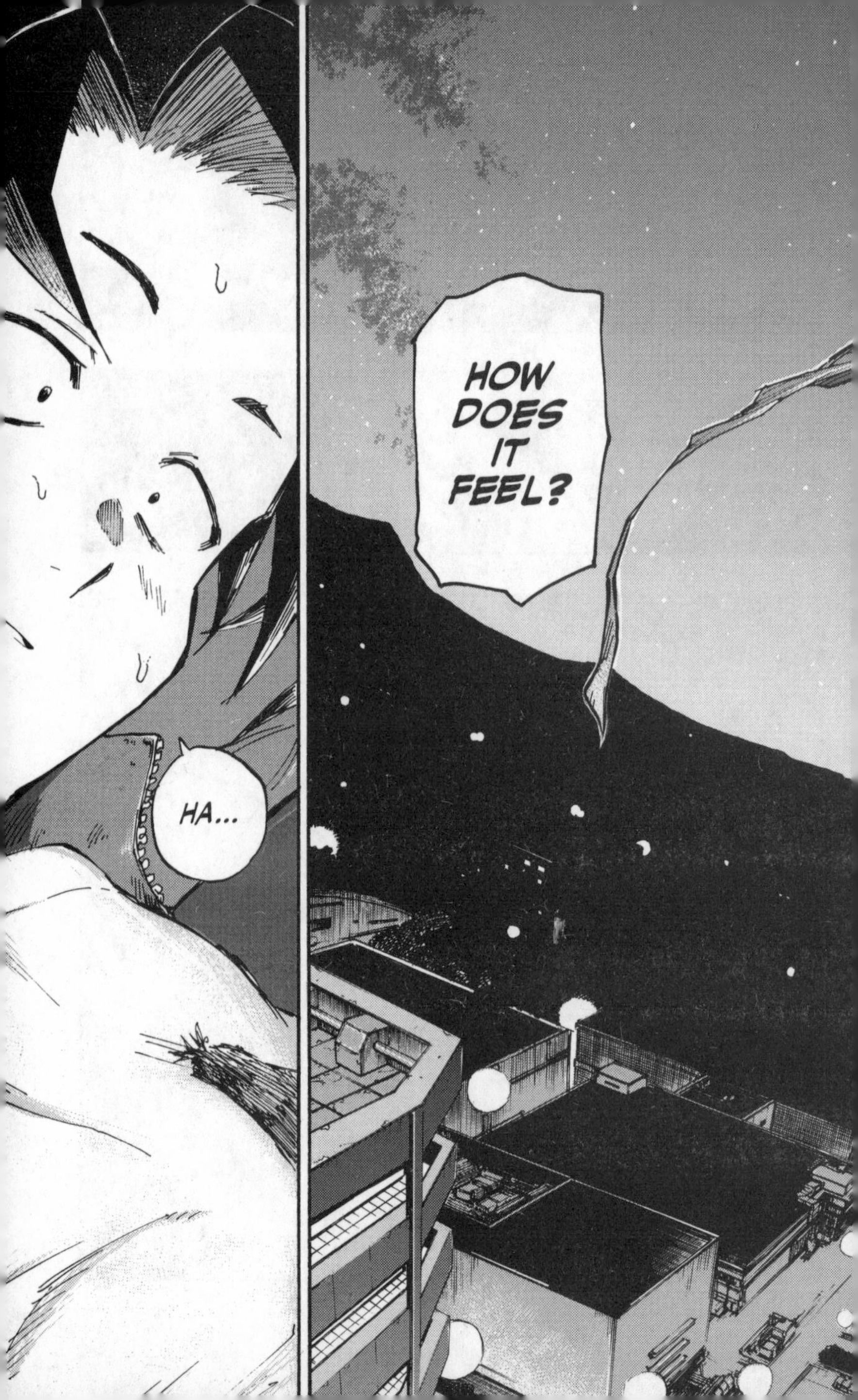
HOW DOES IT FEEL?
HA...

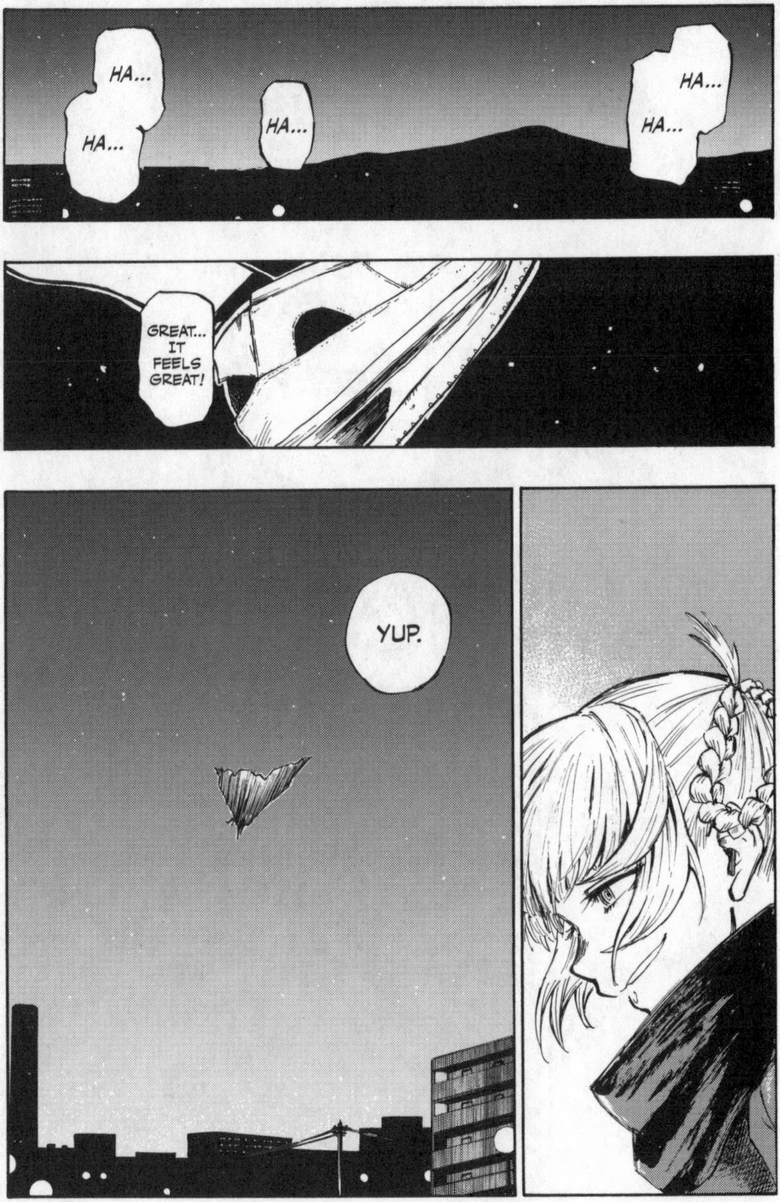
HA... HA...
HA...
HA... HA...
GREAT... IT FEELS GREAT!
YUP.

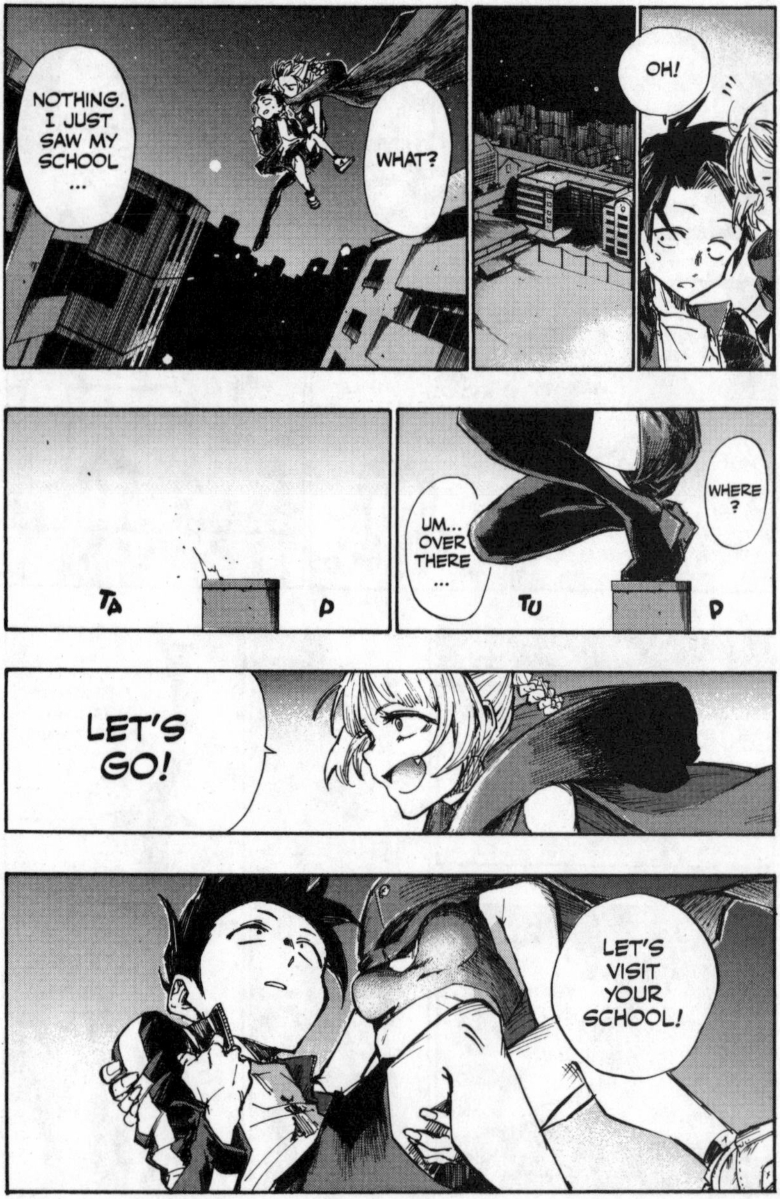
OH!
WHAT?
NOTHING. I JUST SAW MY SCHOOL ...
WHERE ?
UM... OVER THERE ...
TU P
TA P
LET'S GO!
LET'S VISIT YOUR SCHOOL!

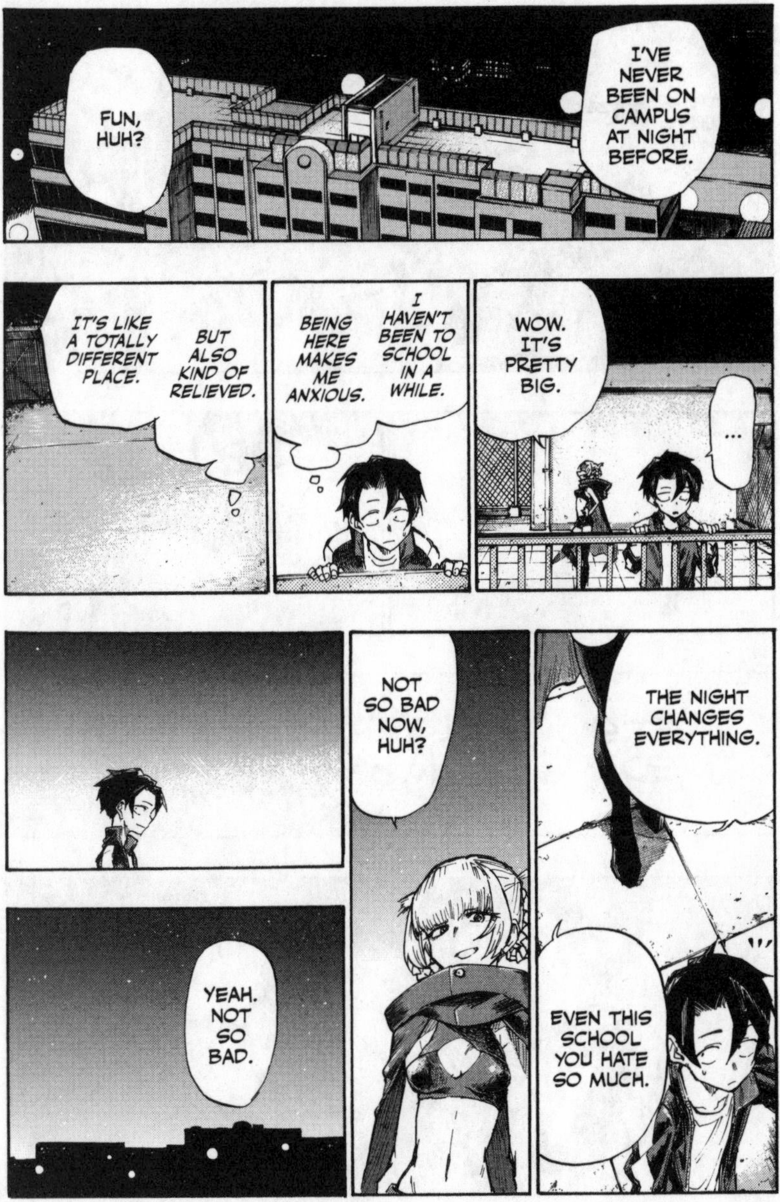

I'VE NEVER BEEN ON CAMPUS AT NIGHT BEFORE.
FUN, HUH?
WOW. IT'S PRETTY BIG.
...
I HAVEN'T BEEN TO SCHOOL IN A WHILE.
BEING HERE MAKES ME ANXIOUS.
BUT ALSO KIND OF RELIEVED.
IT'S LIKE A TOTALLY DIFFERENT PLACE.
THE NIGHT CHANGES EVERYTHING.
EVEN THIS SCHOOL YOU HATE SO MUCH.
NOT SO BAD NOW, HUH?
YEAH. NOT SO BAD.

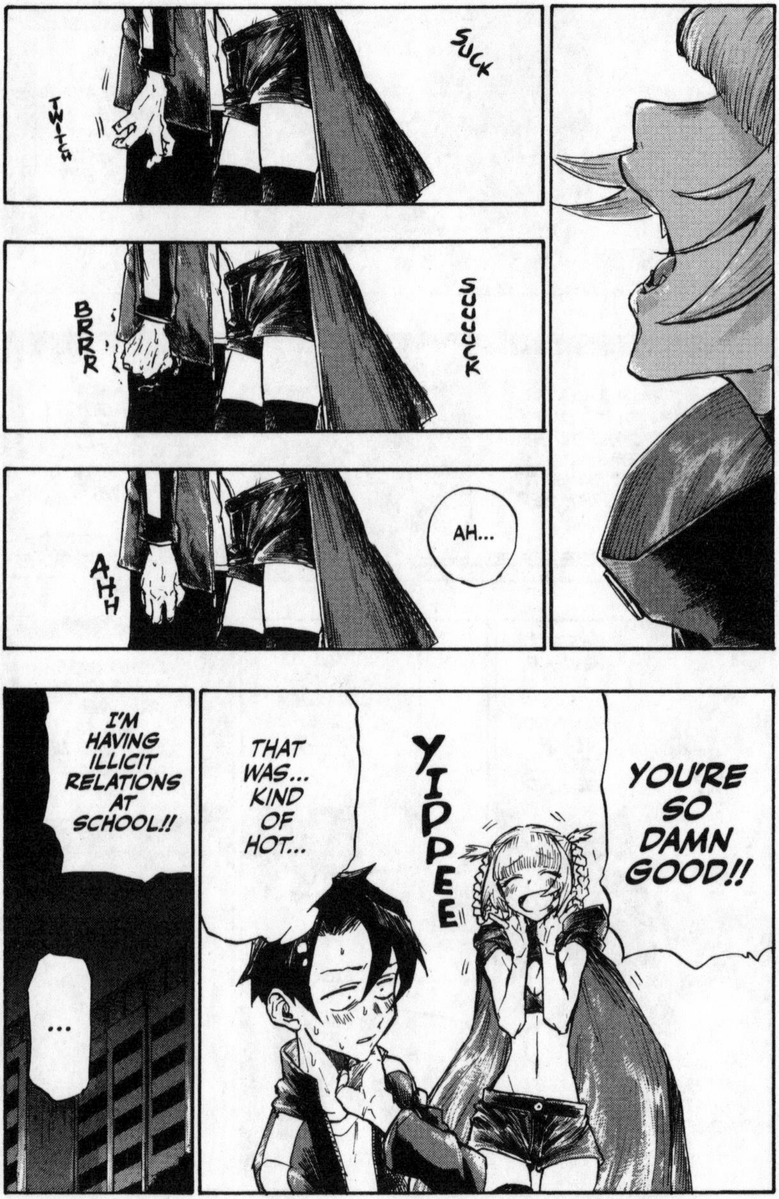
SUCK
TWITCH
SUUUCK
BRRR
AH...
AHH
YOU'RE SO DAMN GOOD!!
YIPPEE
THAT WAS... KIND OF HOT...
I'M HAVING ILLICIT RELATIONS AT SCHOOL!!
...

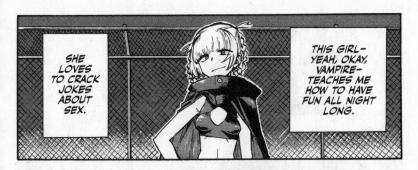

THIS GIRL— YEAH, OKAY, VAMPIRE— TEACHES ME HOW TO HAVE FUN ALL NIGHT LONG.
SHE LOVES TO CRACK JOKES ABOUT SEX.
I DON'T KNOW MUCH ABOUT FUN, NIGHT OR SEX, SO I'M KIND OF AT A DISADVANTAGE.
I HAVE A VAGUE IDEA THAT LOVE'S SUPPOSED TO BE BETWEEN EQUALS, SO I'M TRYING TO KEEP UP WITH HER.
OTHERWISE, INSTEAD OF FALLING IN LOVE, I'LL JUST END UP ADMIRING HER.
?
WHAT IS LOVE, ANYWAY?
COME TO THINK OF IT, NANAKUSA JOKES ABOUT SEX...
...BUT TALKING ABOUT LOVE FREAKS HER OUT.
SHE'S A VAMPIRE WHO DOESN'T WANT TO MAKE MORE OF HER KIND.
DOES THAT MEAN SHE'S NEVER...
...BEEN IN LOVE BEFORE?

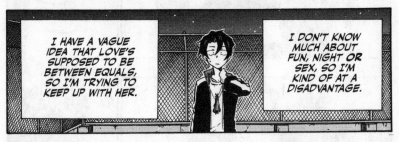

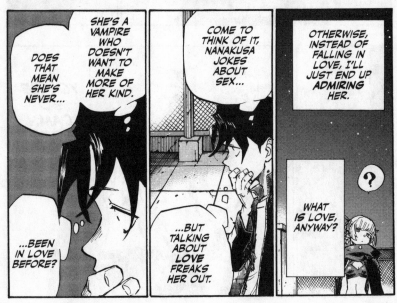

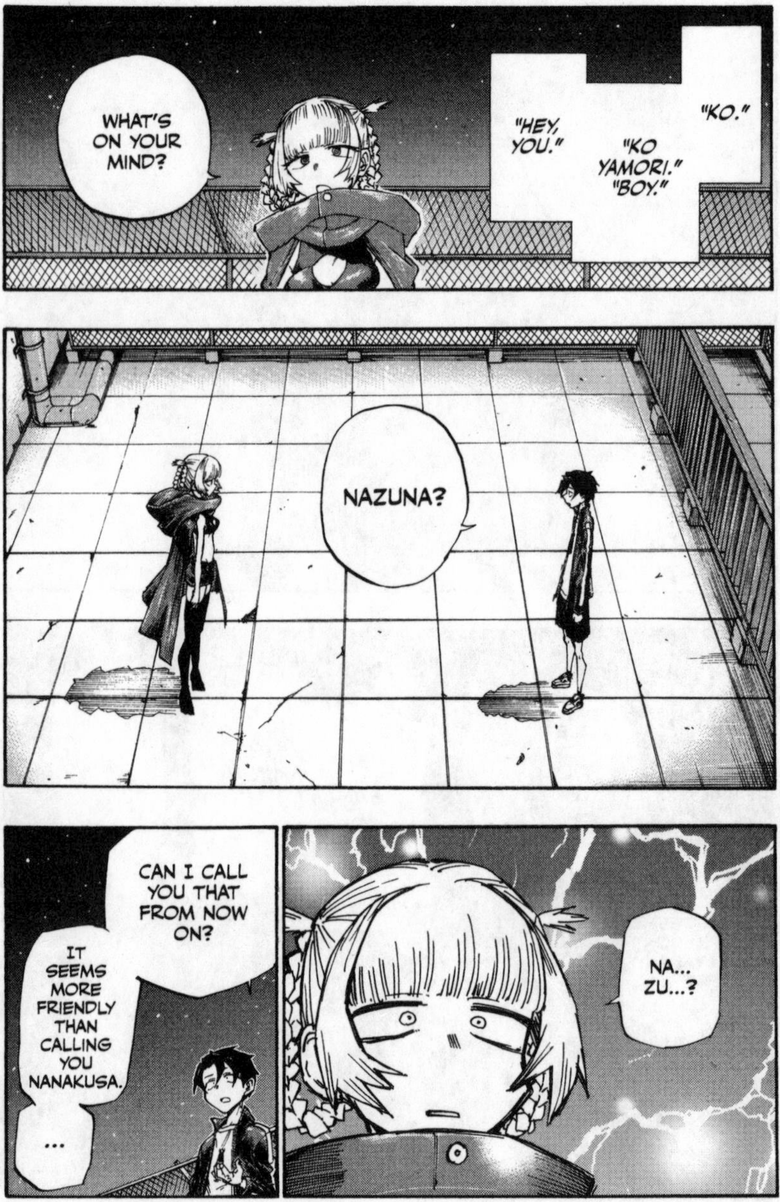
"KO."
"KO YAMORI."
"BOY."
"HEY, YOU."
WHAT'S ON YOUR MIND?
NAZUNA?
NA... ZU...?
CAN I CALL YOU THAT FROM NOW ON?
IT SEEMS MORE FRIENDLY THAN CALLING YOU NANAKUSA.
...

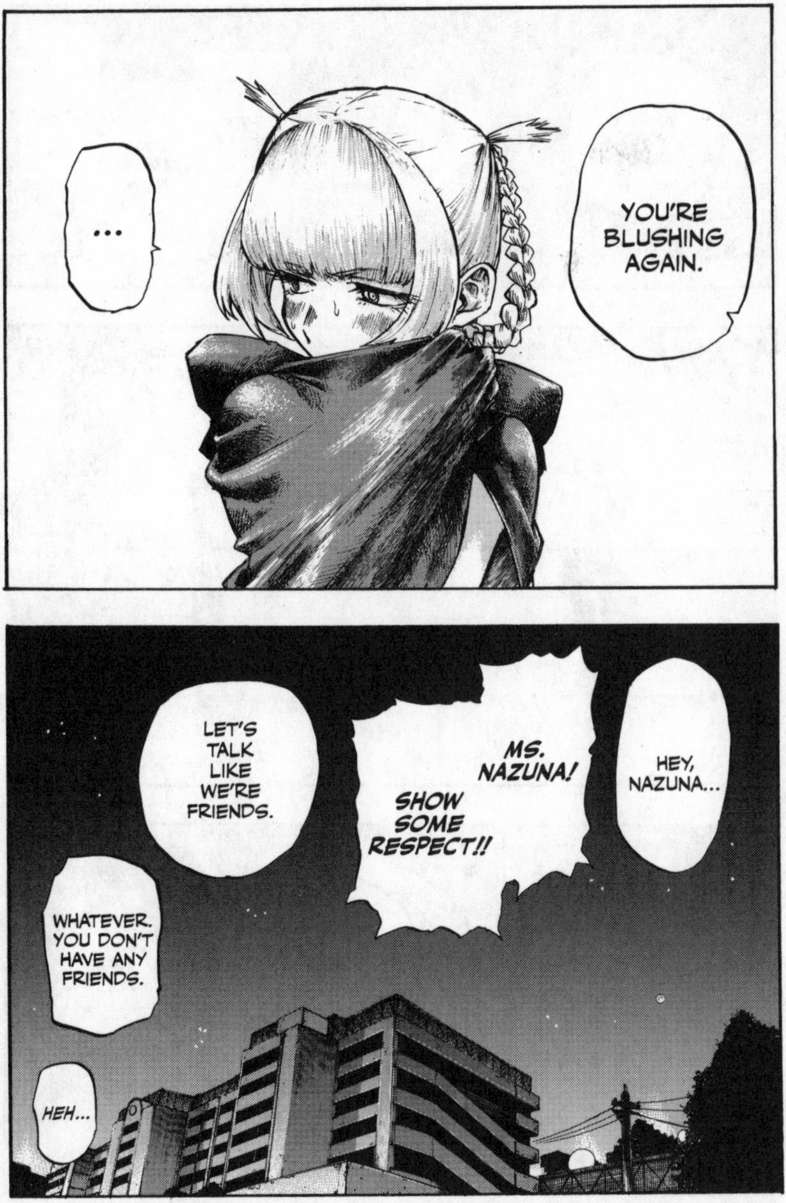
YOU'RE BLUSHING AGAIN.
...
HEY, NAZUNA...
MS. NAZUNA!
SHOW SOME RESPECT!!
LET'S TALK LIKE WE'RE FRIENDS.
WHATEVER. YOU DON'T HAVE ANY FRIENDS.
HEH...

NIGHT 4: DO YOU DO LINE?

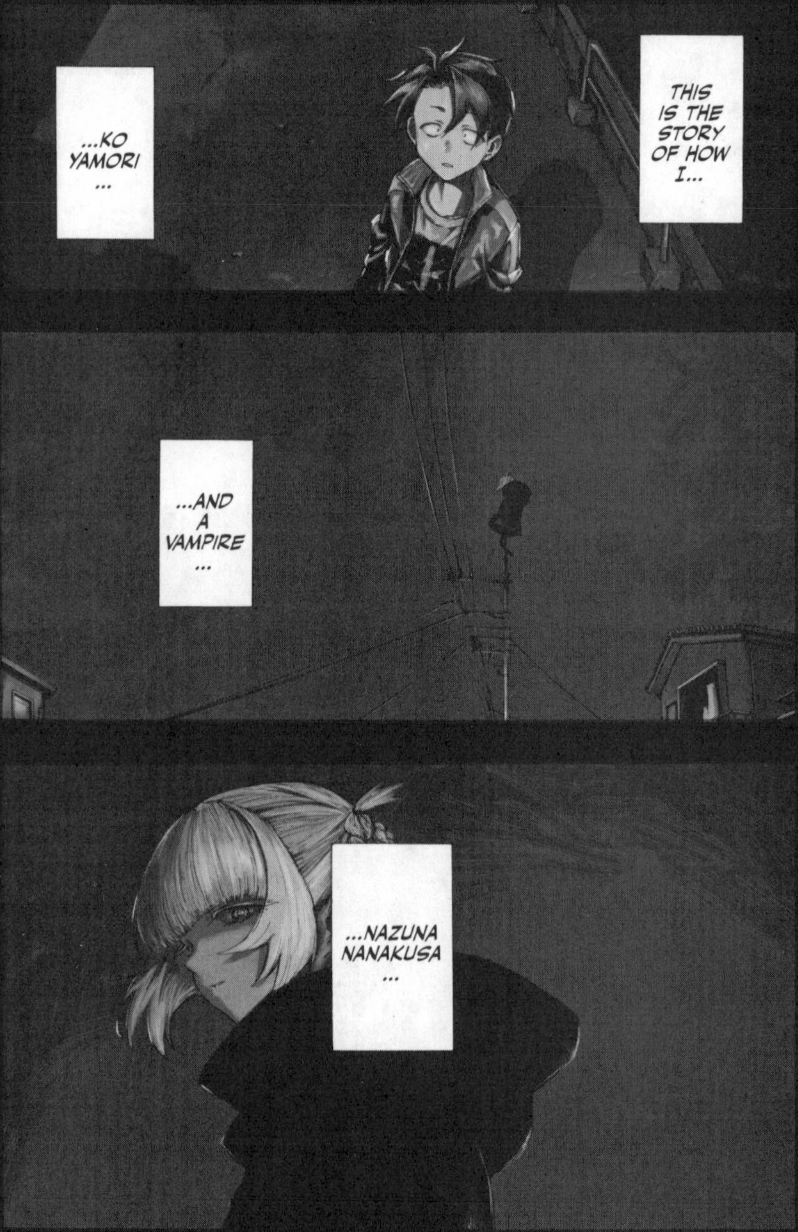
THIS IS THE STORY OF HOW I...
...KO YAMORI ...
...AND A VAMPIRE ...
...NAZUNA NANAKUSA ...

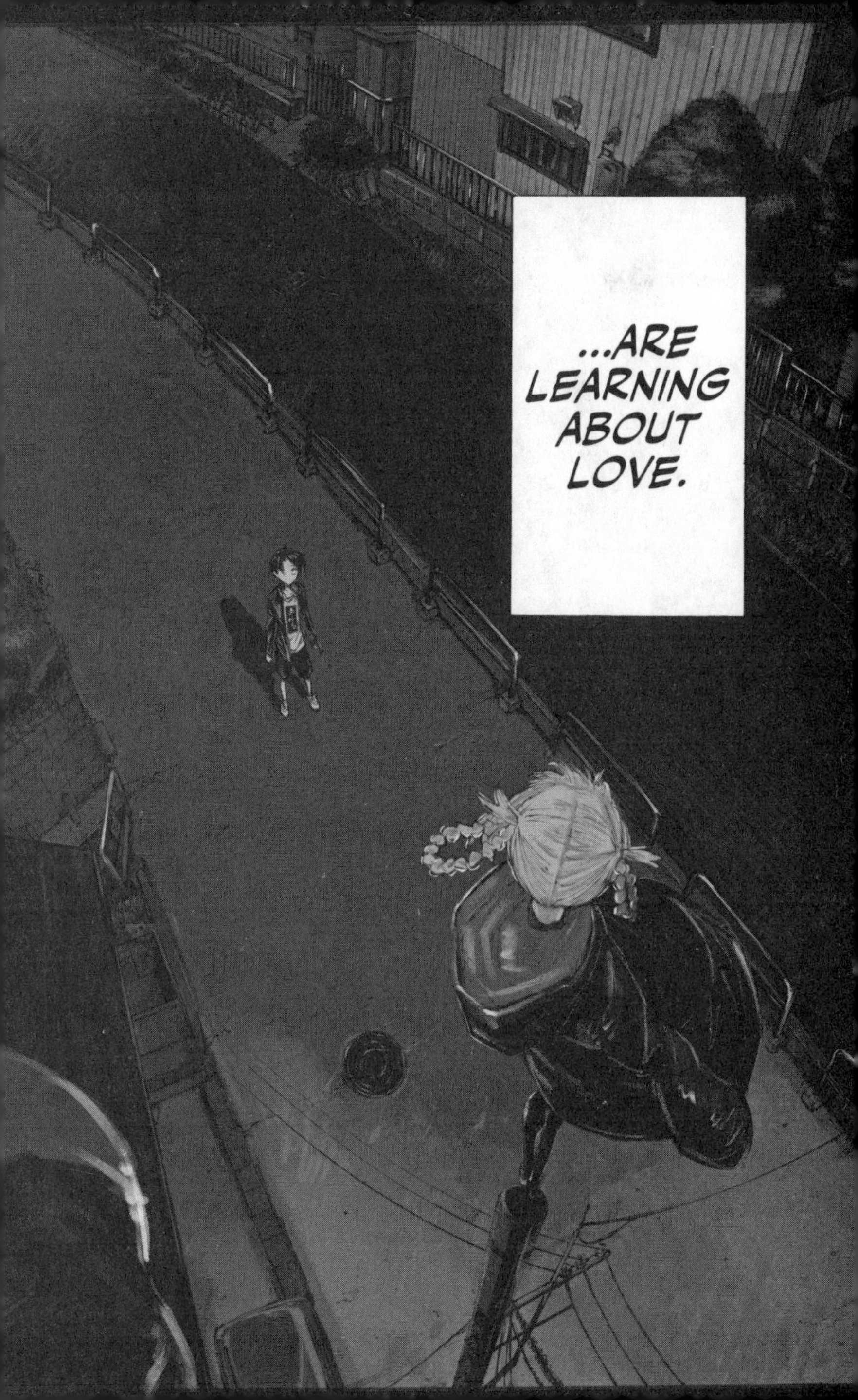
...ARE LEARNING ABOUT LOVE.

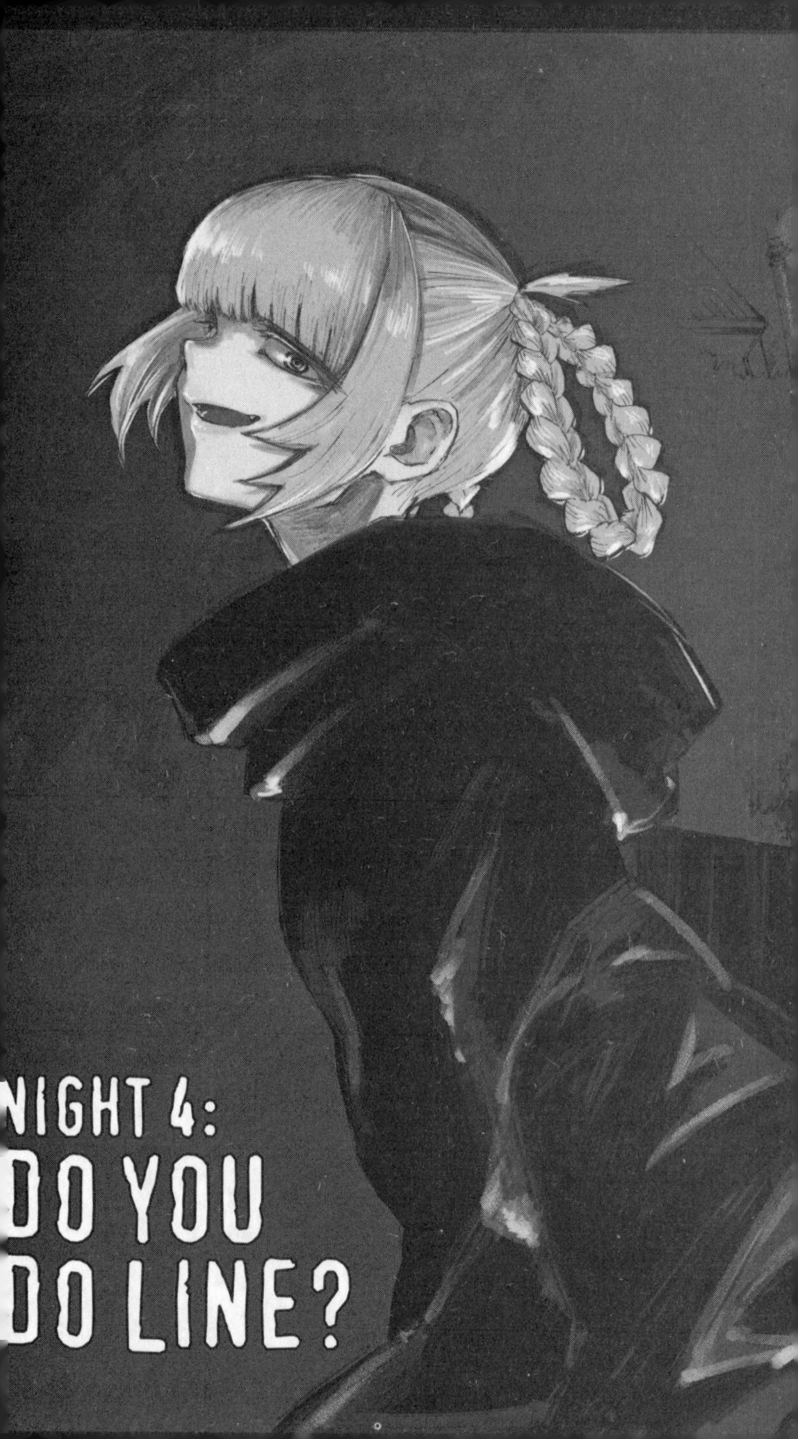
NIGHT 4:
DO YOU
DO LINE?

Call of the Night

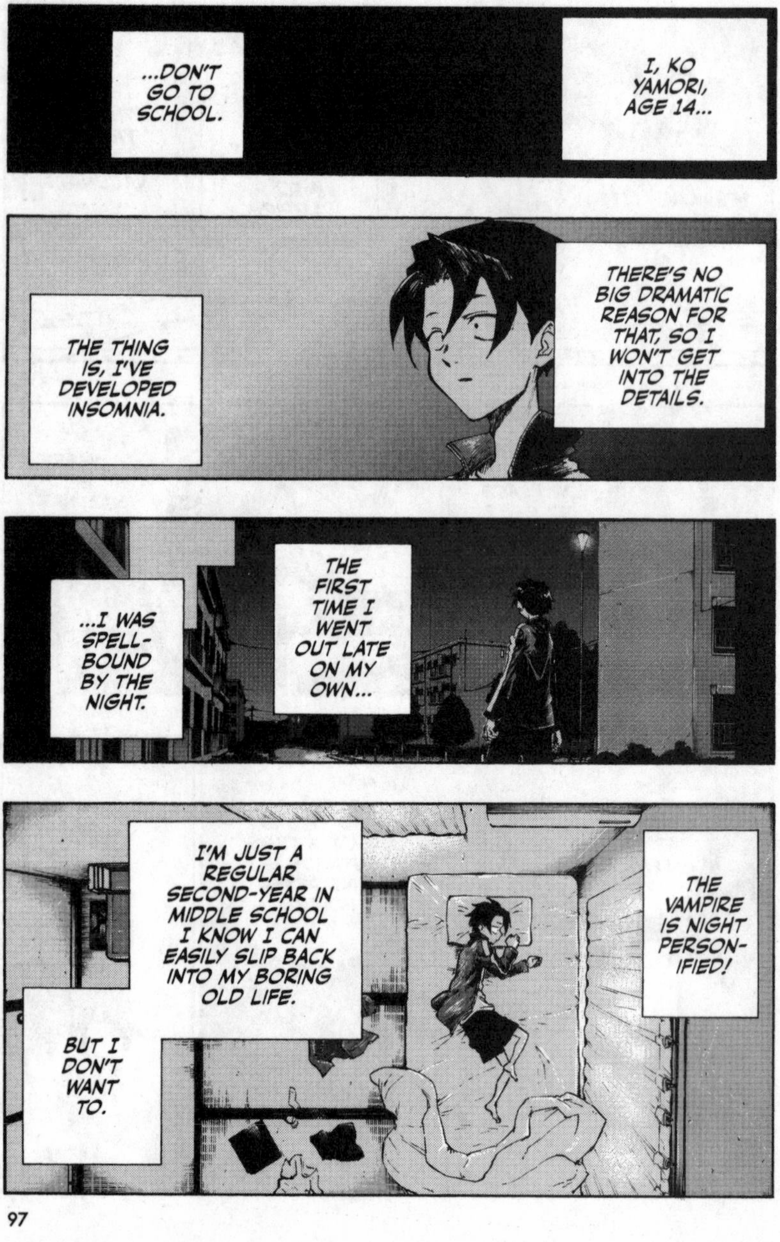
I, KO YAMORI, AGE 14...
...DON'T GO TO SCHOOL.
THERE'S NO BIG DRAMATIC REASON FOR THAT, SO I WON'T GET INTO THE DETAILS.
THE THING IS, I'VE DEVELOPED INSOMNIA.
THE FIRST TIME I WENT OUT LATE ON MY OWN...
...I WAS SPELL-BOUND BY THE NIGHT.
THE VAMPIRE IS NIGHT PERSON-IFIED!
I'M JUST A REGULAR SECOND-YEAR IN MIDDLE SCHOOL I KNOW I CAN EASILY SLIP BACK INTO MY BORING OLD LIFE.
BUT I DON'T WANT TO.

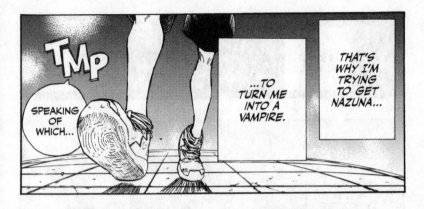

THAT'S WHY I'M TRYING TO GET NAZUNA...
...TO TURN ME INTO A VAMPIRE.
TMP
SPEAKING OF WHICH...
...WHERE IS NAZUNA?
I CAN'T FIND HER ANY-WHERE.
WE NEVER SET A TIME OR PLACE TO MEET OTHER THAN "AT NIGHT."
I'M ALL THE WAY OUT BY THE STATION.
...
SO THIS IS WHAT A TRAIN STATION IS LIKE AFTER HOURS...
NO STUDENTS OR FAMILIES.
ROWSON
EVERYTHING'S DARK EXCEPT FOR THE LIQUOR STORES.

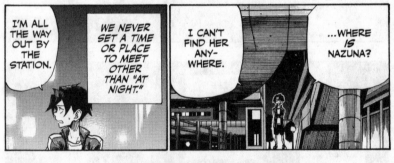

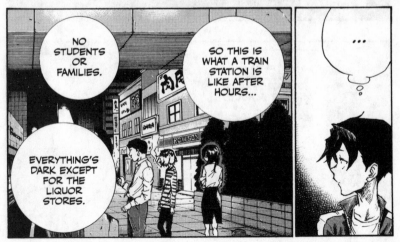

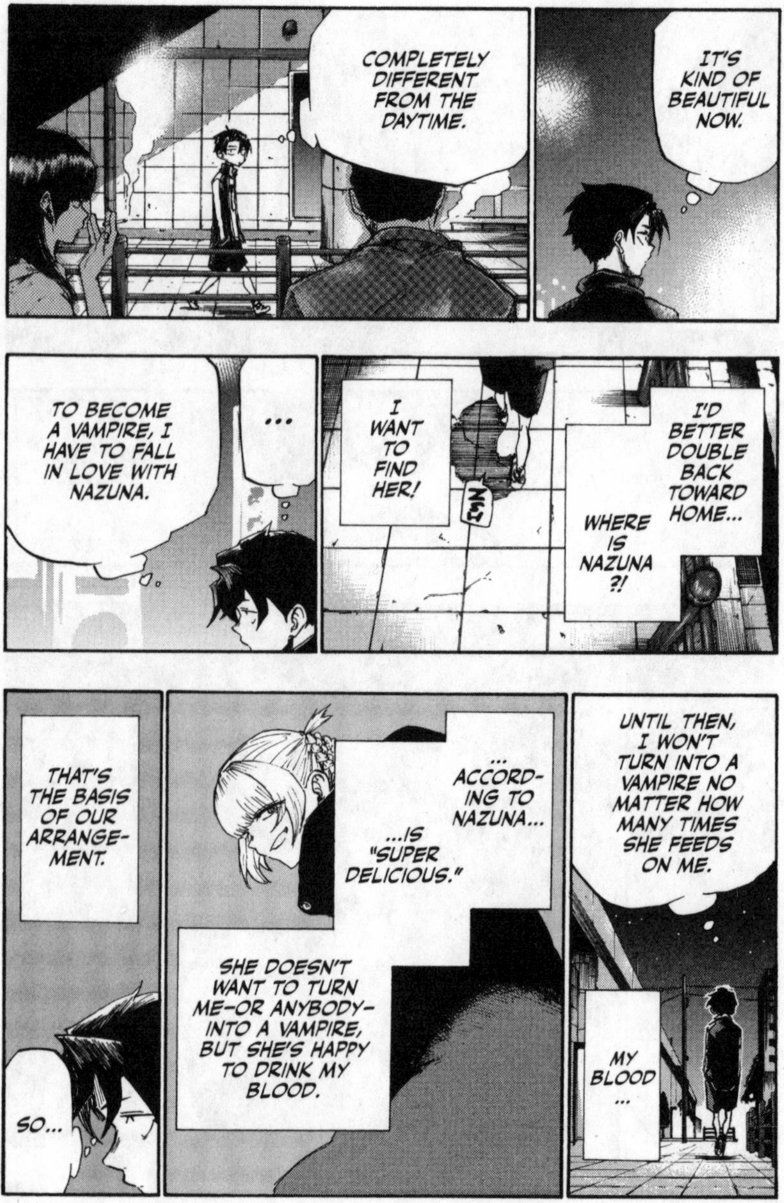
IT'S KIND OF BEAUTIFUL NOW.
COMPLETELY DIFFERENT FROM THE DAYTIME.
I'D BETTER DOUBLE BACK TOWARD HOME...
WHERE IS NAZUNA?!
I WANT TO FIND HER!
...
TO BECOME A VAMPIRE, I HAVE TO FALL IN LOVE WITH NAZUNA.
UNTIL THEN, I WON'T TURN INTO A VAMPIRE NO MATTER HOW MANY TIMES SHE FEEDS ON ME.
MY BLOOD...
...ACCORDING TO NAZUNA...
...IS "SUPER DELICIOUS."
SHE DOESN'T WANT TO TURN ME–OR ANYBODY–INTO A VAMPIRE, BUT SHE'S HAPPY TO DRINK MY BLOOD.
THAT'S THE BASIS OF OUR ARRANGEMENT.
SO...

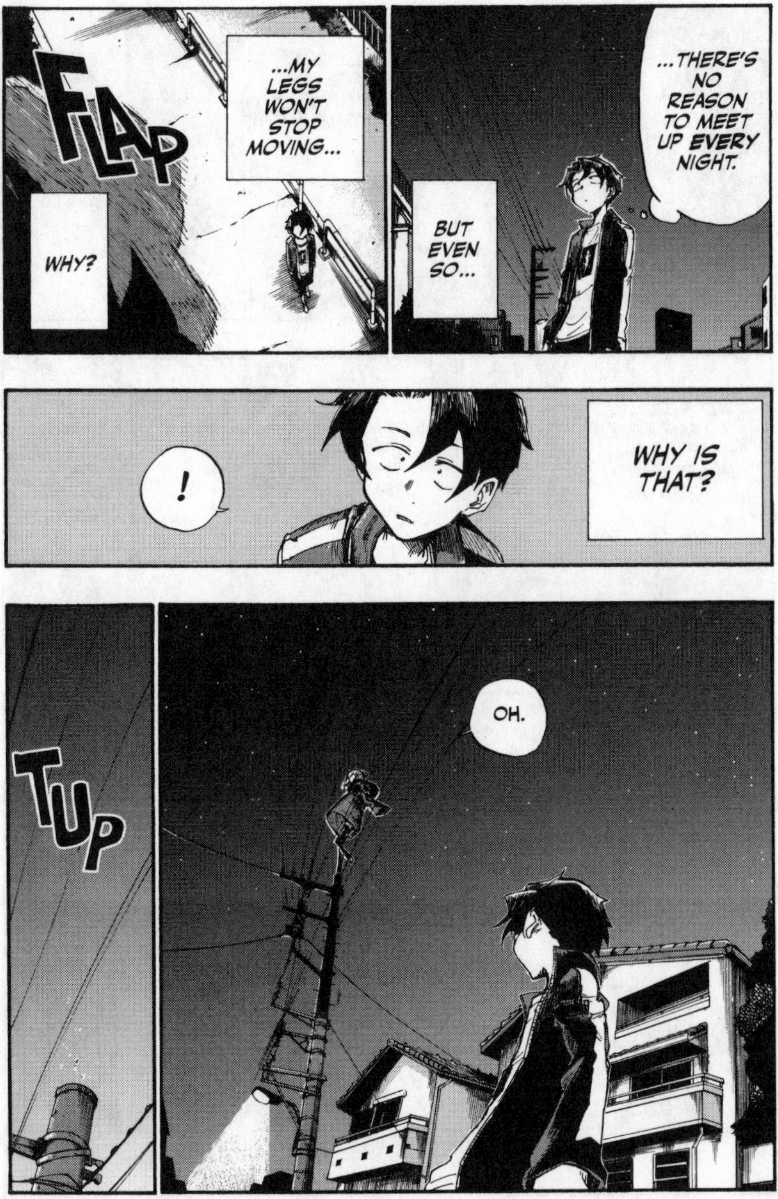
...THERE'S NO REASON TO MEET UP EVERY NIGHT.
BUT EVEN SO...
...MY LEGS WON'T STOP MOVING...
FLAP
WHY?
WHY IS THAT?
!
OH.
TUP

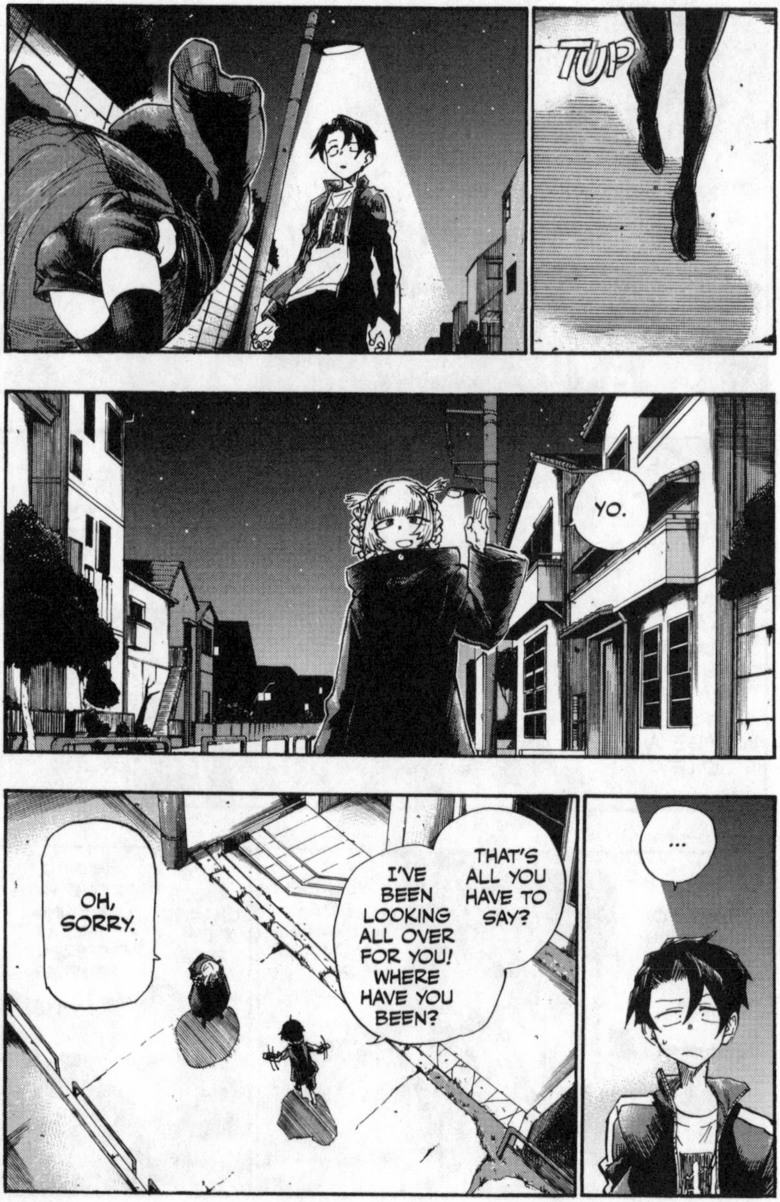
TUP
YO.
...
THAT'S ALL YOU HAVE TO SAY?
I'VE BEEN LOOKING ALL OVER FOR YOU! WHERE HAVE YOU BEEN?
OH, SORRY.

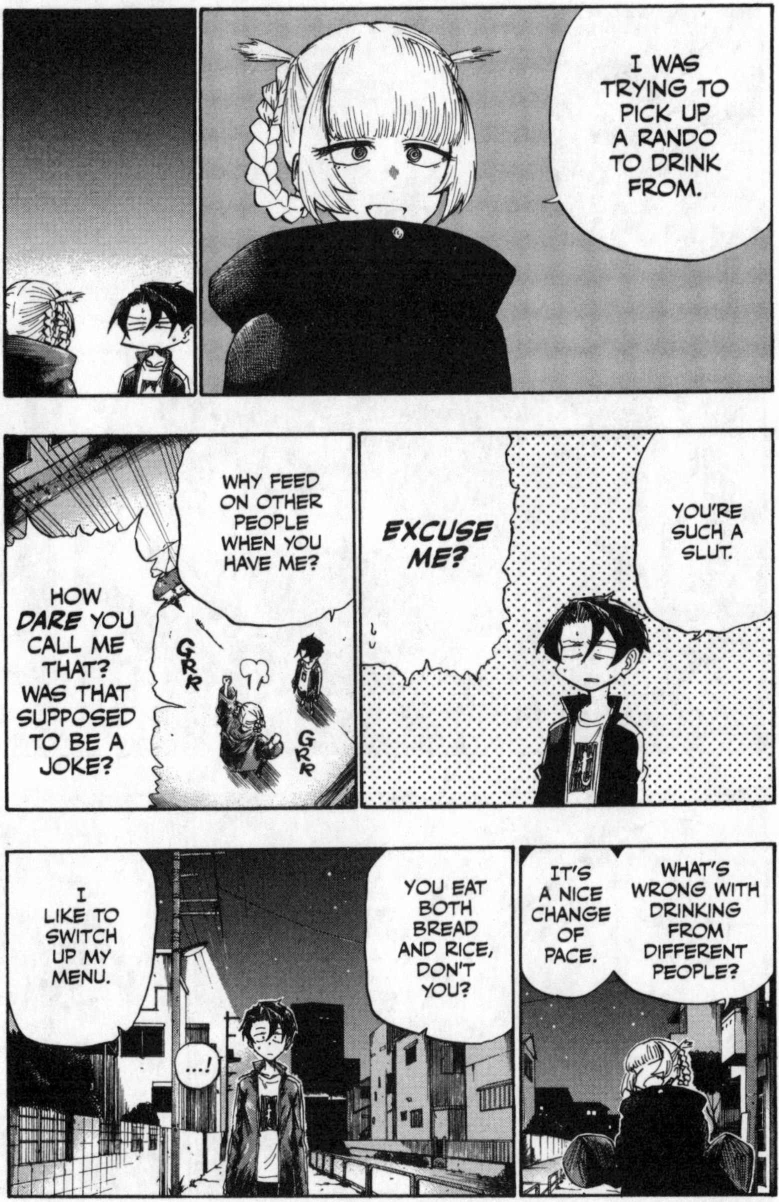
I WAS TRYING TO PICK UP A RANDO TO DRINK FROM.
YOU'RE SUCH A SLUT.
EXCUSE ME?
WHY FEED ON OTHER PEOPLE WHEN YOU HAVE ME?
HOW DARE YOU CALL ME THAT? WAS THAT SUPPOSED TO BE A JOKE?
GRR
GRR
WHAT'S WRONG WITH DRINKING FROM DIFFERENT PEOPLE?
IT'S A NICE CHANGE OF PACE.
YOU EAT BOTH BREAD AND RICE, DON'T YOU?
I LIKE TO SWITCH UP MY MENU.
...!

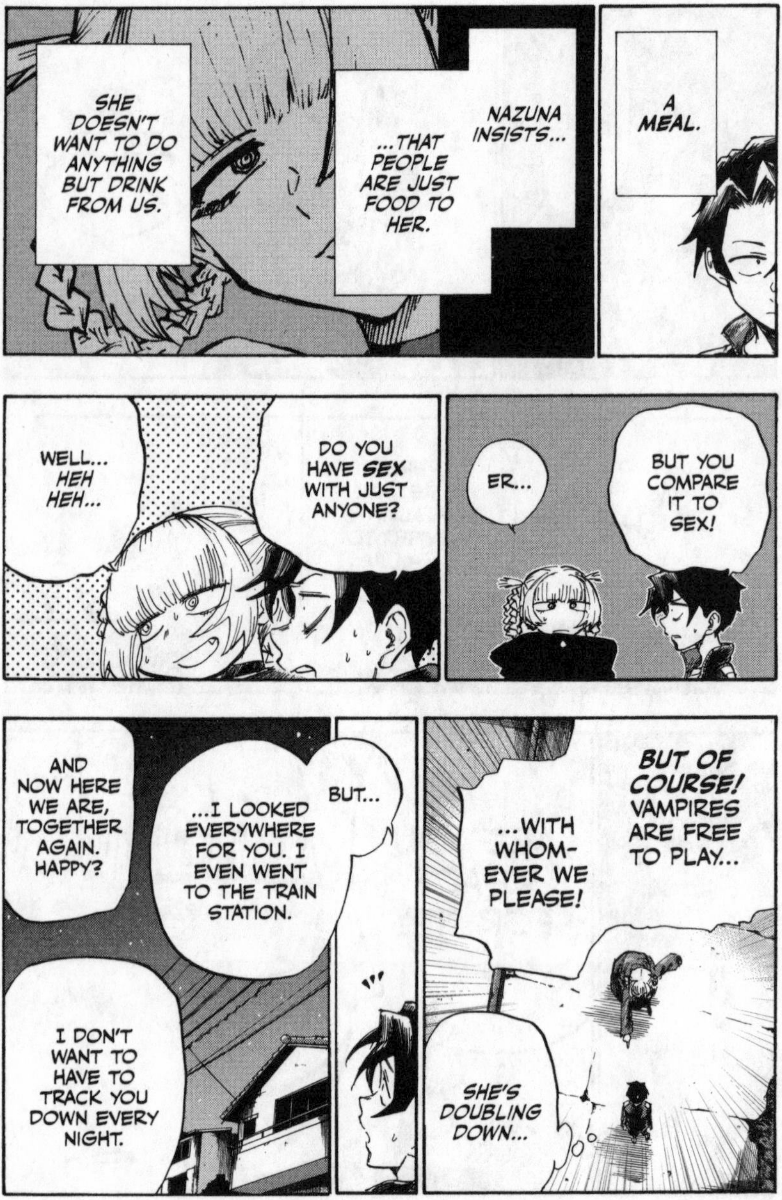
A MEAL.
NAZUNA INSISTS...
...THAT PEOPLE ARE JUST FOOD TO HER.
SHE DOESN'T WANT TO DO ANYTHING BUT DRINK FROM US.
BUT YOU COMPARE IT TO SEX!
ER...
DO YOU HAVE SEX WITH JUST ANYONE?
WELL... HEH HEH...
BUT OF COURSE! VAMPIRES ARE FREE TO PLAY...
...WITH WHOM-EVER WE PLEASE!
SHE'S DOUBLING DOWN...
BUT...
...I LOOKED EVERYWHERE FOR YOU. I EVEN WENT TO THE TRAIN STATION.
AND NOW HERE WE ARE, TOGETHER AGAIN. HAPPY?
I DON'T WANT TO HAVE TO TRACK YOU DOWN EVERY NIGHT.

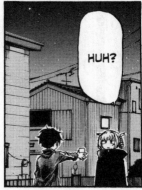

HUH?

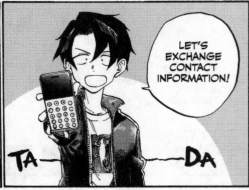

LET'S EXCHANGE CONTACT INFORMATION!

TA — DA

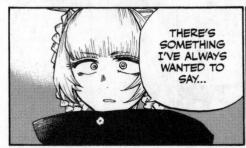

THERE'S SOMETHING I'VE ALWAYS WANTED TO SAY...

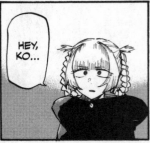

HEY, KO...

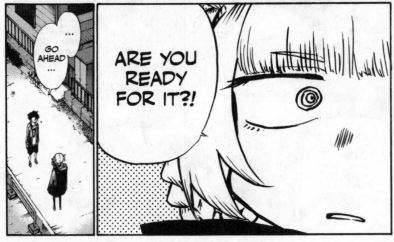

... GO AHEAD ...

ARE YOU READY FOR IT?!

104

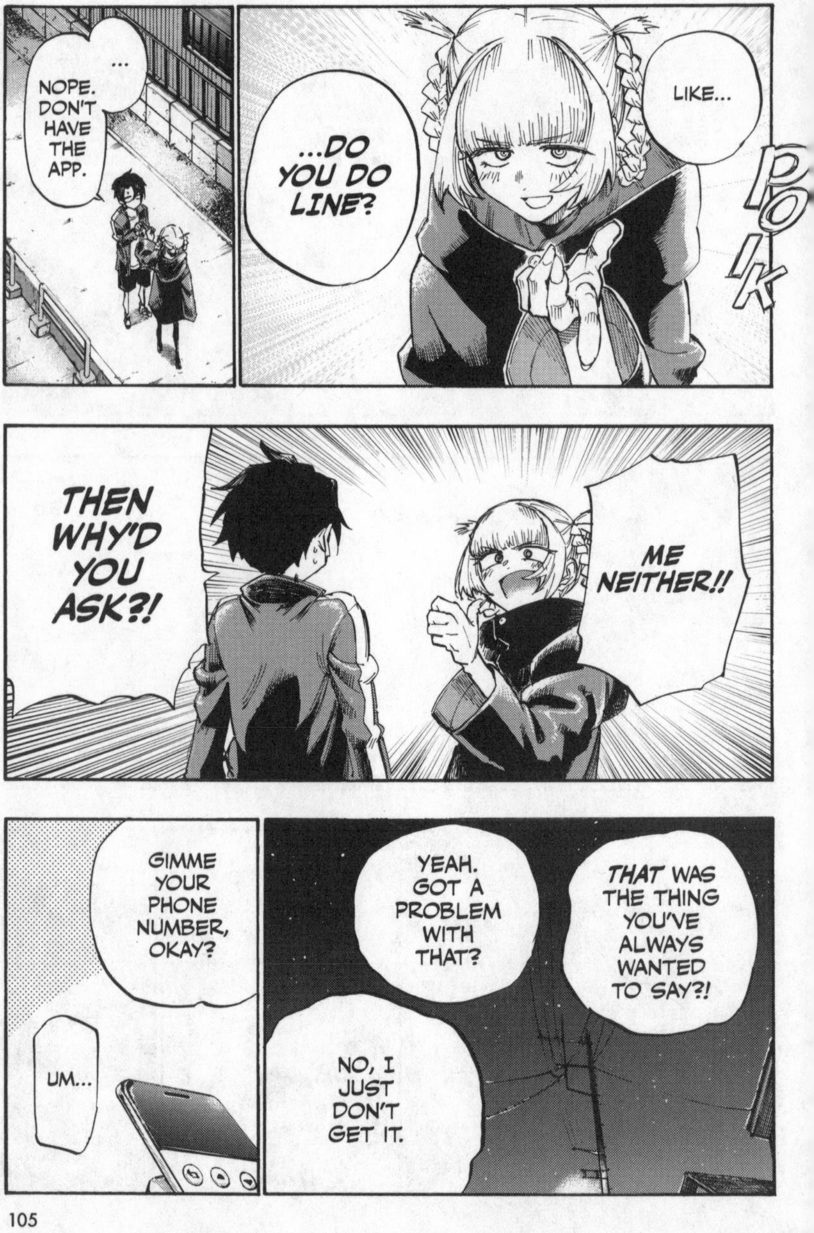
LIKE...
POIK
...DO YOU DO LINE?
...
NOPE. DON'T HAVE THE APP.
ME NEITHER!!
THEN WHY'D YOU ASK?!
THAT WAS THE THING YOU'VE ALWAYS WANTED TO SAY?!
YEAH. GOT A PROBLEM WITH THAT?
NO, I JUST DON'T GET IT.
GIMME YOUR PHONE NUMBER, OKAY?
UM...

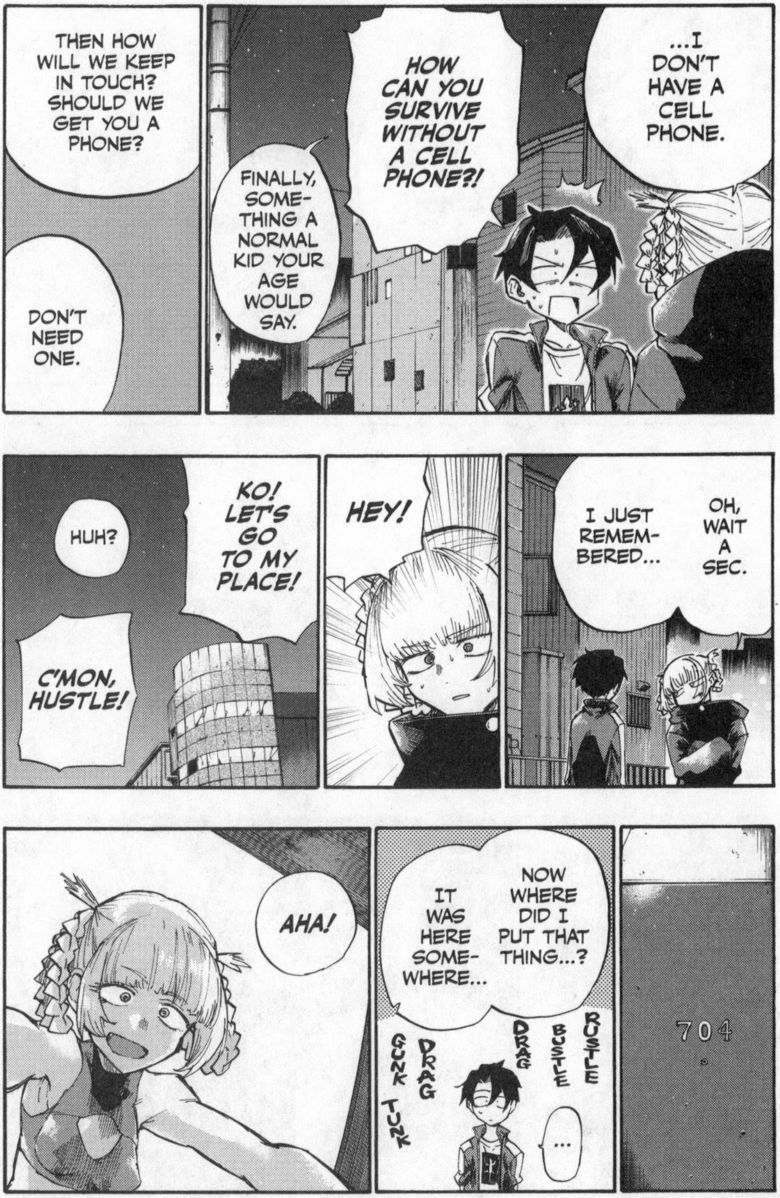
...I DON'T HAVE A CELL PHONE.
HOW CAN YOU SURVIVE WITHOUT A CELL PHONE?!
FINALLY, SOME-THING A NORMAL KID YOUR AGE WOULD SAY.
THEN HOW WILL WE KEEP IN TOUCH? SHOULD WE GET YOU A PHONE?
DON'T NEED ONE.
OH, WAIT A SEC.
I JUST REMEM-BERED...
HEY!
KO! LET'S GO TO MY PLACE!
HUH?
C'MON, HUSTLE!
704
NOW WHERE DID I PUT THAT THING...?
IT WAS HERE SOME-WHERE...
RUSTLE
BUSTLE
DRAG
DRAG
GUNK
TUNK
...
AHA!

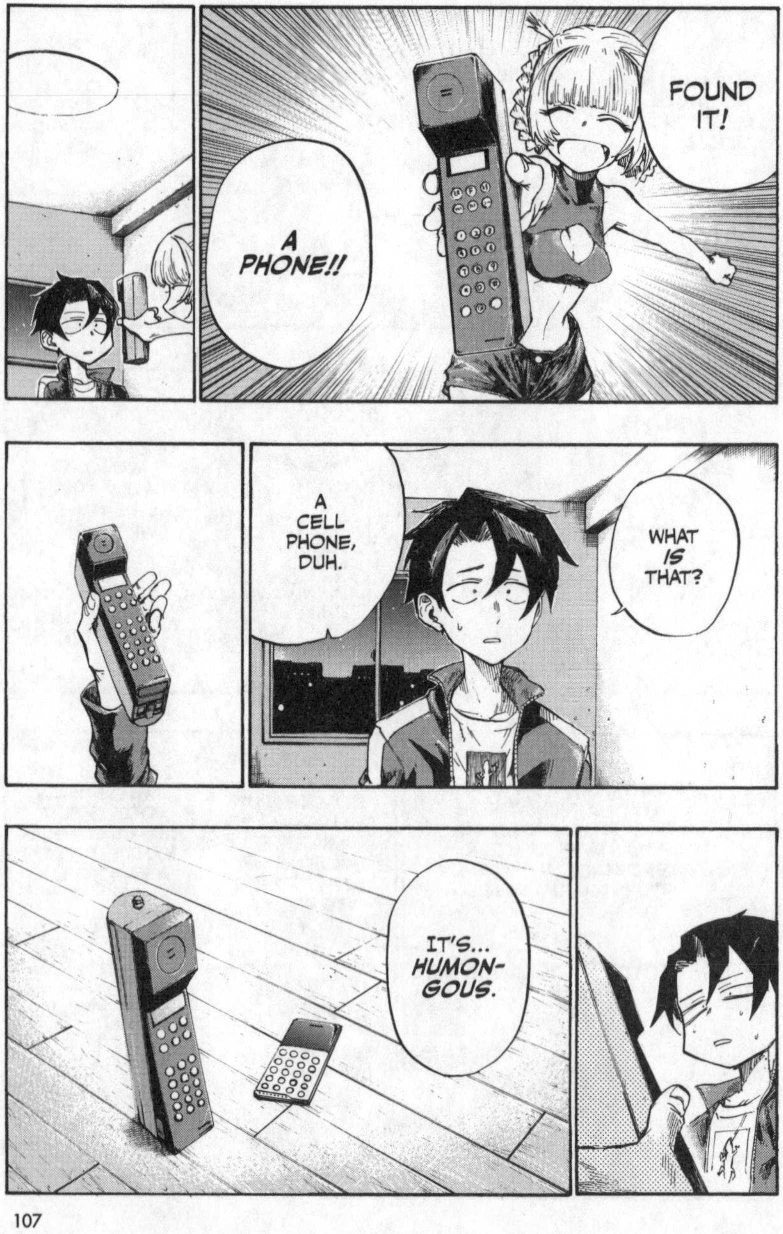
FOUND IT!
A PHONE!!
WHAT IS THAT?
A CELL PHONE, DUH.
IT'S... HUMONGOUS.

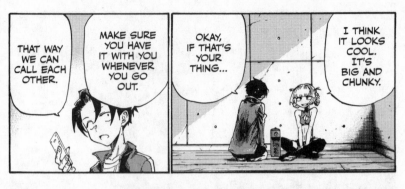

I THINK IT LOOKS COOL. IT'S BIG AND CHUNKY.
OKAY, IF THAT'S YOUR THING...
MAKE SURE YOU HAVE IT WITH YOU WHENEVER YOU GO OUT.
THAT WAY WE CAN CALL EACH OTHER.
I DON'T WANNA CARRY THIS HUGE THING WITH ME!
WHAT DO YOU THINK IT'S FOR?!
I BOUGHT THIS A WHILE BACK. THOUGHT IT MIGHT COME IN HANDY. BUT IT'S A PAIN TO LUG AROUND.
AND THEY KEEP COMING OUT WITH SMALLER MODELS. KEEPING UP WITH TRENDS PISSES ME OFF.
There are even mini ones now!
I... SEE...
I DON'T NEED A PHONE. ANYWAY, I HEAR THESE DAYS RETAILERS TAKE ADVANTAGE OF YOUR IGNORANCE AND LOCK YOU INTO BUM DEALS.
WHERE DOES SHE LEARN THIS STUFF?

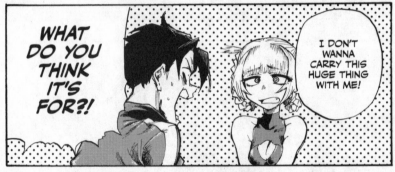

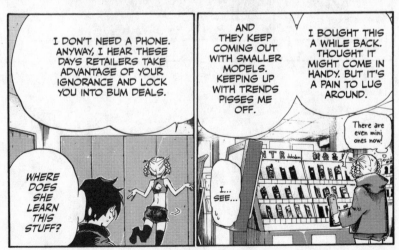

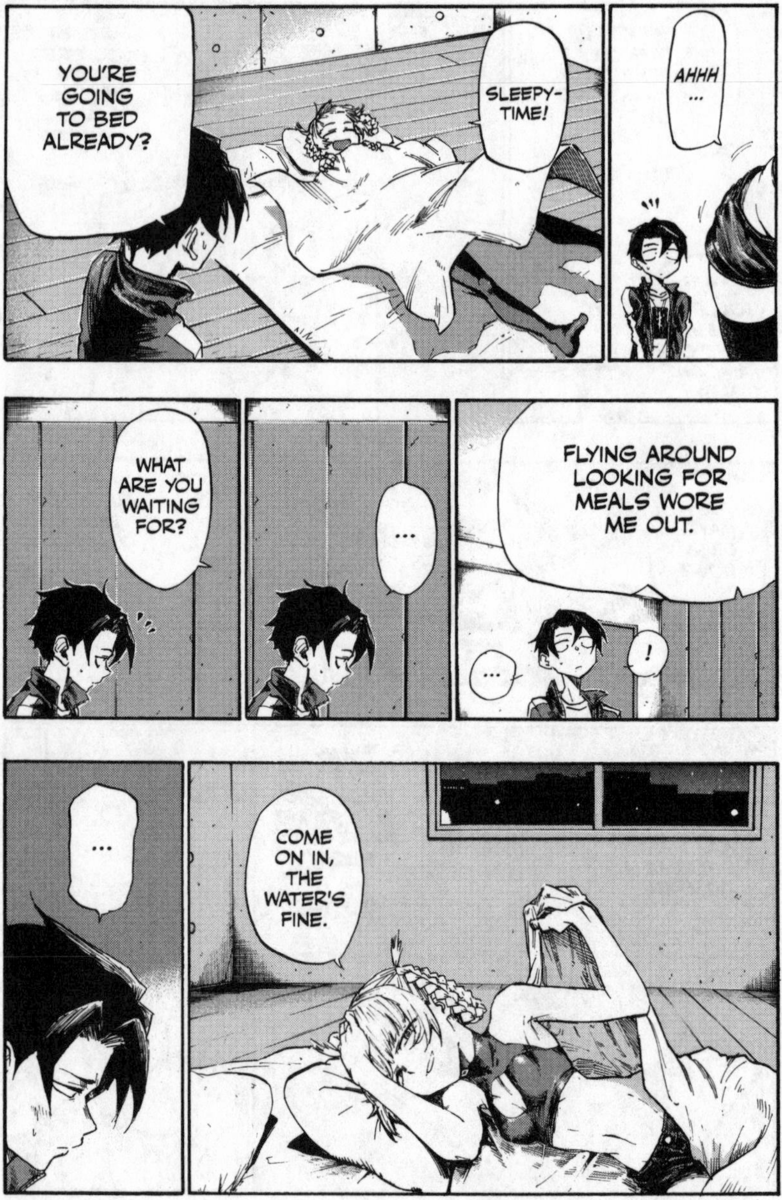
AHHH ...
SLEEPY-TIME!
YOU'RE GOING TO BED ALREADY?
FLYING AROUND LOOKING FOR MEALS WORE ME OUT.
!
...
...
WHAT ARE YOU WAITING FOR?
COME ON IN, THE WATER'S FINE.
...

AREN'T YOU TIRED FROM WALKING ALL NIGHT?
AND SLEEPY?
A LITTLE...
THOUGHT SO.
WHAT'S UP WITH ME? I DON'T THINK I'M IN LOVE WITH HER YET...
...BUT WOULDN'T A REGULAR PERSON BE PANICKING NOW?
I'M CUDDLING WITH A VAMPIRE.
THERE'S NO WAY THIS IS NORMAL.
HEY.
HEY, KO.
KOOO...
MAY I DRINK NOW?
...
NO.
HUH?!
WHY NOT? YOU PROMISED TO LET ME DRINK YOUR BLOOD!
LIAR!
DON'T YOU WANNA BECOME A VAMPIRE?
...

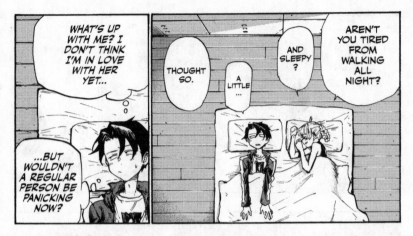

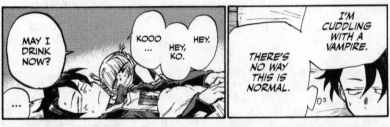

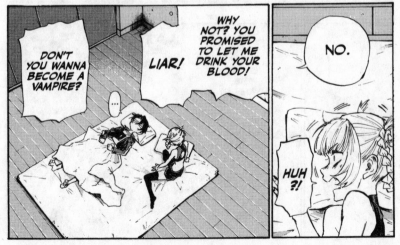

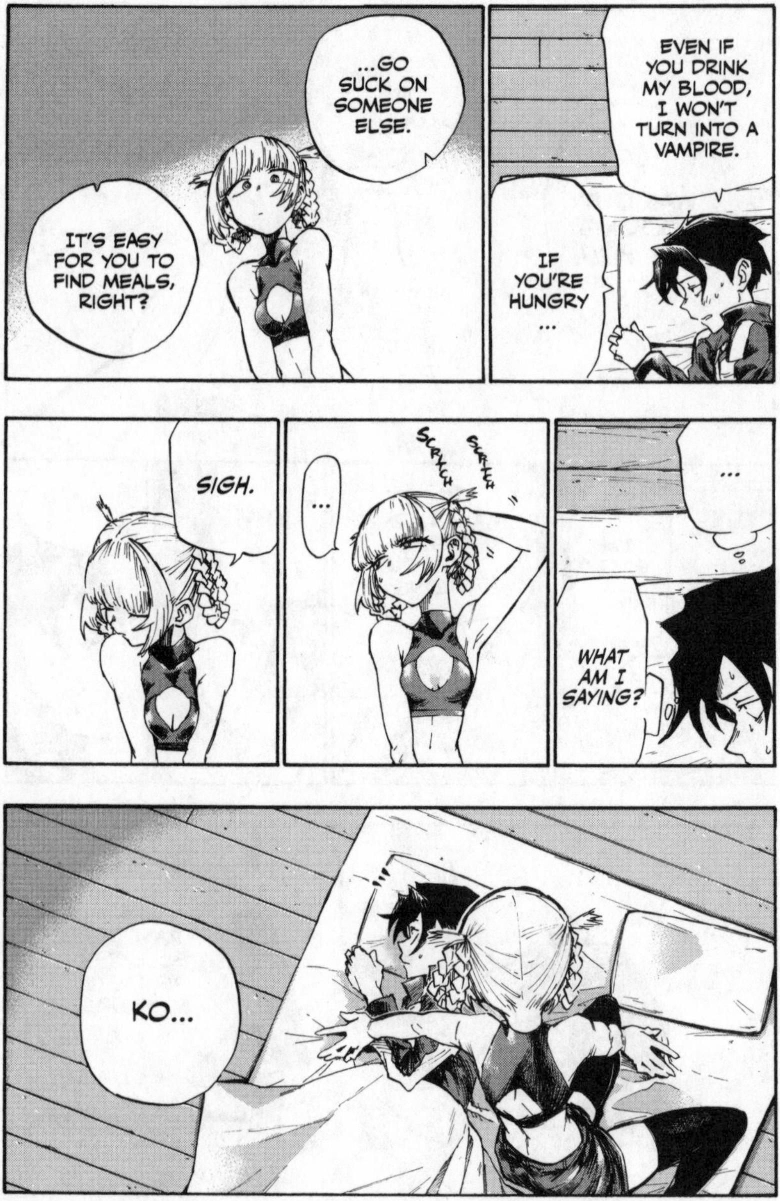
EVEN IF YOU DRINK MY BLOOD, I WON'T TURN INTO A VAMPIRE.
IF YOU'RE HUNGRY...
...GO SUCK ON SOMEONE ELSE.
IT'S EASY FOR YOU TO FIND MEALS, RIGHT?
...
WHAT AM I SAYING?
SCRTCH SCRTCH
...
SIGH.
KO...

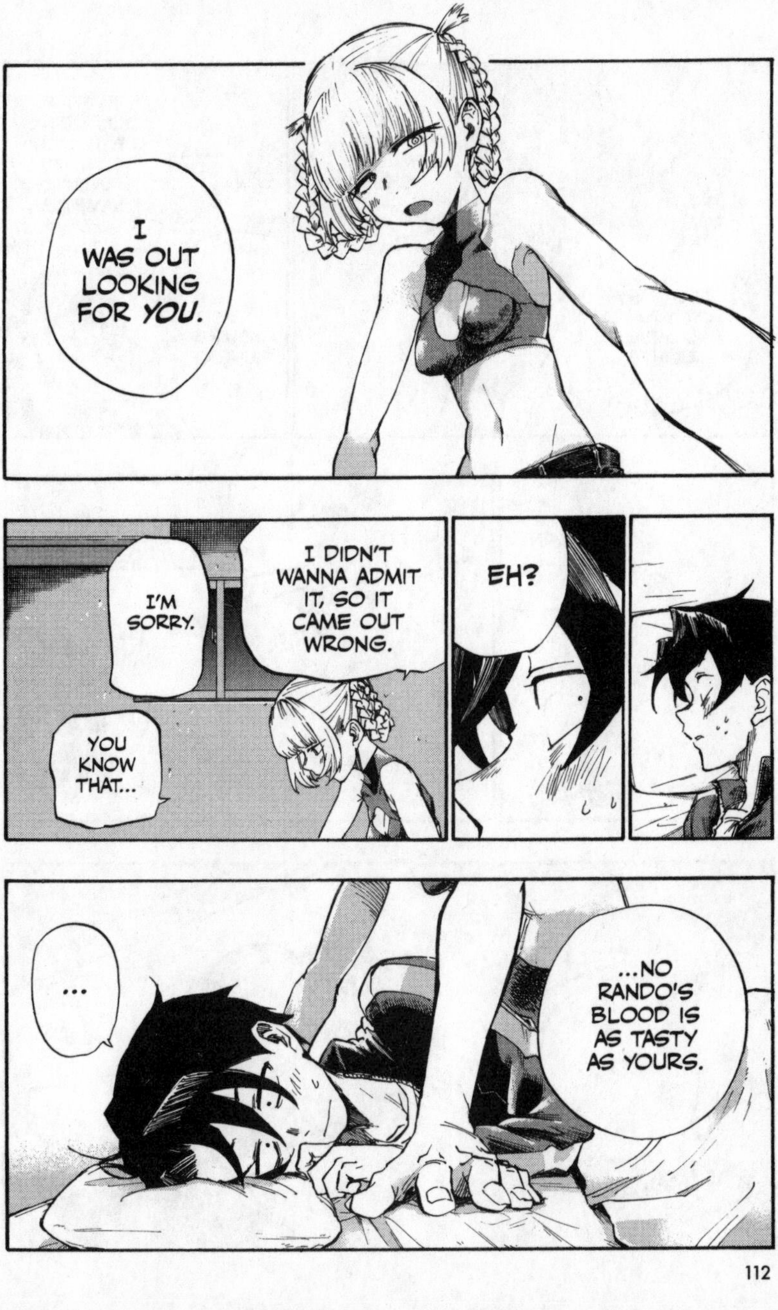
I WAS OUT LOOKING FOR YOU.
EH?
I DIDN'T WANNA ADMIT IT, SO IT CAME OUT WRONG.
I'M SORRY.
YOU KNOW THAT...
...NO RANDO'S BLOOD IS AS TASTY AS YOURS.
...

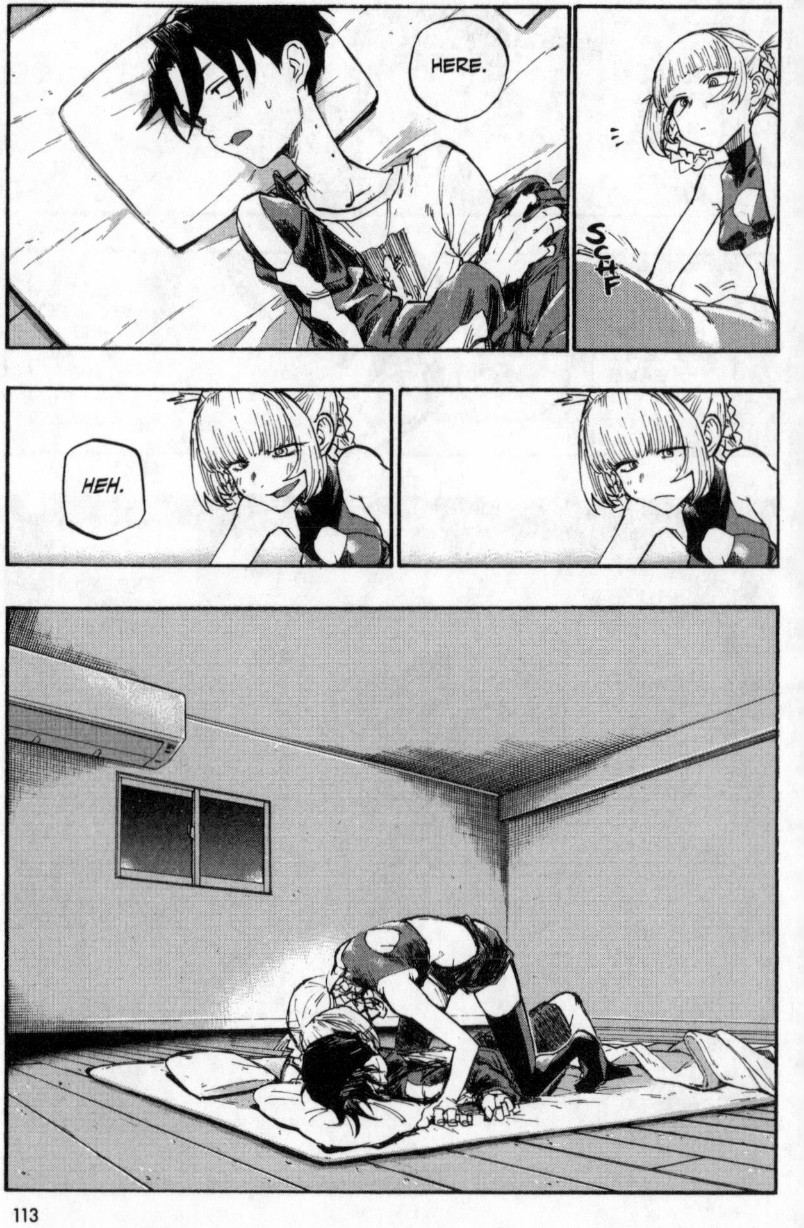
SCHF
HERE.
HEH.

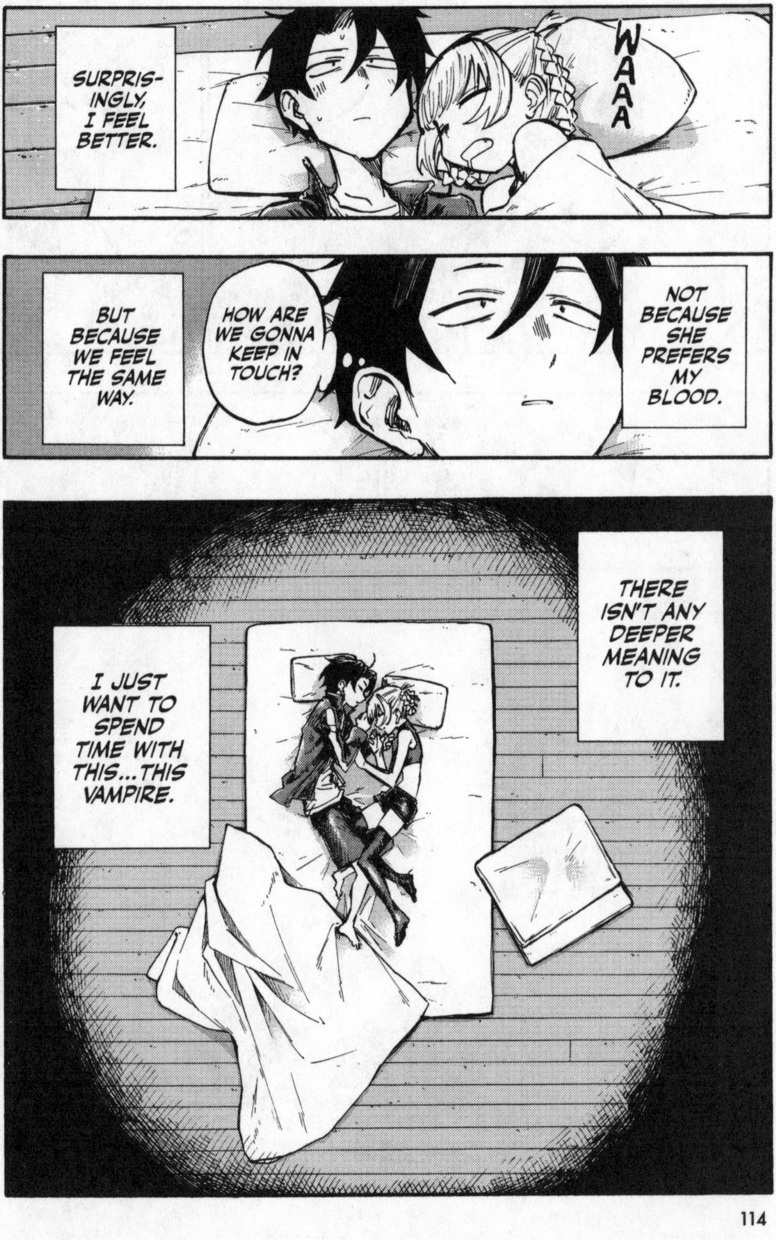
WAAA
SURPRISINGLY, I FEEL BETTER.
NOT BECAUSE SHE PREFERS MY BLOOD.
HOW ARE WE GONNA KEEP IN TOUCH?
BUT BECAUSE WE FEEL THE SAME WAY.
THERE ISN'T ANY DEEPER MEANING TO IT.
I JUST WANT TO SPEND TIME WITH THIS...THIS VAMPIRE.

NIGHT 5: GOOD EVENING, SADNESS

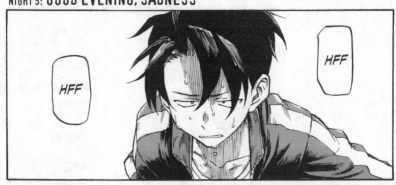

HFF
HFF
ONCE AGAIN ...
...I CAN'T FIND NAZUNA.

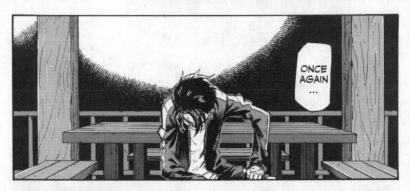

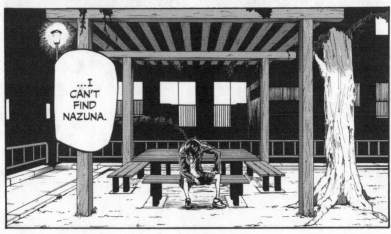

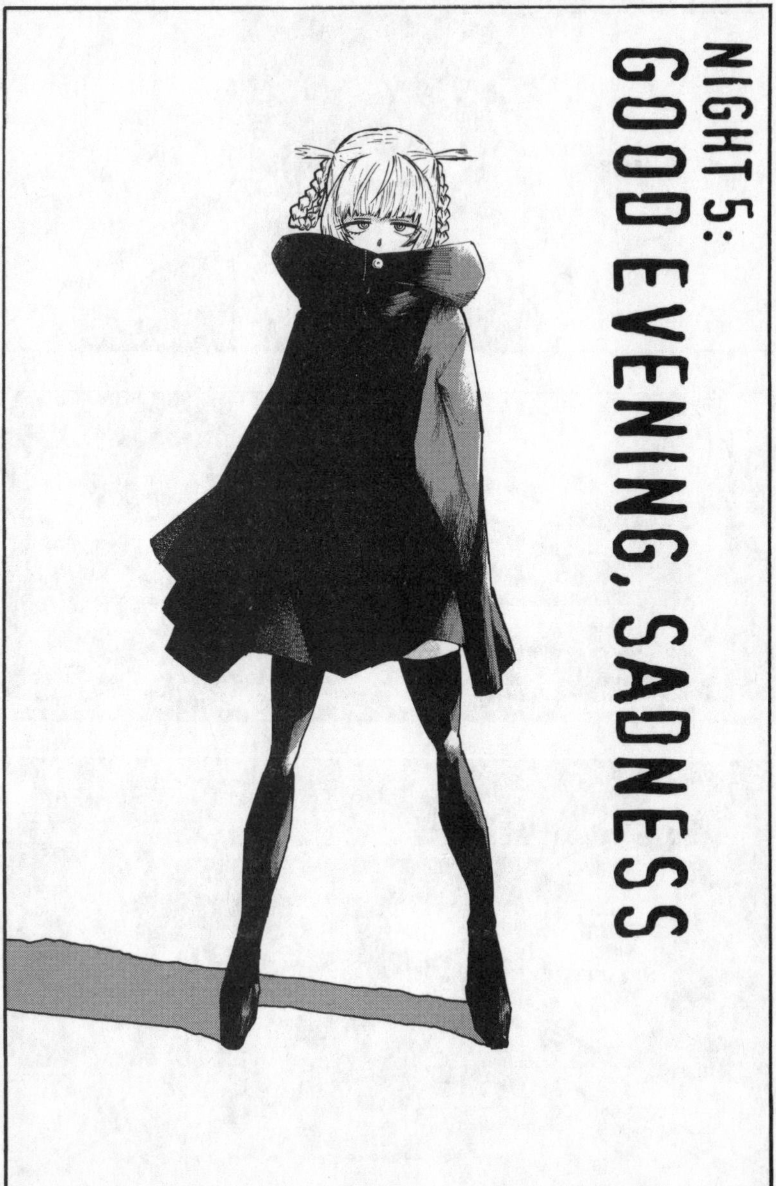
NIGHT 5:
GOOD EVENING, SADNESS

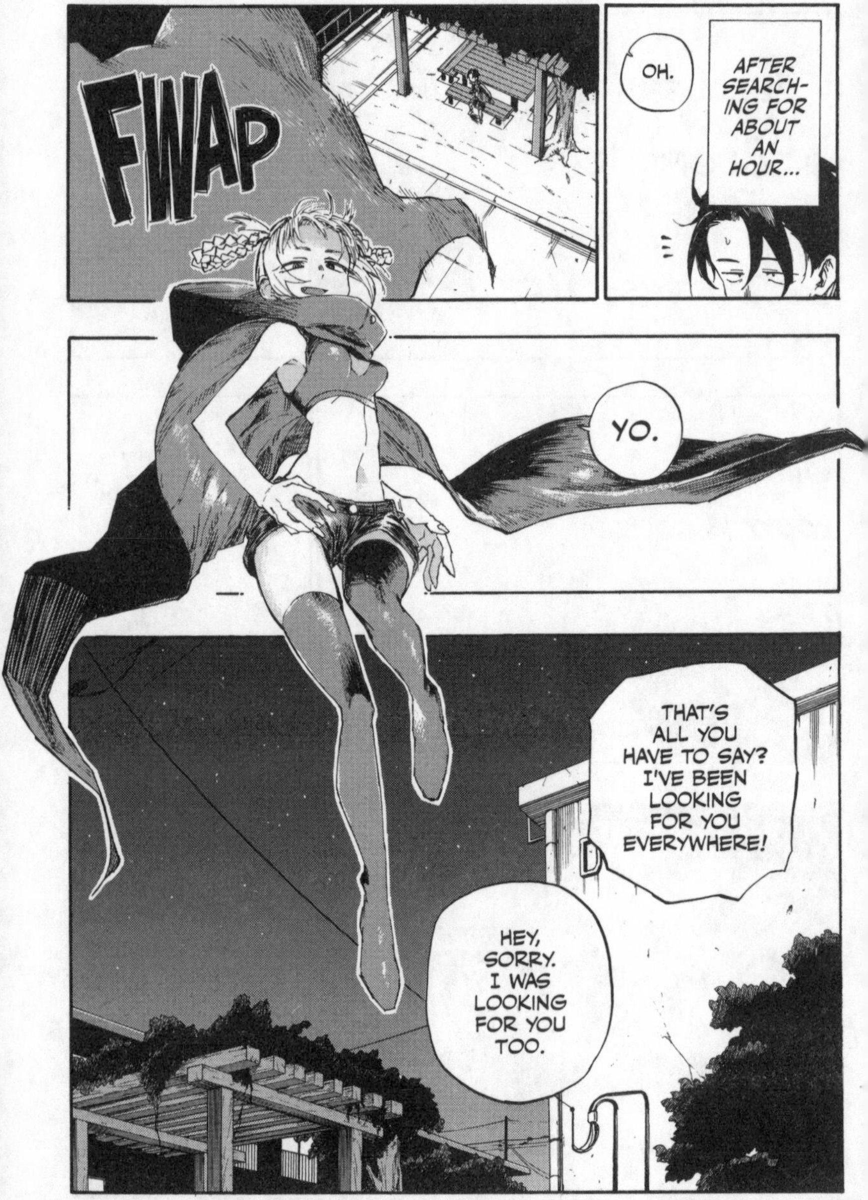
AFTER SEARCHING FOR ABOUT AN HOUR...
OH.
FWAP
YO.
THAT'S ALL YOU HAVE TO SAY? I'VE BEEN LOOKING FOR YOU EVERYWHERE!
HEY, SORRY. I WAS LOOKING FOR YOU TOO.

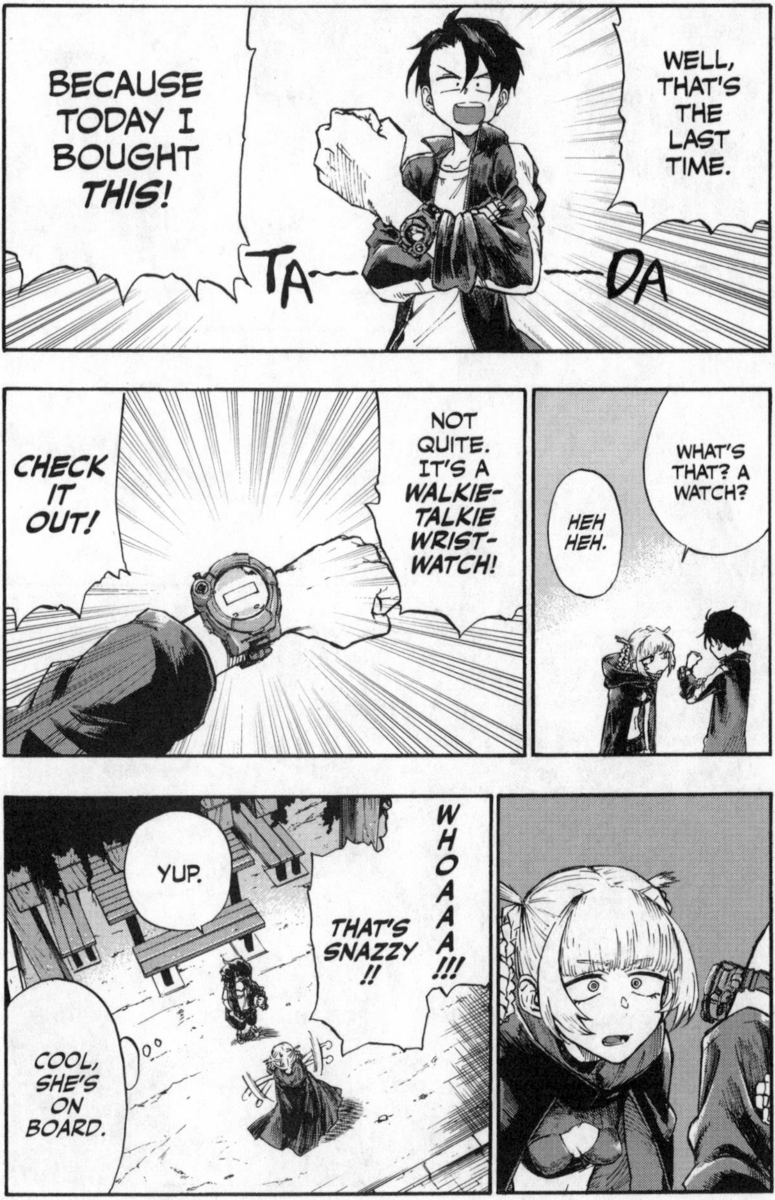
WELL, THAT'S THE LAST TIME.
BECAUSE TODAY I BOUGHT *THIS!*
TA——DA
WHAT'S THAT? A WATCH?
HEH HEH.
NOT QUITE. IT'S A *WALKIE-TALKIE WRIST-WATCH!*
CHECK IT OUT!
WHOAAAA!!!
THAT'S SNAZZY!!
YUP.
COOL, SHE'S ON BOARD.

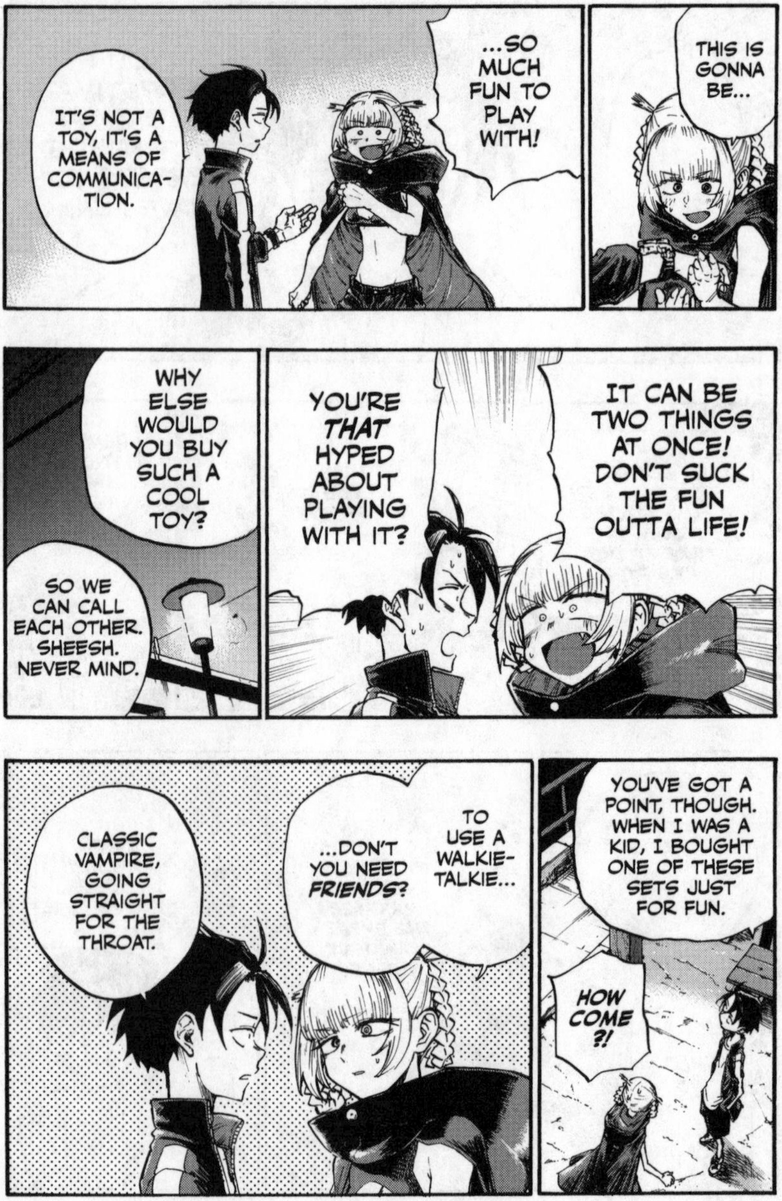
THIS IS GONNA BE...
...SO MUCH FUN TO PLAY WITH!
IT'S NOT A TOY, IT'S A MEANS OF COMMUNICATION.
IT CAN BE TWO THINGS AT ONCE! DON'T SUCK THE FUN OUTTA LIFE!
YOU'RE *THAT* HYPED ABOUT PLAYING WITH IT?
WHY ELSE WOULD YOU BUY SUCH A COOL TOY?
SO WE CAN CALL EACH OTHER. SHEESH. NEVER MIND.
YOU'VE GOT A POINT, THOUGH. WHEN I WAS A KID, I BOUGHT ONE OF THESE SETS JUST FOR FUN.
HOW COME?!
TO USE A WALKIE-TALKIE...
...DON'T YOU NEED *FRIENDS?*
CLASSIC VAMPIRE, GOING STRAIGHT FOR THE THROAT.

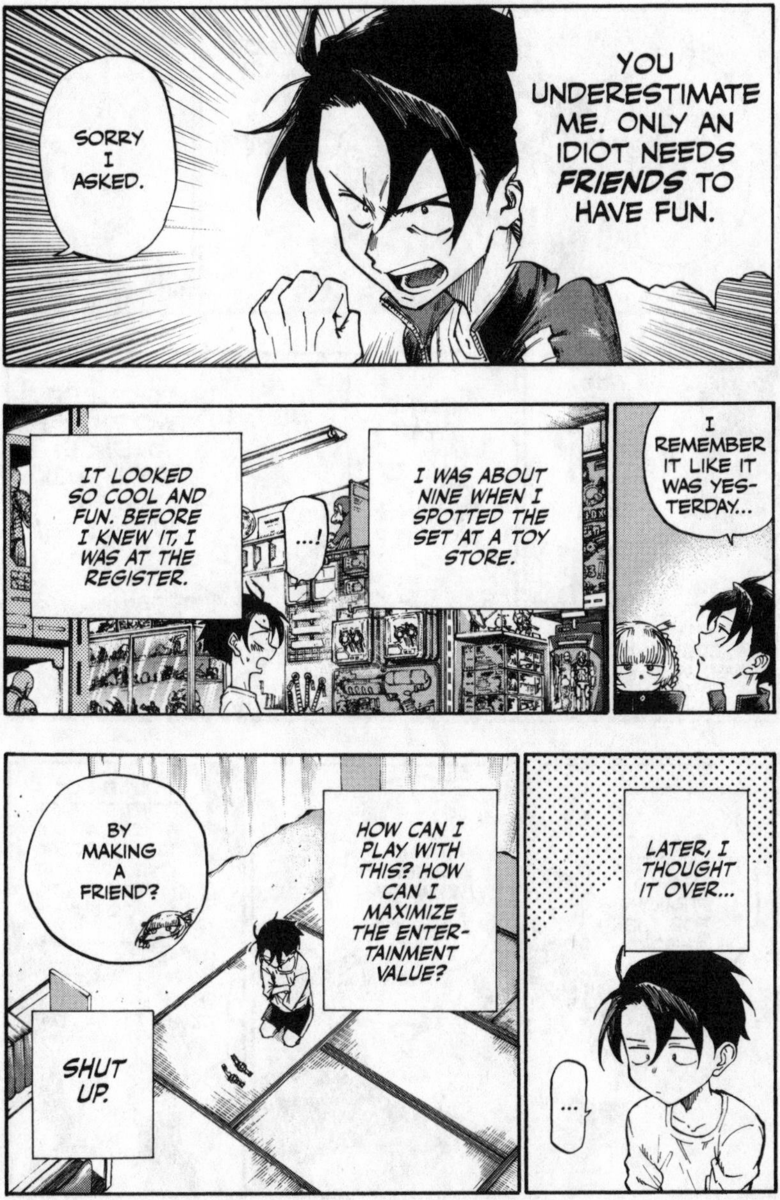
YOU UNDERESTIMATE ME. ONLY AN IDIOT NEEDS FRIENDS TO HAVE FUN.
SORRY I ASKED.
I REMEMBER IT LIKE IT WAS YES-TERDAY...
I WAS ABOUT NINE WHEN I SPOTTED THE SET AT A TOY STORE.
...!
IT LOOKED SO COOL AND FUN. BEFORE I KNEW IT, I WAS AT THE REGISTER.
LATER, I THOUGHT IT OVER...
...
HOW CAN I PLAY WITH THIS? HOW CAN I MAXIMIZE THE ENTER-TAINMENT VALUE?
BY MAKING A FRIEND?
SHUT UP.

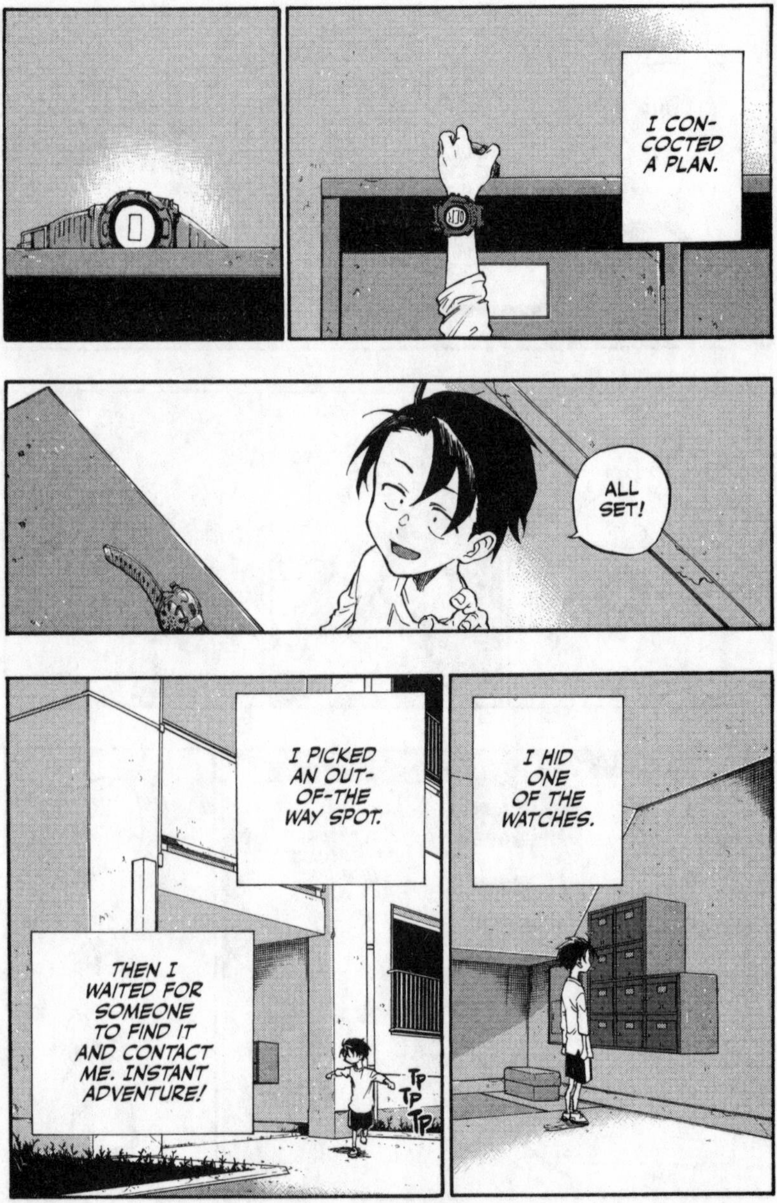
I CONCOCTED A PLAN.
ALL SET!
I HID ONE OF THE WATCHES.
I PICKED AN OUT-OF-THE WAY SPOT.
THEN I WAITED FOR SOMEONE TO FIND IT AND CONTACT ME. INSTANT ADVENTURE!
TP TP TP

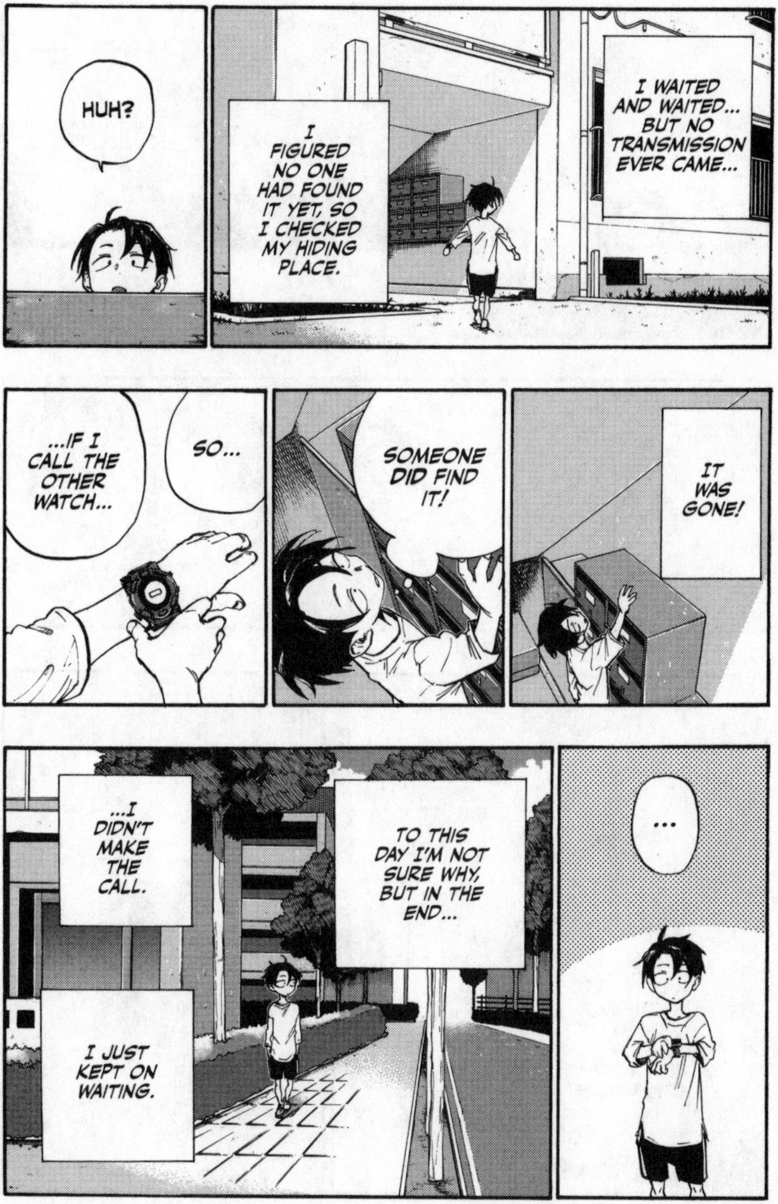
I WAITED AND WAITED... BUT NO TRANSMISSION EVER CAME...
I FIGURED NO ONE HAD FOUND IT YET, SO I CHECKED MY HIDING PLACE.
HUH?
IT WAS GONE!
SOMEONE DID FIND IT!
SO...
...IF I CALL THE OTHER WATCH...
...
TO THIS DAY I'M NOT SURE WHY, BUT IN THE END...
...I DIDN'T MAKE THE CALL.
I JUST KEPT ON WAITING.

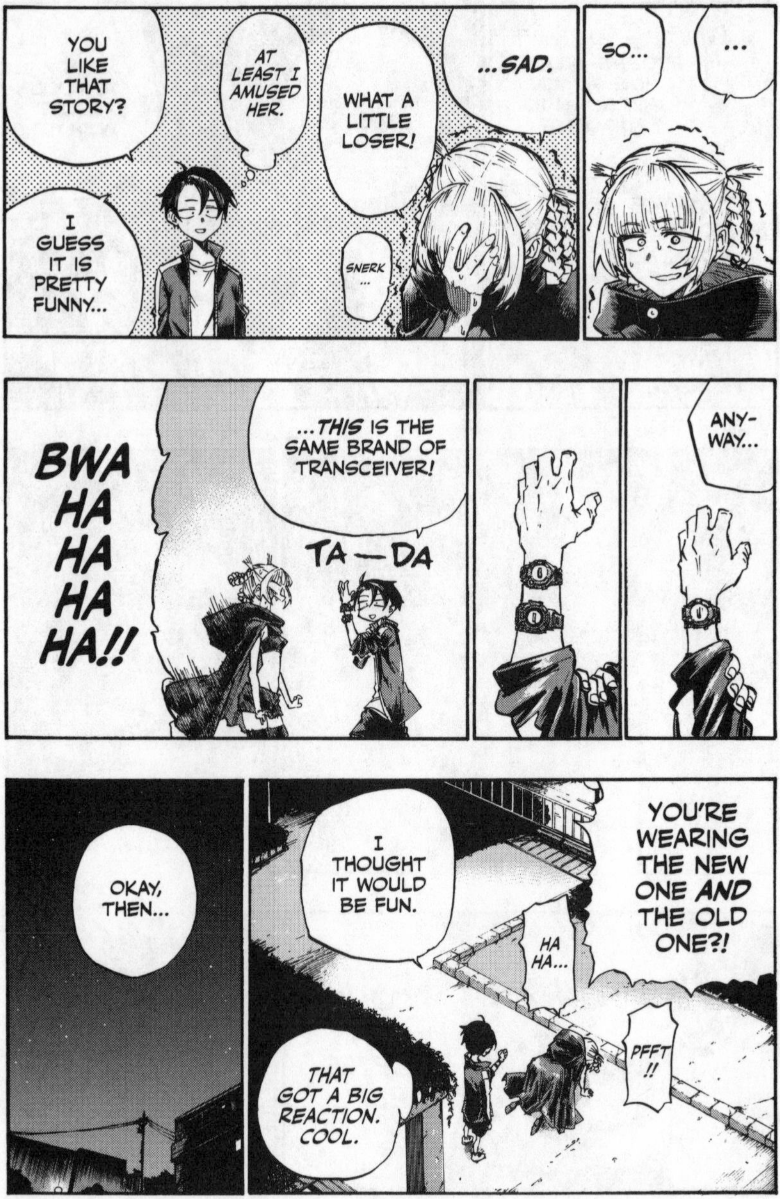
...
SO...
...SAD.
WHAT A LITTLE LOSER!
AT LEAST I AMUSED HER.
YOU LIKE THAT STORY?
SNERK...
I GUESS IT IS PRETTY FUNNY...
ANYWAY...
...*THIS* IS THE SAME BRAND OF TRANSCEIVER!
TA—DA
BWA HA HA HA HA!!
YOU'RE WEARING THE NEW ONE *AND* THE OLD ONE?!
I THOUGHT IT WOULD BE FUN.
HA HA...
PFFT!!
THAT GOT A BIG REACTION. COOL.
OKAY, THEN...

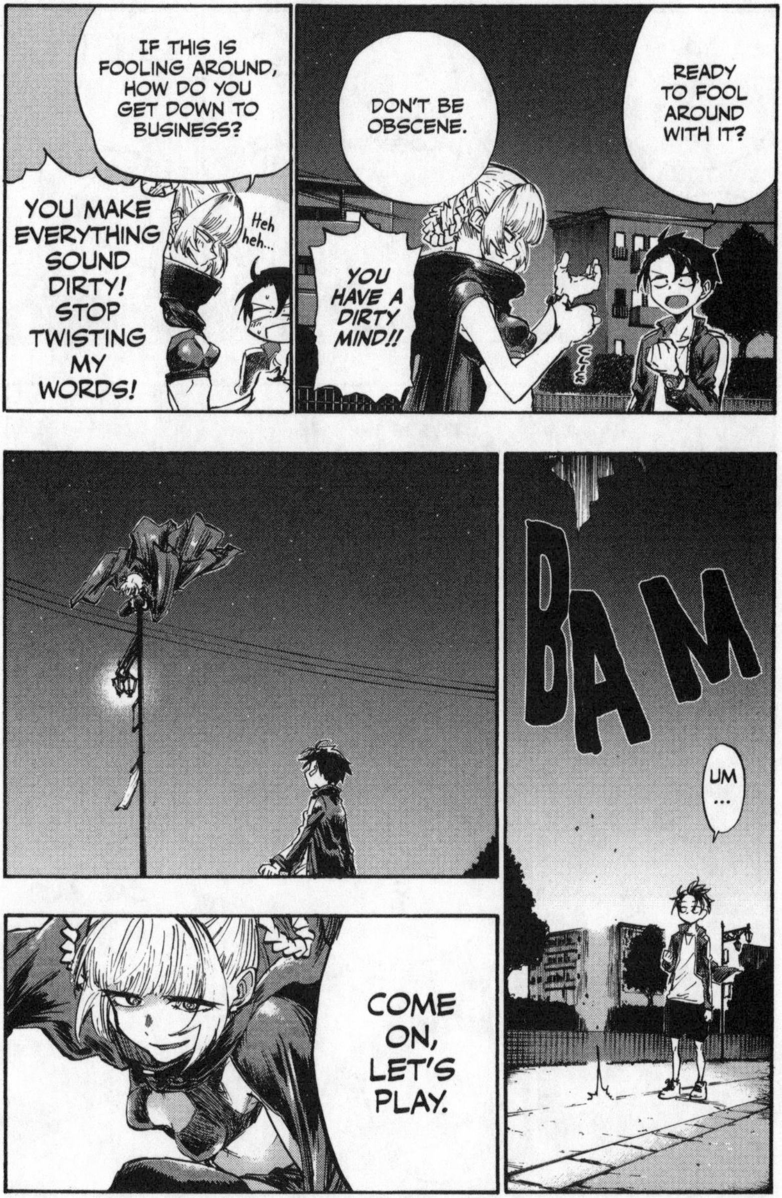
READY TO FOOL AROUND WITH IT?
DON'T BE OBSCENE.
YOU HAVE A DIRTY MIND!!
IF THIS IS FOOLING AROUND, HOW DO YOU GET DOWN TO BUSINESS?
Heh heh...
YOU MAKE EVERYTHING SOUND DIRTY! STOP TWISTING MY WORDS!
BAM
UM ...
COME ON, LET'S PLAY.

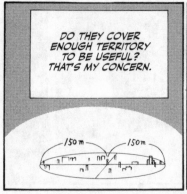

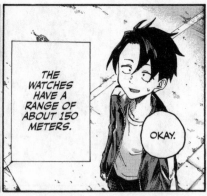

THE WATCHES HAVE A RANGE OF ABOUT 150 METERS.
OKAY.
DO THEY COVER ENOUGH TERRITORY TO BE USEFUL? THAT'S MY CONCERN.
150m
150m
IF WE'RE NOT FAIRLY CLOSE TO EACH OTHER, THE SIGNAL WON'T REACH FAR ENOUGH.
Call
...
ALSO...
...ALL THE SIGNAL TELLS YOU IS THAT THE OTHER PERSON IS NEARBY. YOU CAN'T HOME IN ON THEM.
Call
BIP
I GUESS IT'S BETTER THAN NOTHING.
AT LEAST WE'LL BE LESS LIKELY TO PASS EACH OTHER LIKE SHIPS IN THE NIGHT.

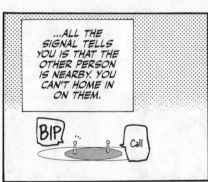

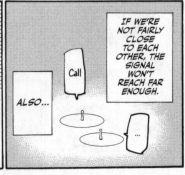

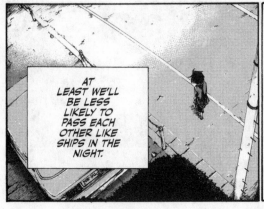

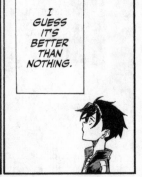

...
I'M ALONE.
THIS IS DIFFERENT FROM WANDERING AROUND...
...LOOKING FOR NAZUNA.
I DON'T USUALLY FEEL LONELY WHEN I'M ALONE.
I FEEL LONELY WHEN I'M WITH PEOPLE.
IS IT LIKE THAT FOR OTHER PEOPLE?
MAYBE...
...THIS FEELS DIFFERENT...
...BECAUSE IT ISN'T RANDOM.
IT'S A MEANINGFUL SOLITUDE.

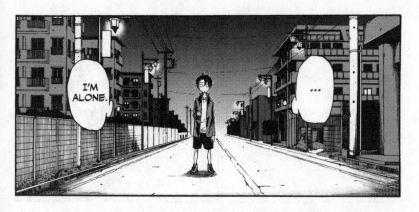

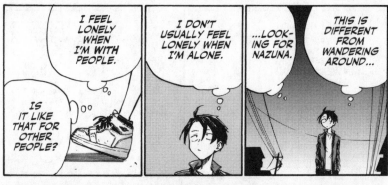

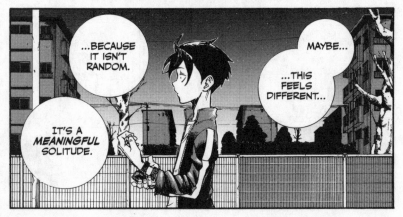

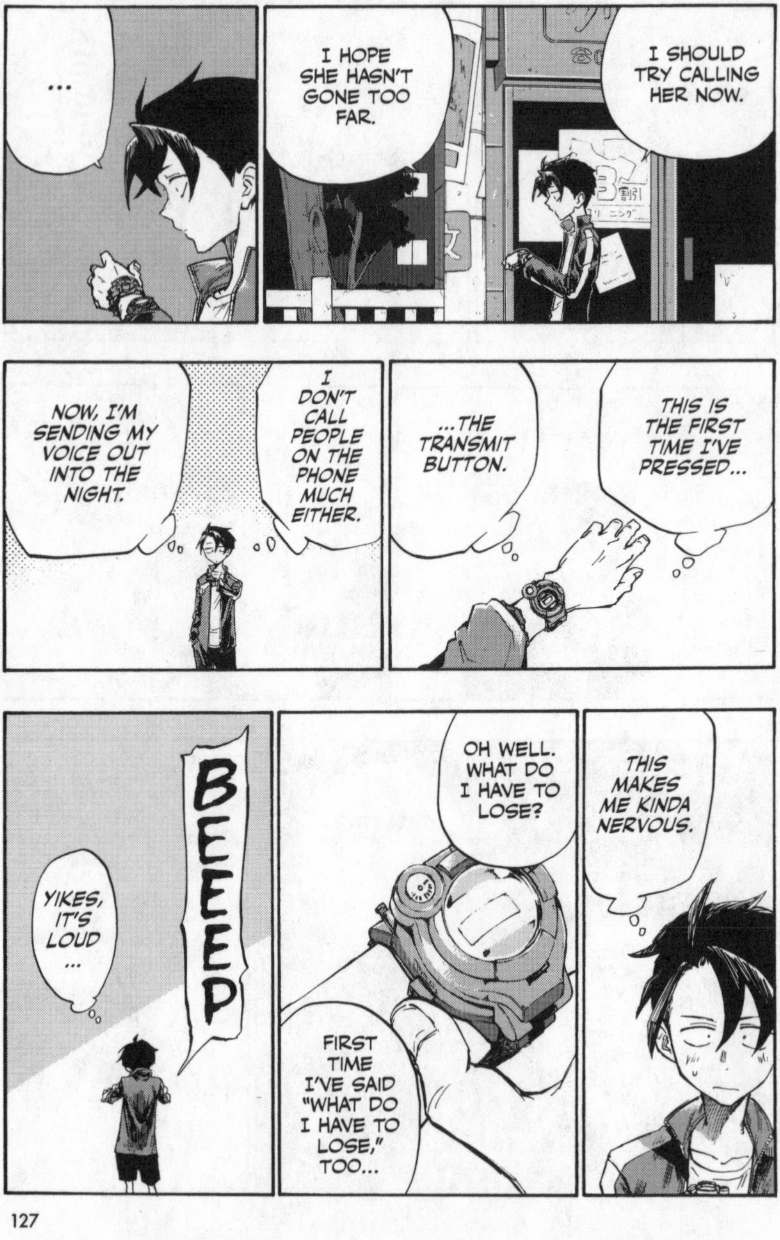
I SHOULD TRY CALLING HER NOW.
I HOPE SHE HASN'T GONE TOO FAR.
...
THIS IS THE FIRST TIME I'VE PRESSED...
...THE TRANSMIT BUTTON.
I DON'T CALL PEOPLE ON THE PHONE MUCH EITHER.
NOW, I'M SENDING MY VOICE OUT INTO THE NIGHT.
THIS MAKES ME KINDA NERVOUS.
OH WELL. WHAT DO I HAVE TO LOSE?
FIRST TIME I'VE SAID "WHAT DO I HAVE TO LOSE," TOO...
BEEEP
YIKES, IT'S LOUD...

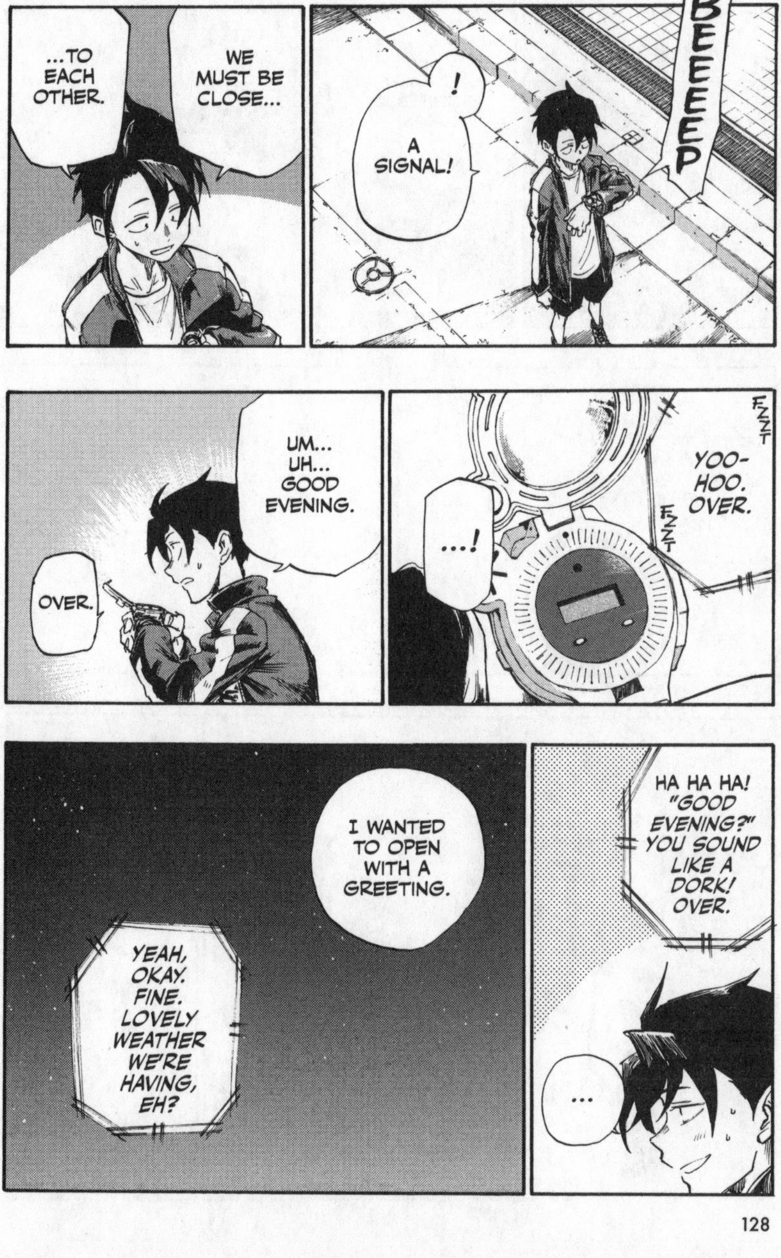
BEEEEEP
!
A SIGNAL!
WE MUST BE CLOSE...
...TO EACH OTHER.
FZZT
YOO-HOO. OVER.
FZZT
...!
UM... UH... GOOD EVENING.
OVER.
HA HA HA! "GOOD EVENING?" YOU SOUND LIKE A DORK! OVER.
...
I WANTED TO OPEN WITH A GREETING.
YEAH, OKAY. FINE. LOVELY WEATHER WE'RE HAVING, EH?

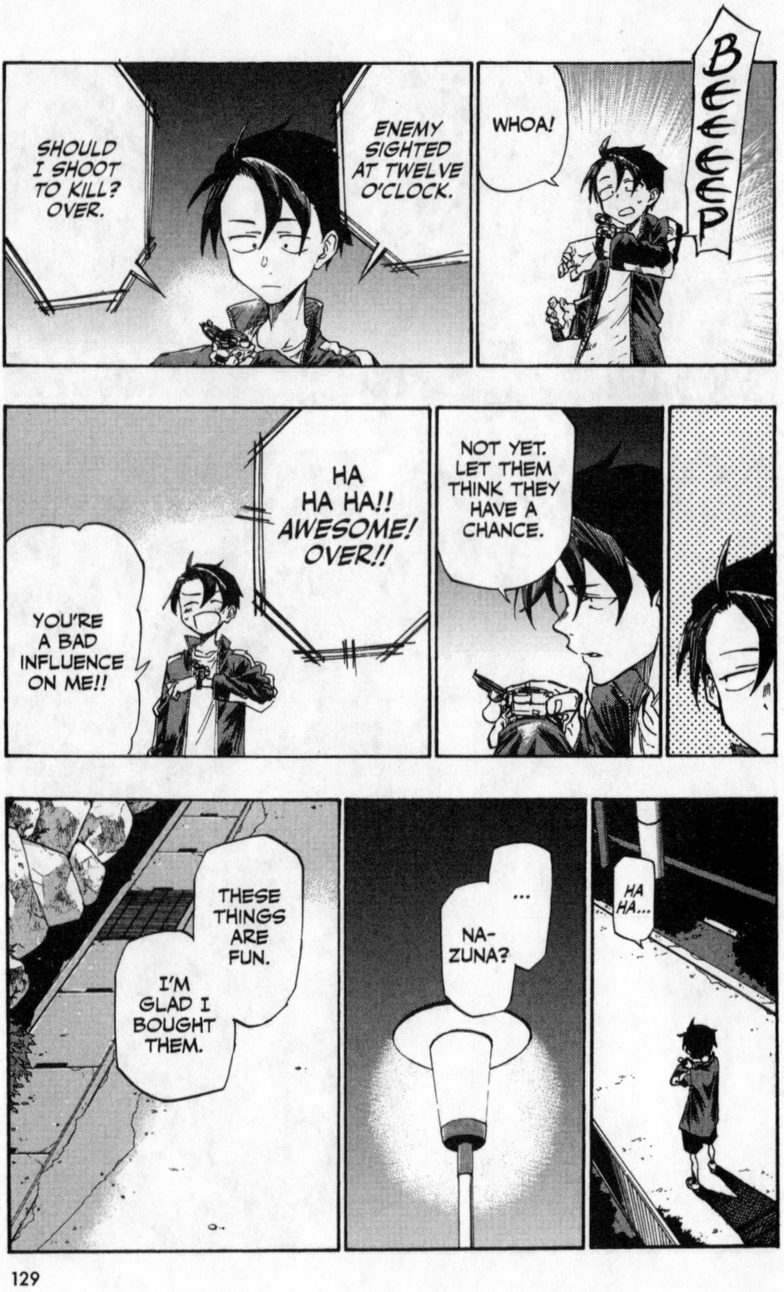
BEEEEP
WHOA!
ENEMY SIGHTED AT TWELVE O'CLOCK.
SHOULD I SHOOT TO KILL? OVER.
NOT YET. LET THEM THINK THEY HAVE A CHANCE.
HA HA HA!! AWESOME! OVER!!
YOU'RE A BAD INFLUENCE ON ME!!
HA HA...
...
NA-ZUNA?
THESE THINGS ARE FUN.
I'M GLAD I BOUGHT THEM.

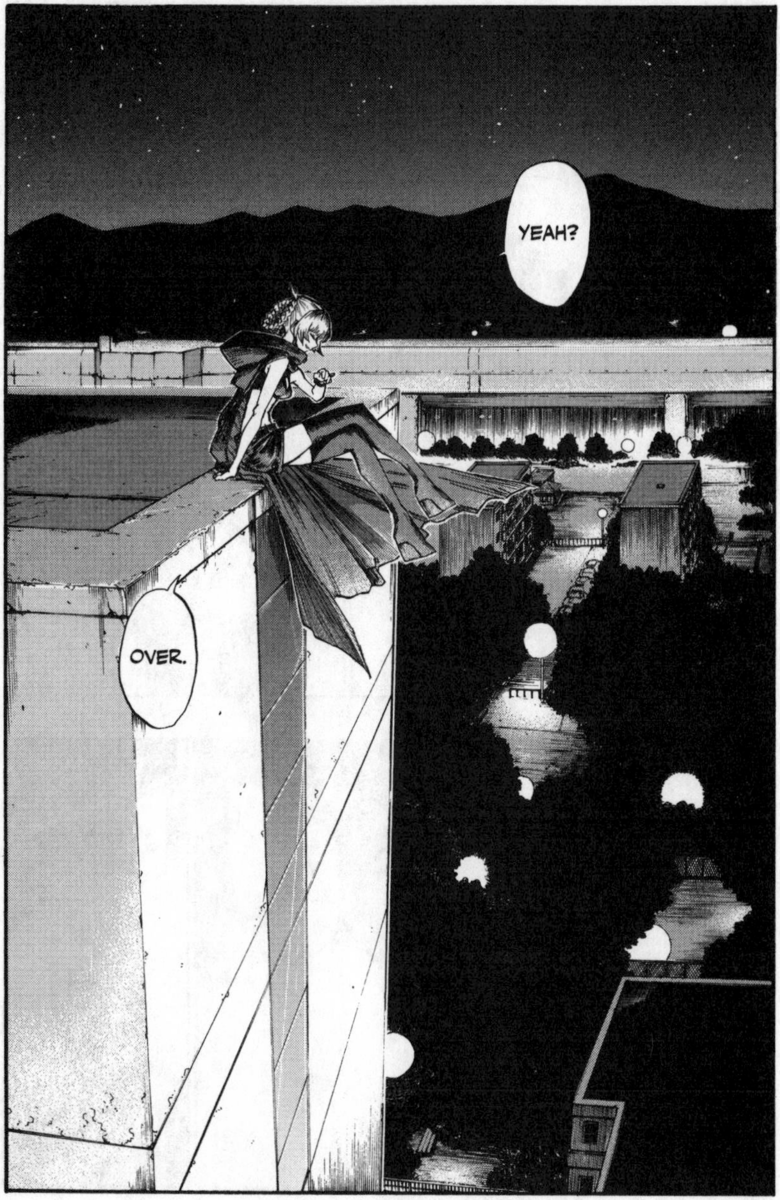
YEAH?
OVER.

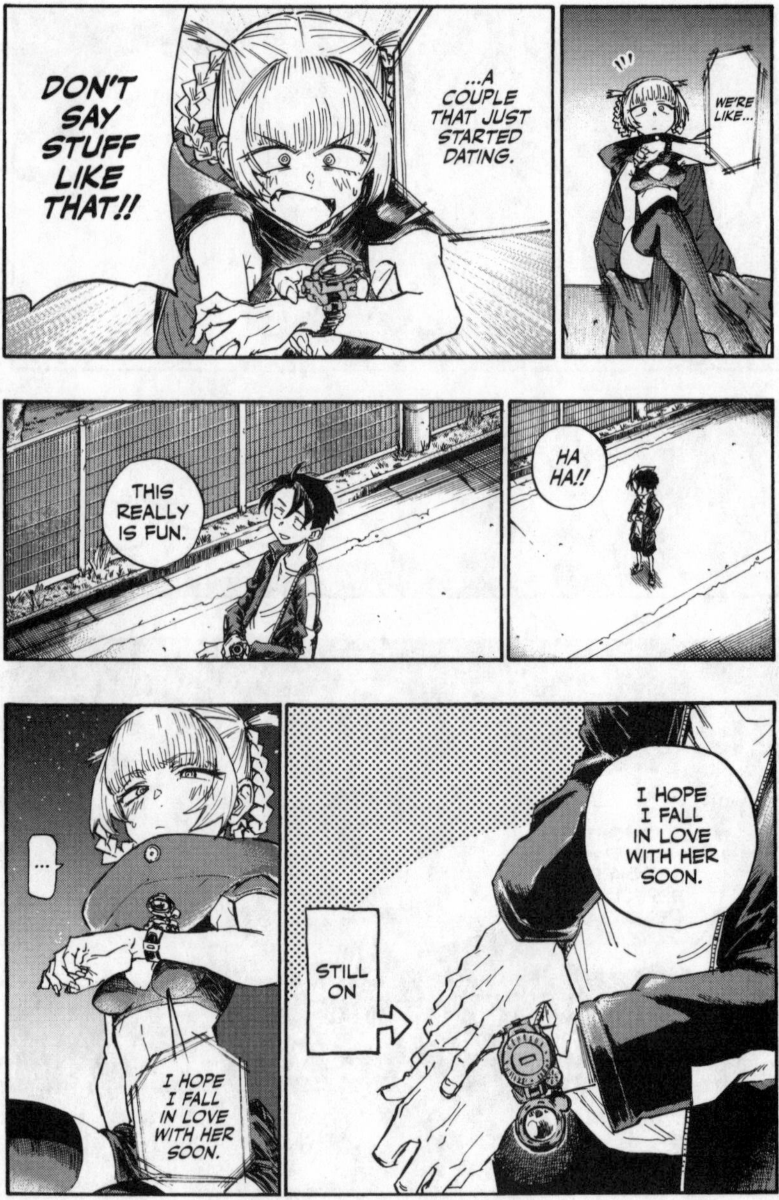
!!
WE'RE LIKE...
...A COUPLE THAT JUST STARTED DATING.
DON'T SAY STUFF LIKE THAT!!
HA HA!!
THIS REALLY IS FUN.
I HOPE I FALL IN LOVE WITH HER SOON.
STILL ON
...
I HOPE I FALL IN LOVE WITH HER SOON.

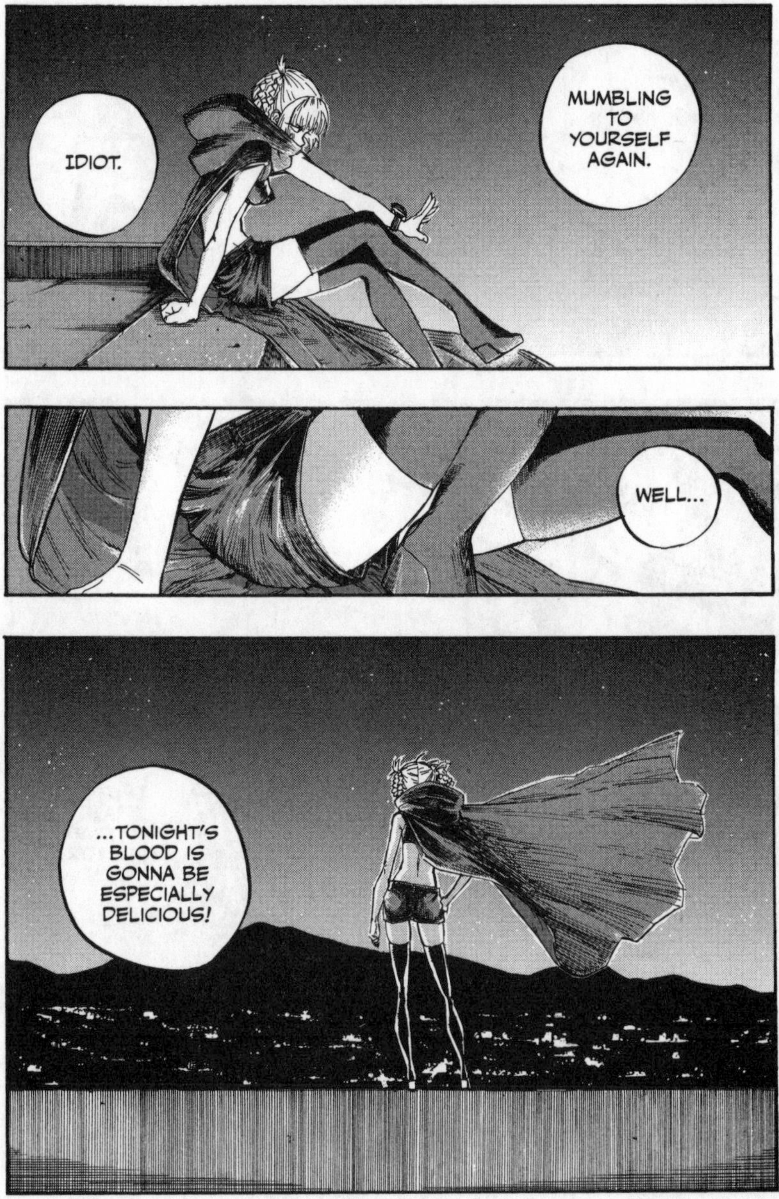
MUMBLING TO YOURSELF AGAIN.
IDIOT.
WELL...
...TONIGHT'S BLOOD IS GONNA BE ESPECIALLY DELICIOUS!

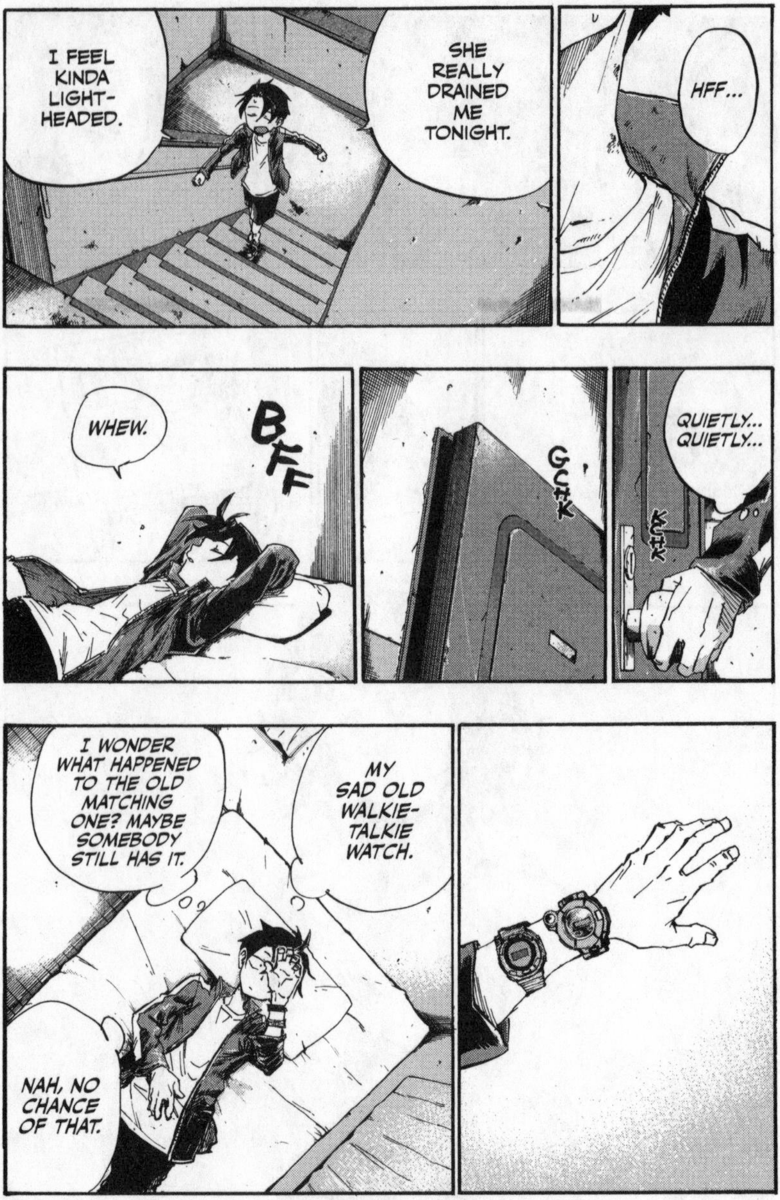
HFF...
SHE REALLY DRAINED ME TONIGHT.
I FEEL KINDA LIGHT-HEADED.
QUIETLY... QUIETLY...
KCHK
GCHK
BFF
WHEW.
MY SAD OLD WALKIE-TALKIE WATCH.
I WONDER WHAT HAPPENED TO THE OLD MATCHING ONE? MAYBE SOMEBODY STILL HAS IT.
NAH, NO CHANCE OF THAT.

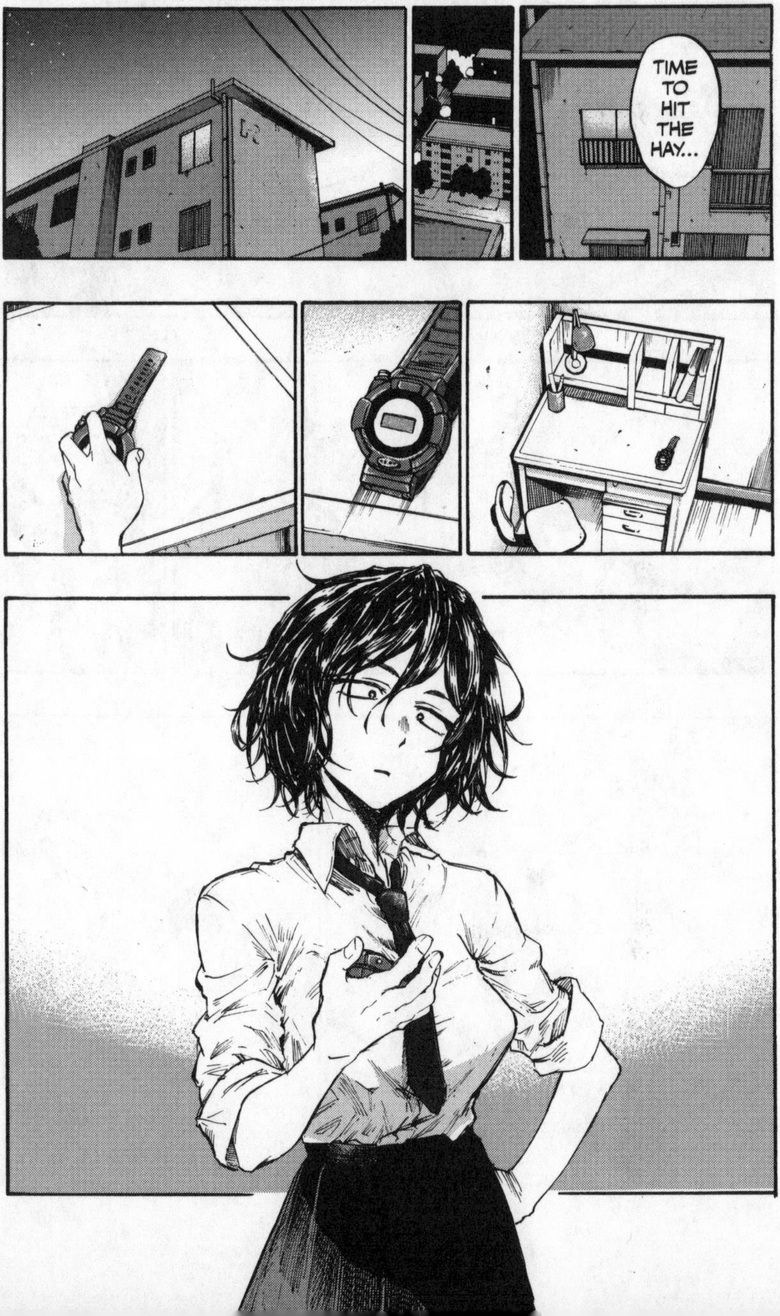
TIME TO HIT THE HAY...

Call of the Night

Call of the **Night**

NIGHT 6: AKIRA

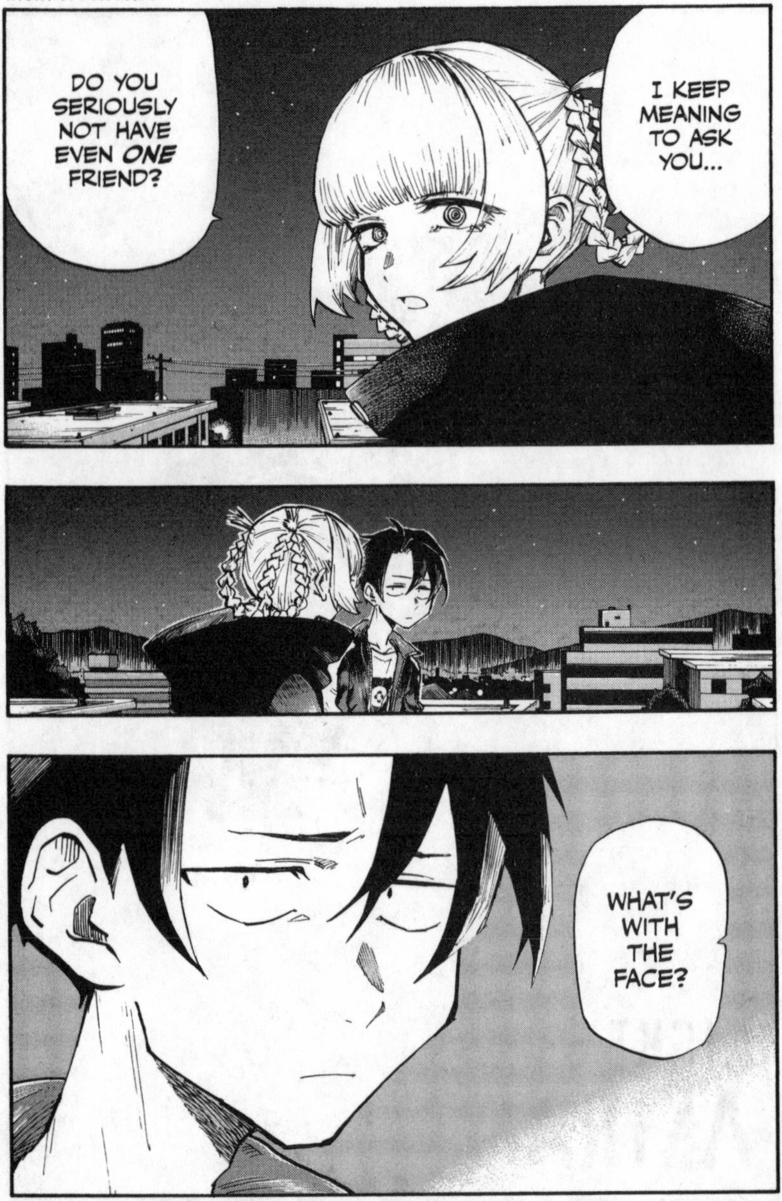
I KEEP MEANING TO ASK YOU...
DO YOU SERIOUSLY NOT HAVE EVEN *ONE* FRIEND?
WHAT'S WITH THE FACE?

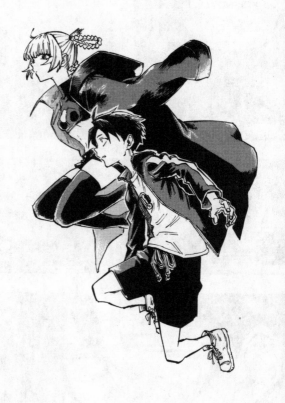

NIGHT 6:
AKIRA

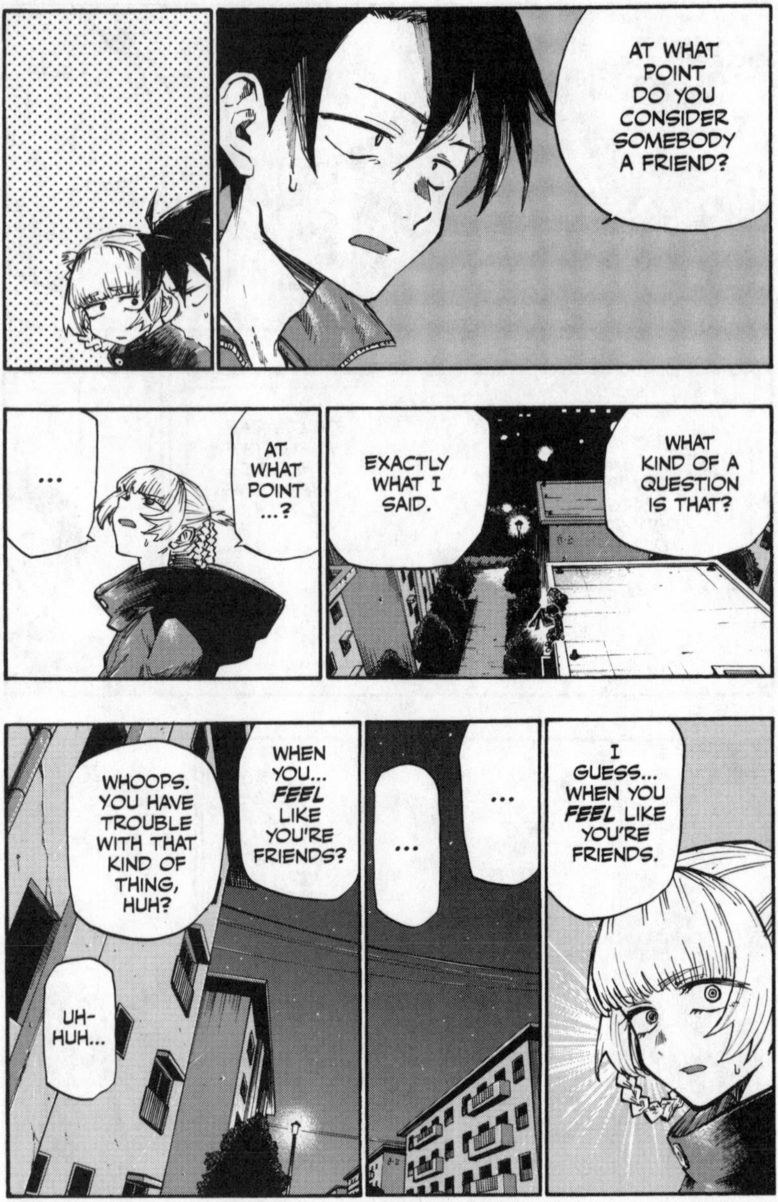
AT WHAT POINT DO YOU CONSIDER SOMEBODY A FRIEND?
WHAT KIND OF A QUESTION IS THAT?
EXACTLY WHAT I SAID.
AT WHAT POINT ...?
...
I GUESS... WHEN YOU FEEL LIKE YOU'RE FRIENDS.
...
...
WHEN YOU... FEEL LIKE YOU'RE FRIENDS?
WHOOPS. YOU HAVE TROUBLE WITH THAT KIND OF THING, HUH?
UH-HUH...

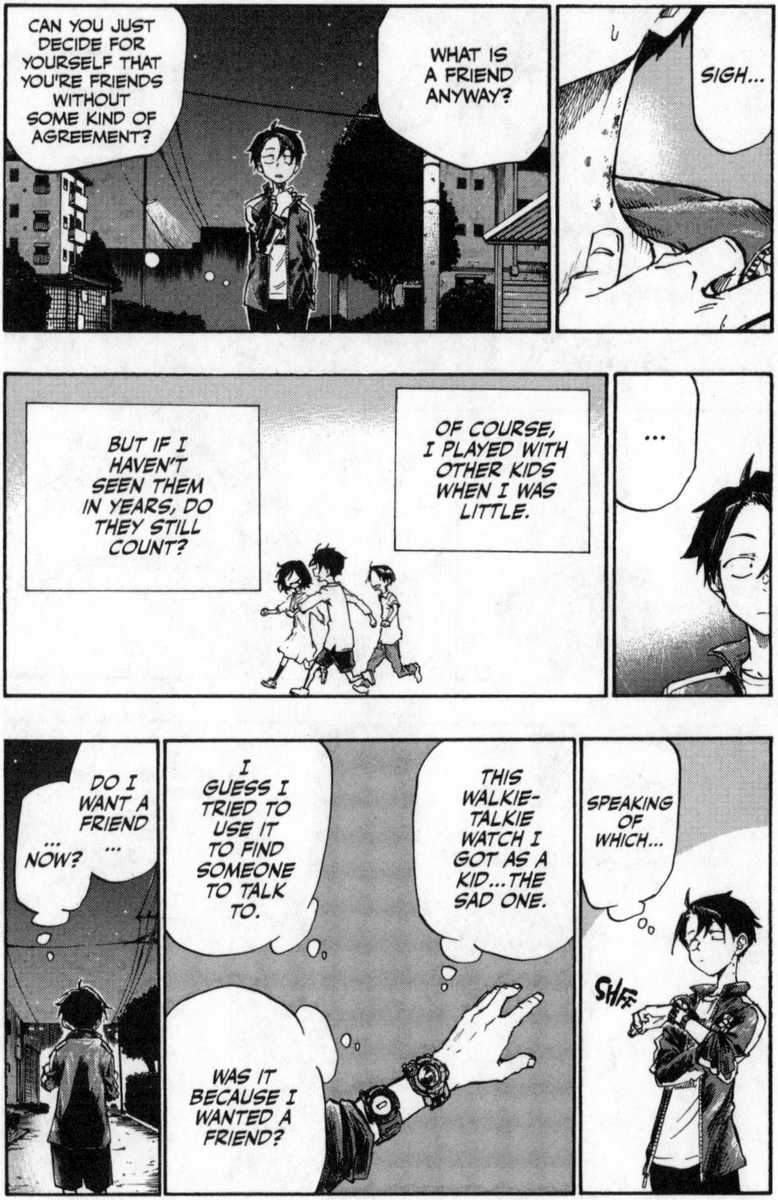
SIGH...
WHAT IS A FRIEND ANYWAY?
CAN YOU JUST DECIDE FOR YOURSELF THAT YOU'RE FRIENDS WITHOUT SOME KIND OF AGREEMENT?
...
OF COURSE, I PLAYED WITH OTHER KIDS WHEN I WAS LITTLE.
BUT IF I HAVEN'T SEEN THEM IN YEARS, DO THEY STILL COUNT?
SPEAKING OF WHICH...
SHFF
THIS WALKIE-TALKIE WATCH I GOT AS A KID...THE SAD ONE.
I GUESS I TRIED TO USE IT TO FIND SOMEONE TO TALK TO.
WAS IT BECAUSE I WANTED A FRIEND?
DO I WANT A FRIEND... ...NOW?

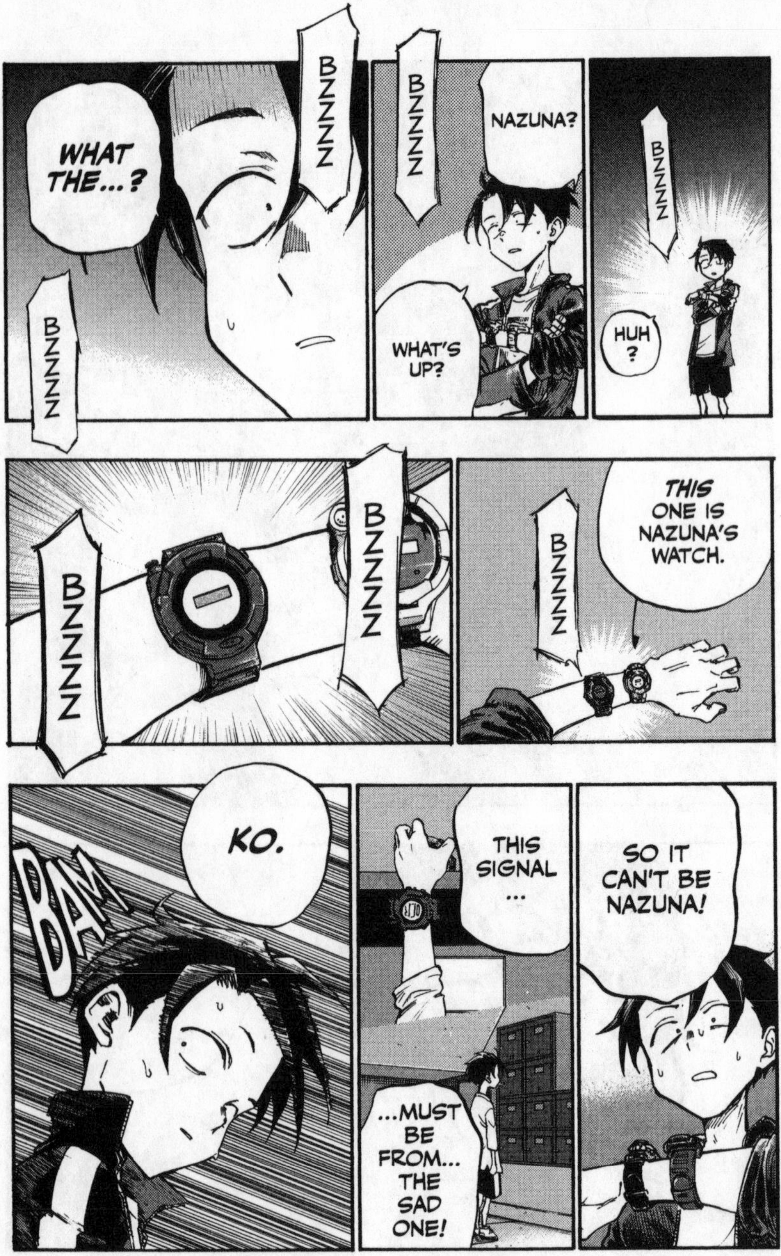
BZZZZ
HUH?
BZZZZ
NAZUNA?
WHAT'S UP?
BZZZZ
WHAT THE...?
BZZZZ
THIS ONE IS NAZUNA'S WATCH.
BZZZZ
BZZZZ
BZZZZZ
SO IT CAN'T BE NAZUNA!
THIS SIGNAL ...
...MUST BE FROM... THE SAD ONE!
KO.
BAM

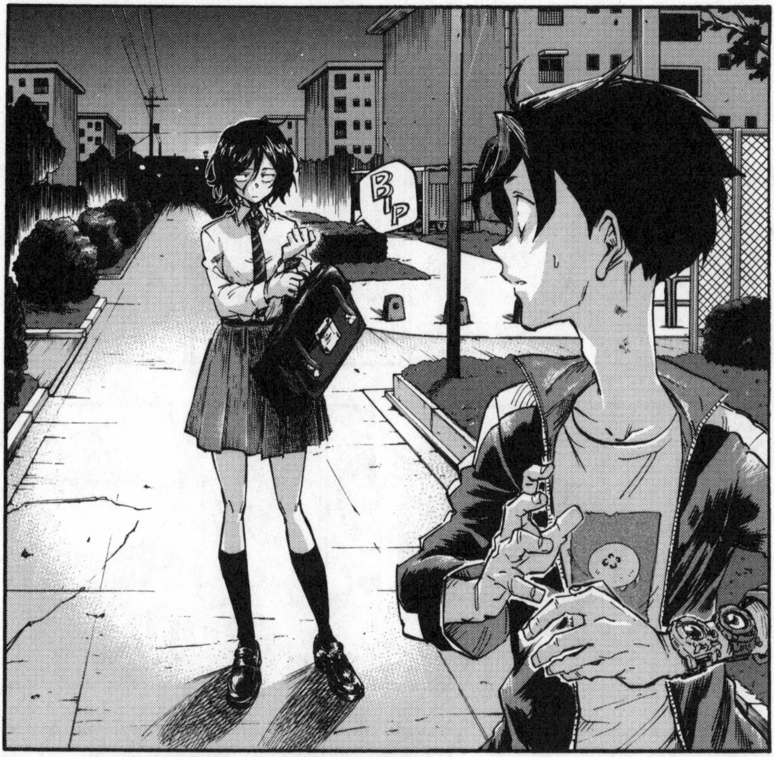
BIP
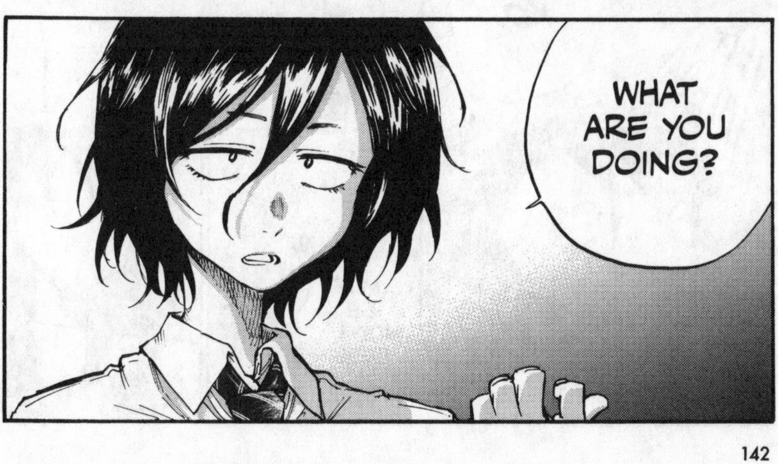
WHAT ARE YOU DOING?

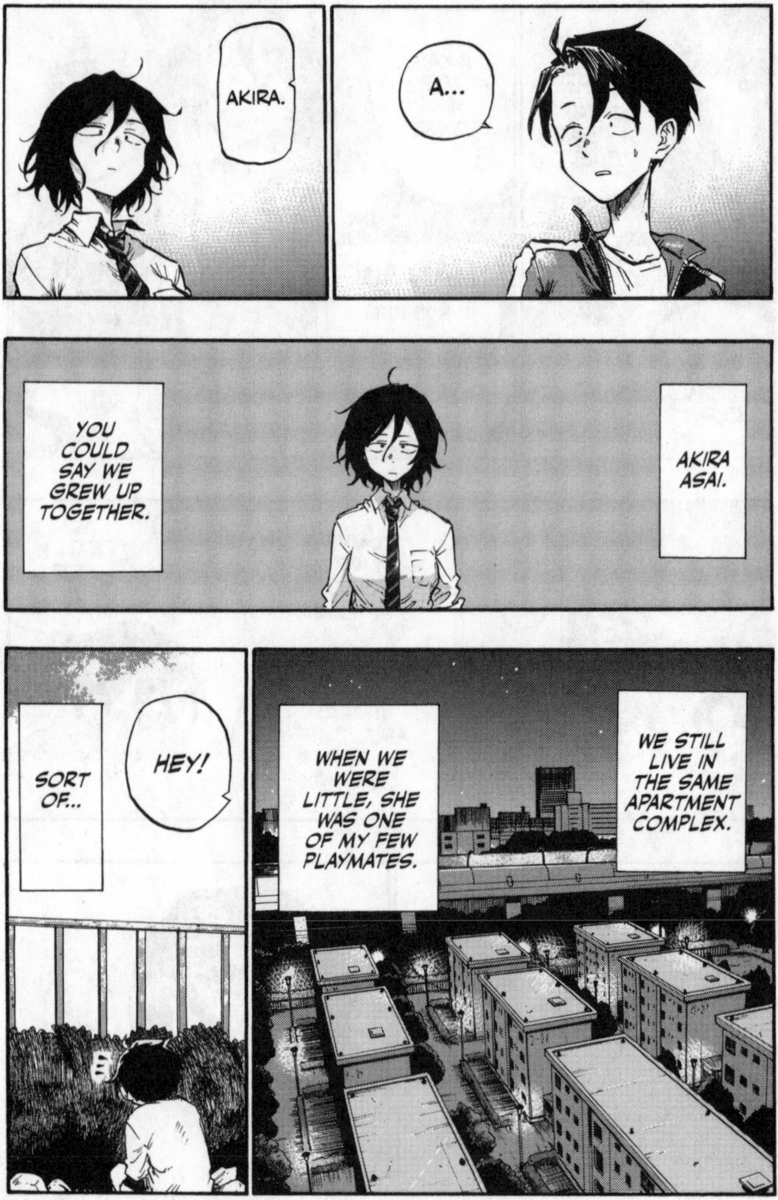
A...
AKIRA.
AKIRA ASAI.
YOU COULD SAY WE GREW UP TOGETHER.
WE STILL LIVE IN THE SAME APARTMENT COMPLEX.
WHEN WE WERE LITTLE, SHE WAS ONE OF MY FEW PLAYMATES.
HEY!
SORT OF...

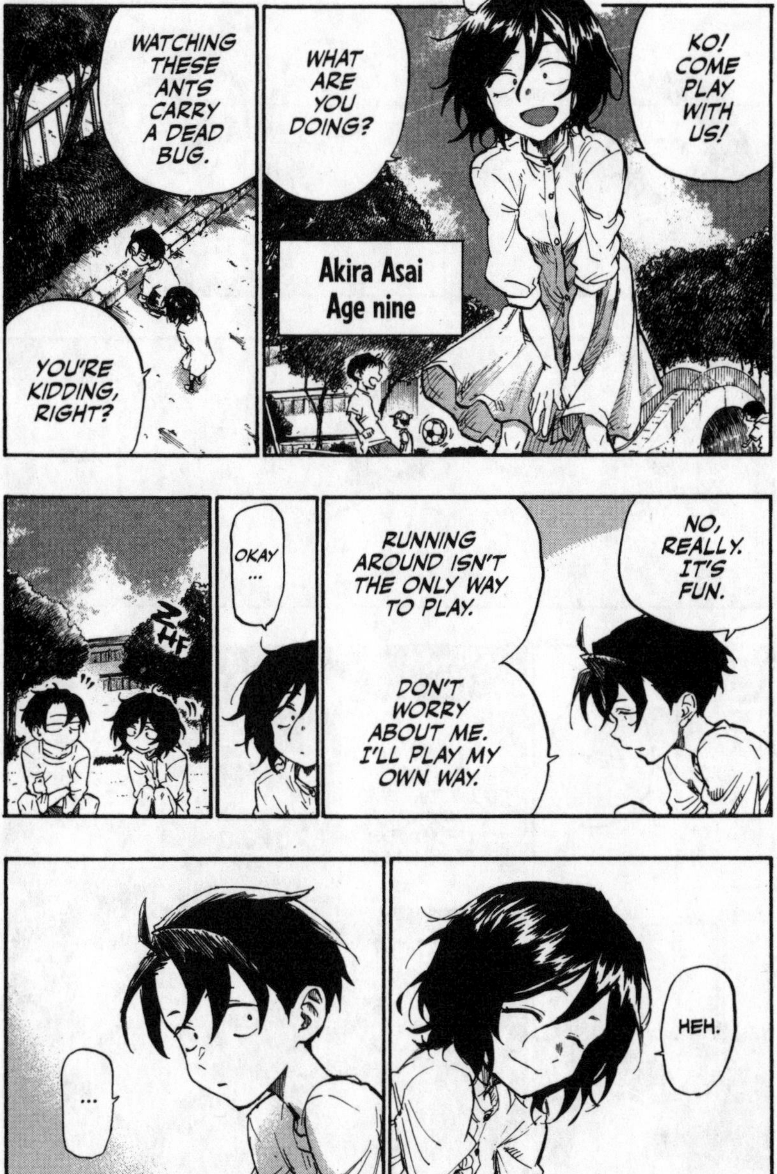
KO! COME PLAY WITH US!
WHAT ARE YOU DOING?
Akira Asai Age nine
WATCHING THESE ANTS CARRY A DEAD BUG.
YOU'RE KIDDING, RIGHT?
NO, REALLY. IT'S FUN.
RUNNING AROUND ISN'T THE ONLY WAY TO PLAY.
DON'T WORRY ABOUT ME. I'LL PLAY MY OWN WAY.
OKAY ...
HEH.
...

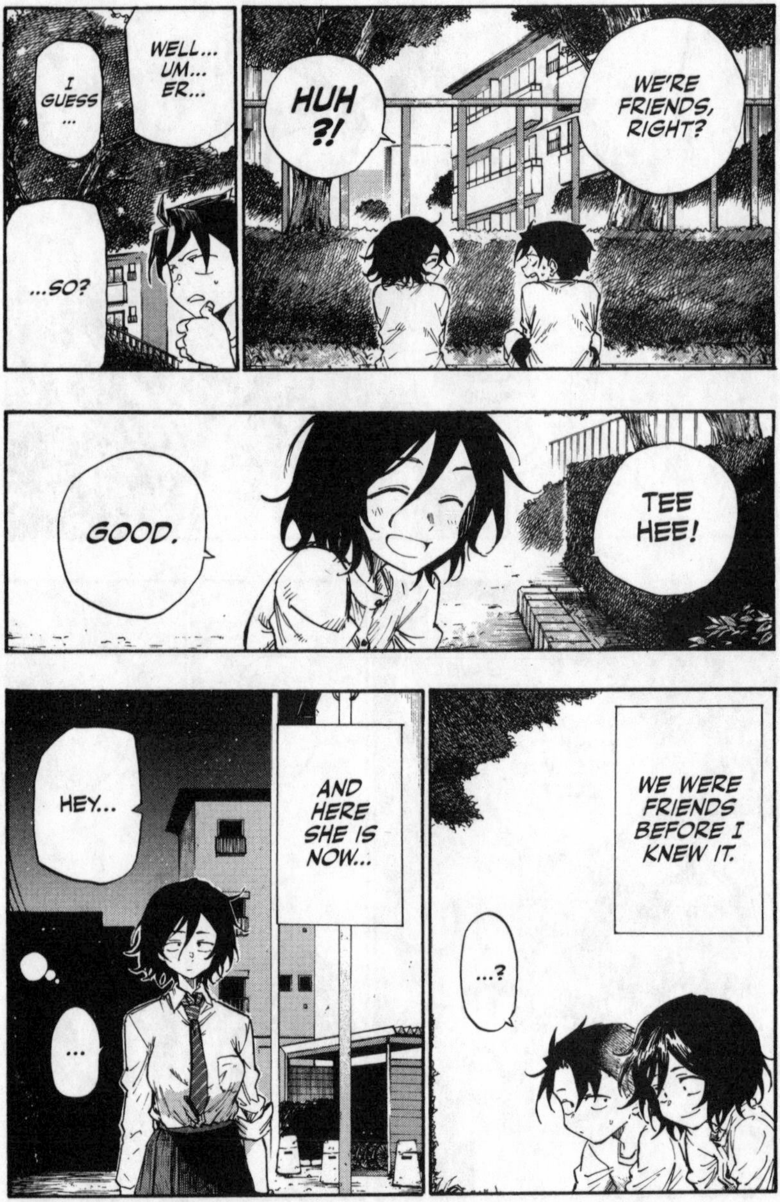
WE'RE FRIENDS, RIGHT?
HUH ?!
WELL... UM... ER...
I GUESS ...
...SO?
TEE HEE!
GOOD.
WE WERE FRIENDS BEFORE I KNEW IT.
...?
AND HERE SHE IS NOW...
HEY...
...

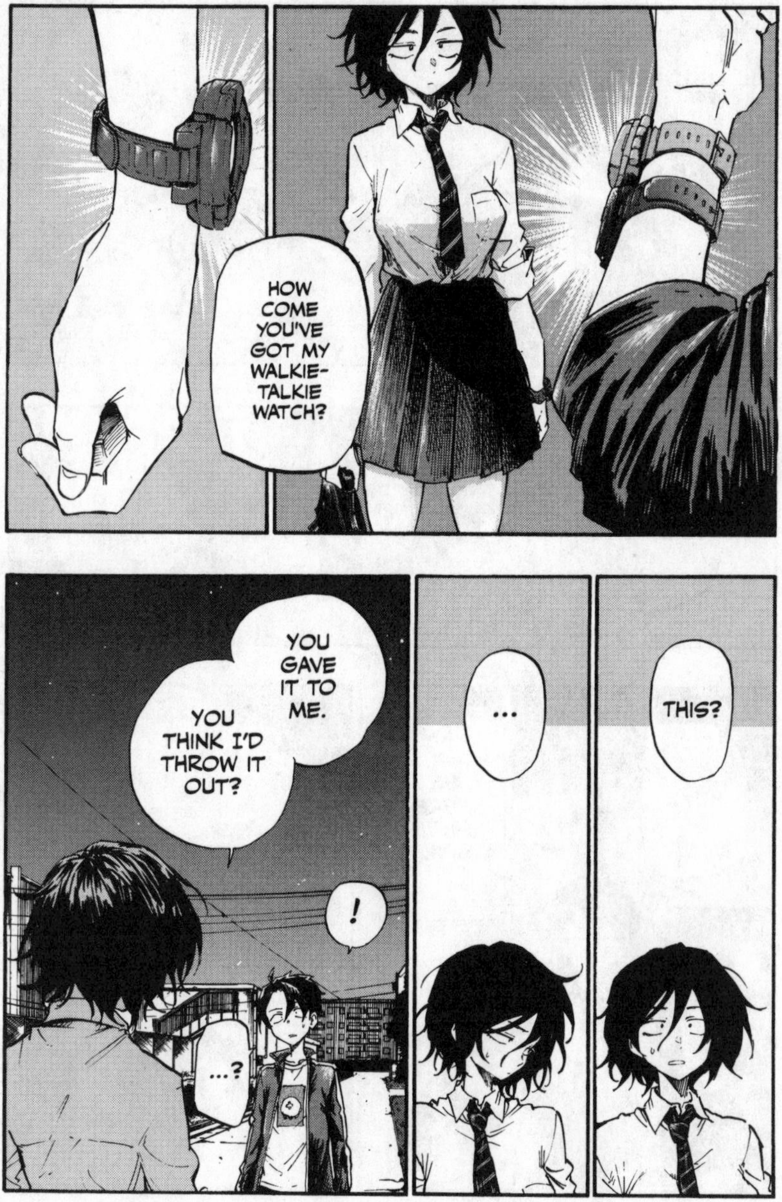
HOW COME YOU'VE GOT MY WALKIE-TALKIE WATCH?
THIS?
...
YOU GAVE IT TO ME.
YOU THINK I'D THROW IT OUT?
!
...?

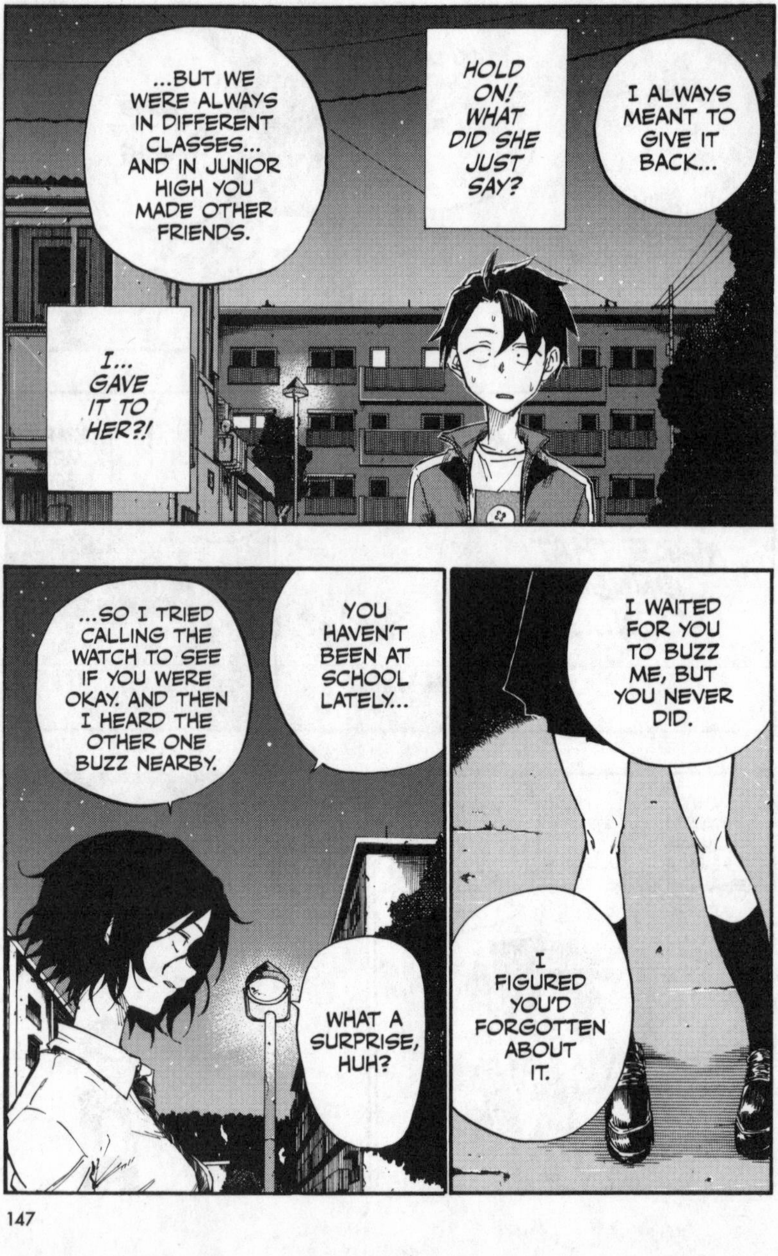
I ALWAYS MEANT TO GIVE IT BACK...
HOLD ON! WHAT DID SHE JUST SAY?
...BUT WE WERE ALWAYS IN DIFFERENT CLASSES... AND IN JUNIOR HIGH YOU MADE OTHER FRIENDS.
I... GAVE IT TO HER?!
I WAITED FOR YOU TO BUZZ ME, BUT YOU NEVER DID.
I FIGURED YOU'D FORGOTTEN ABOUT IT.
YOU HAVEN'T BEEN AT SCHOOL LATELY...
...SO I TRIED CALLING THE WATCH TO SEE IF YOU WERE OKAY. AND THEN I HEARD THE OTHER ONE BUZZ NEARBY.
WHAT A SURPRISE, HUH?

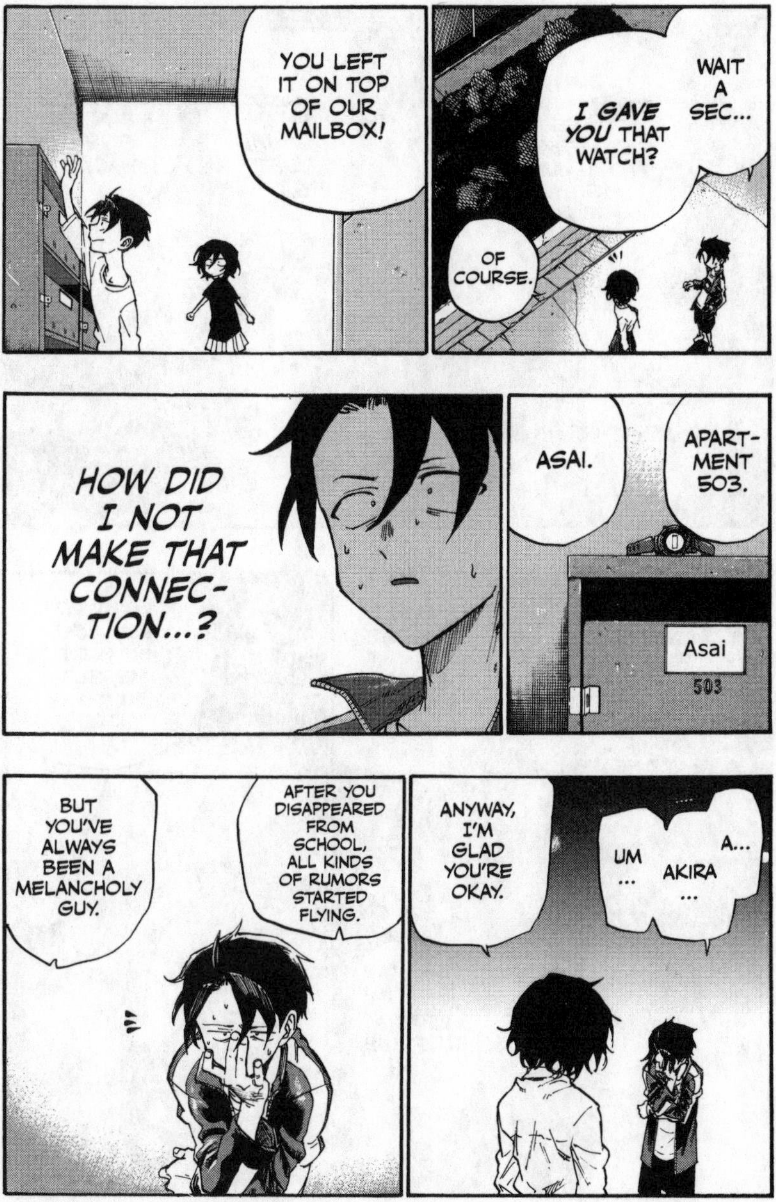
WAIT A SEC...
I GAVE YOU THAT WATCH?
OF COURSE.
YOU LEFT IT ON TOP OF OUR MAILBOX!
APARTMENT 503.
ASAI.
Asai
503
HOW DID I NOT MAKE THAT CONNECTION...?
A... AKIRA...
UM...
ANYWAY, I'M GLAD YOU'RE OKAY.
AFTER YOU DISAPPEARED FROM SCHOOL, ALL KINDS OF RUMORS STARTED FLYING.
BUT YOU'VE ALWAYS BEEN A MELANCHOLY GUY.

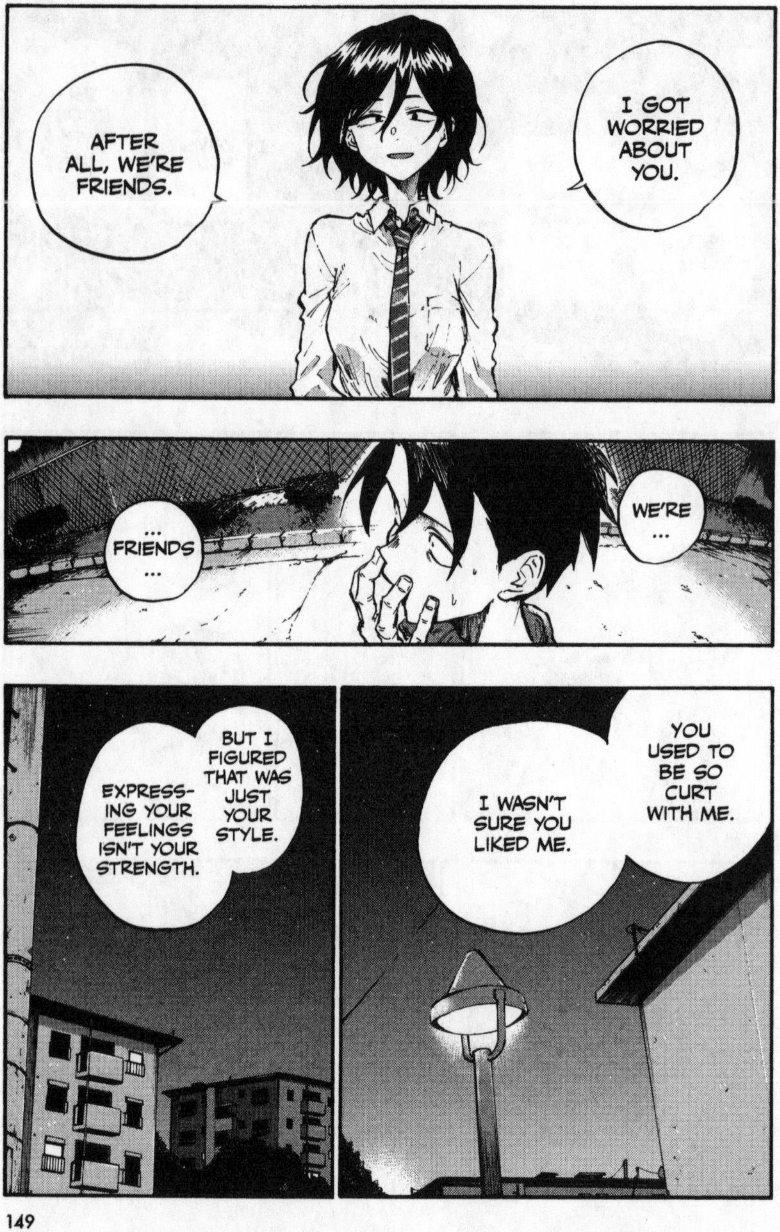
I GOT WORRIED ABOUT YOU.
AFTER ALL, WE'RE FRIENDS.
WE'RE ...
... FRIENDS ...
YOU USED TO BE SO CURT WITH ME.
I WASN'T SURE YOU LIKED ME.
BUT I FIGURED THAT WAS JUST YOUR STYLE.
EXPRESS-ING YOUR FEELINGS ISN'T YOUR STRENGTH.

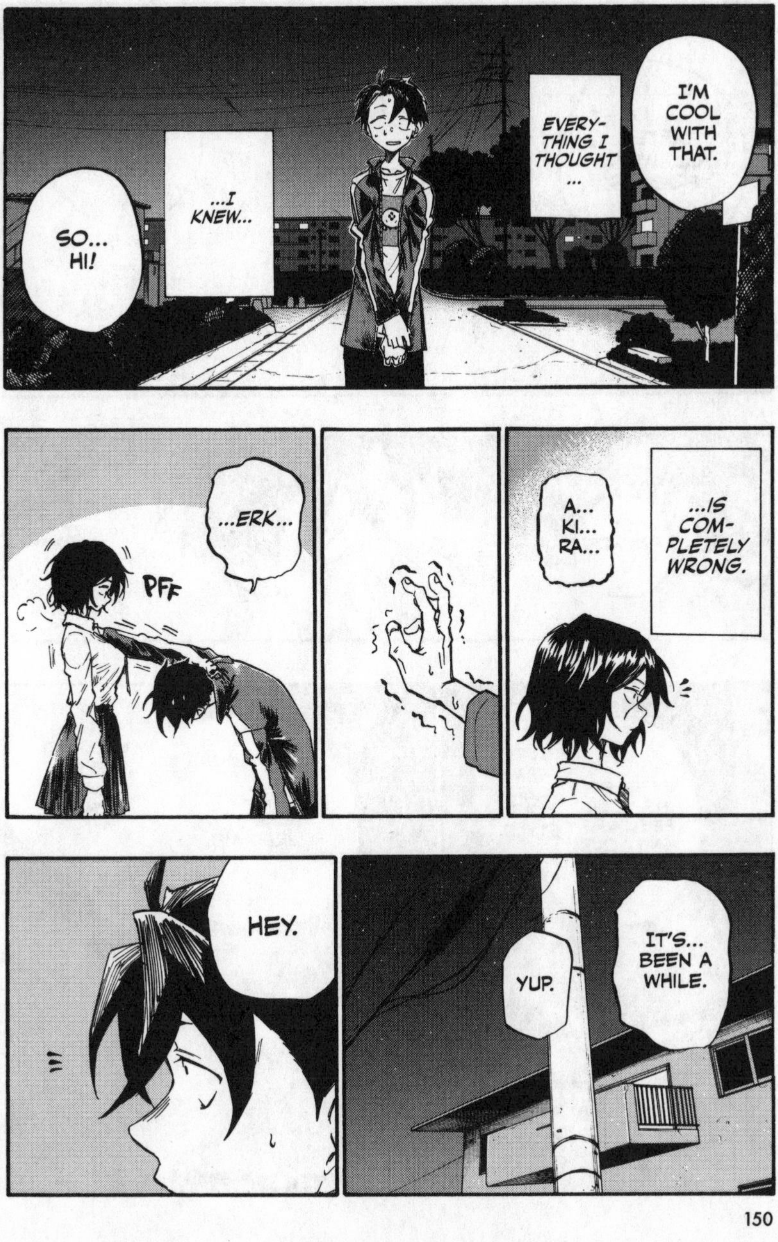
I'M COOL WITH THAT.
EVERY-THING I THOUGHT...
...I KNEW...
SO... HI!
...IS COM-PLETELY WRONG.
A... KI... RA...
...ERK...
PFF
IT'S... BEEN A WHILE.
YUP.
HEY.

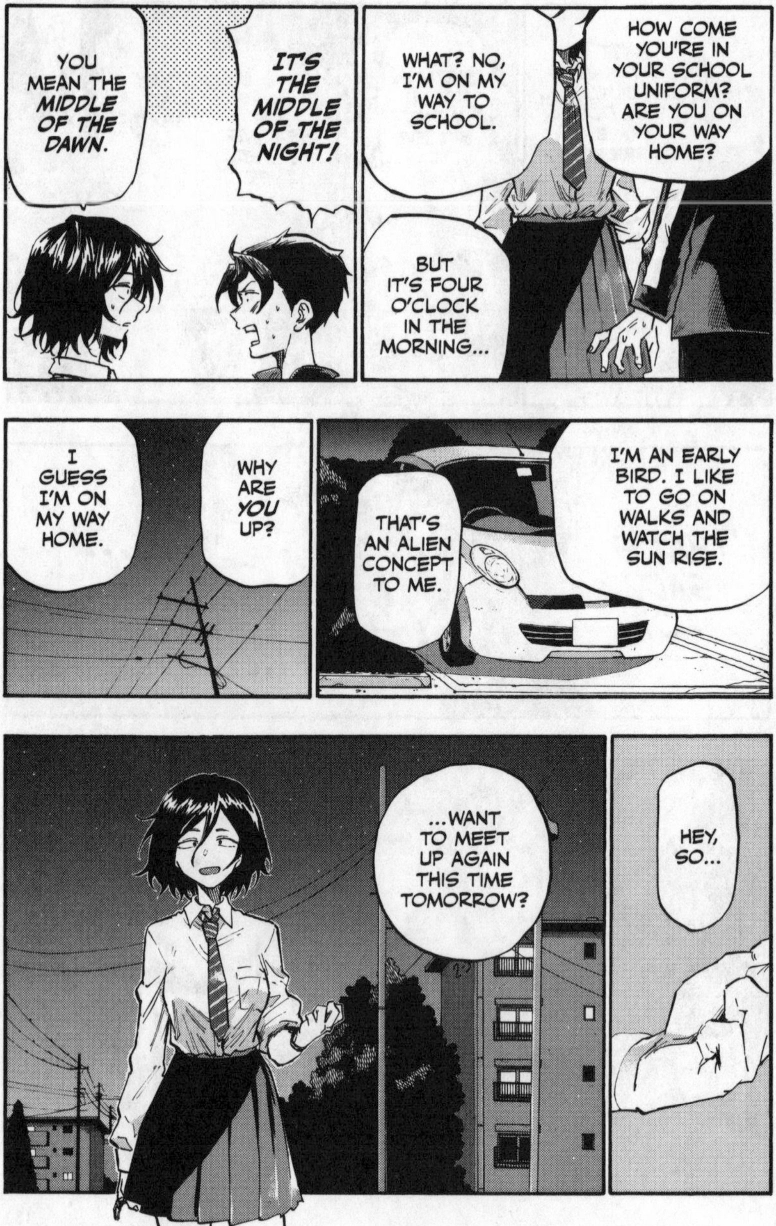
HOW COME YOU'RE IN YOUR SCHOOL UNIFORM? ARE YOU ON YOUR WAY HOME?
WHAT? NO, I'M ON MY WAY TO SCHOOL.
BUT IT'S FOUR O'CLOCK IN THE MORNING...
IT'S THE MIDDLE OF THE NIGHT!
YOU MEAN THE *MIDDLE OF THE DAWN.*
I'M AN EARLY BIRD. I LIKE TO GO ON WALKS AND WATCH THE SUN RISE.
THAT'S AN ALIEN CONCEPT TO ME.
WHY ARE *YOU* UP?
I GUESS I'M ON MY WAY HOME.
HEY, SO...
...WANT TO MEET UP AGAIN THIS TIME TOMORROW?

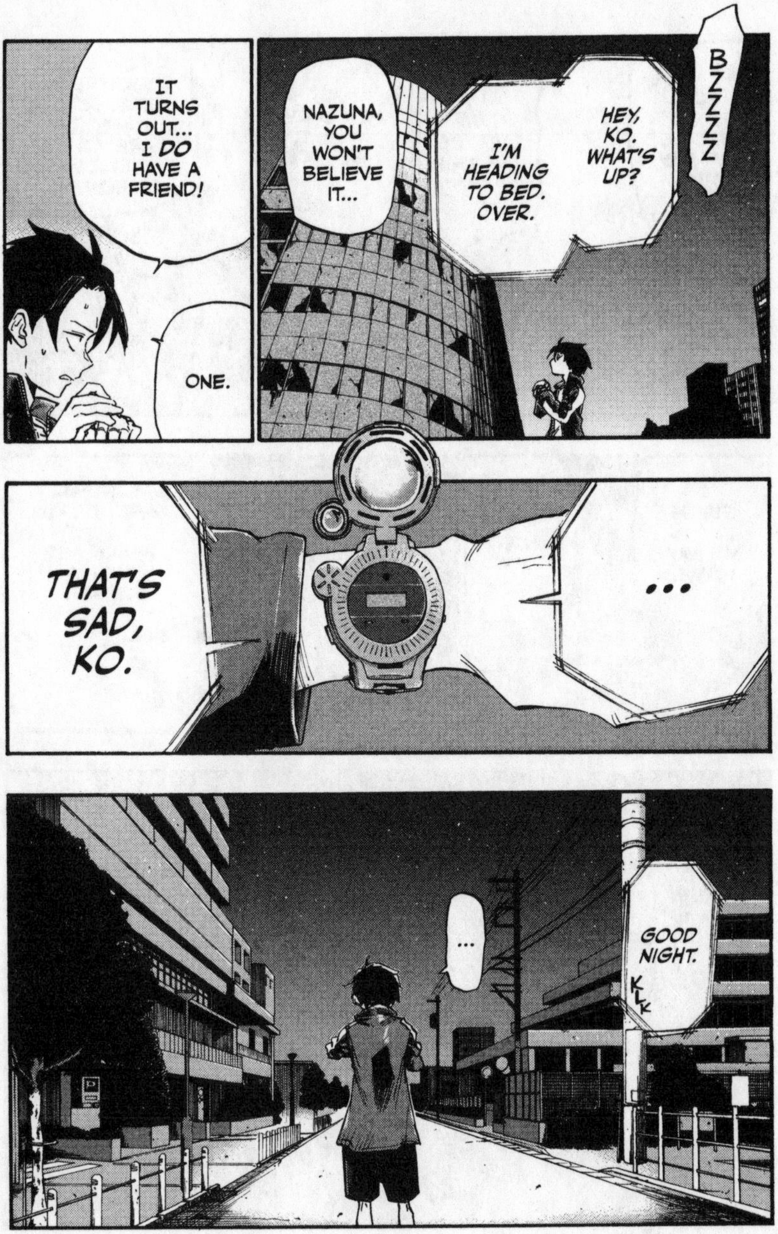
BZZZ
HEY, KO. WHAT'S UP?
I'M HEADING TO BED. OVER.
NAZUNA, YOU WON'T BELIEVE IT...
IT TURNS OUT... I *DO* HAVE A FRIEND!
ONE.
...
THAT'S SAD, KO.
GOOD NIGHT.
KLK
...

NIGHT 7: WHAT'S YOUR NAME?

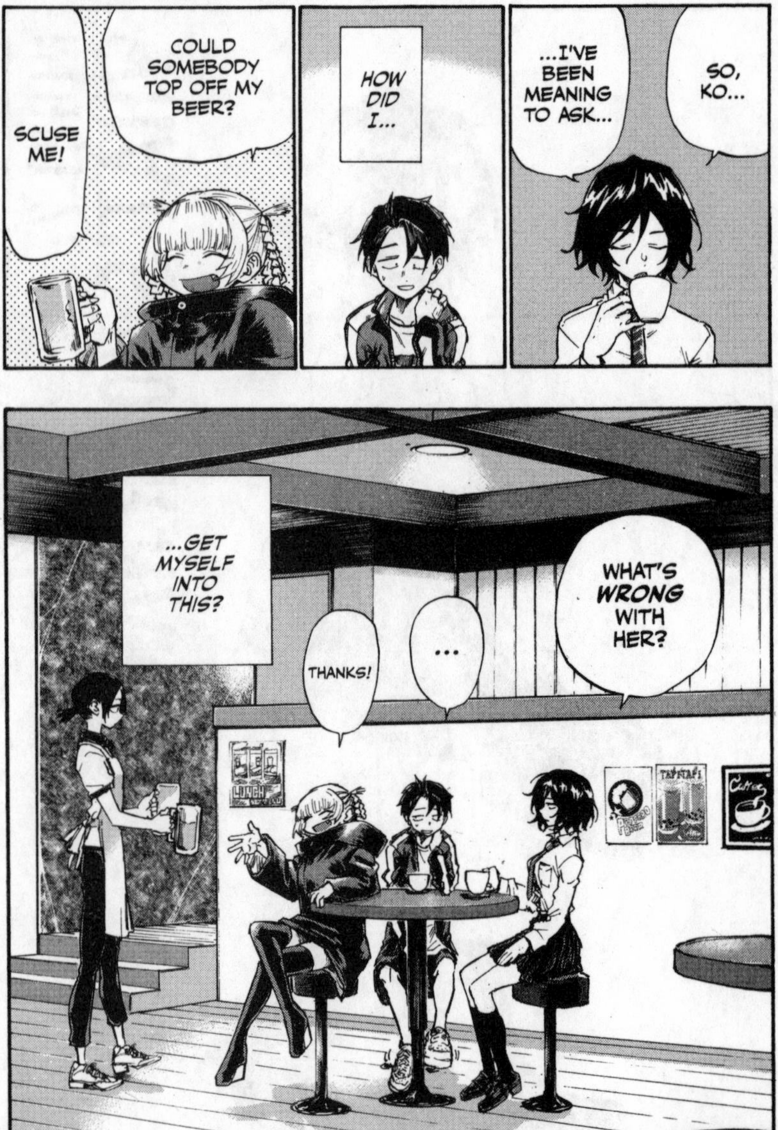
SO, KO...
...I'VE BEEN MEANING TO ASK...
HOW DID I...
COULD SOMEBODY TOP OFF MY BEER?
SCUSE ME!
WHAT'S WRONG WITH HER?
...
THANKS!
...GET MYSELF INTO THIS?

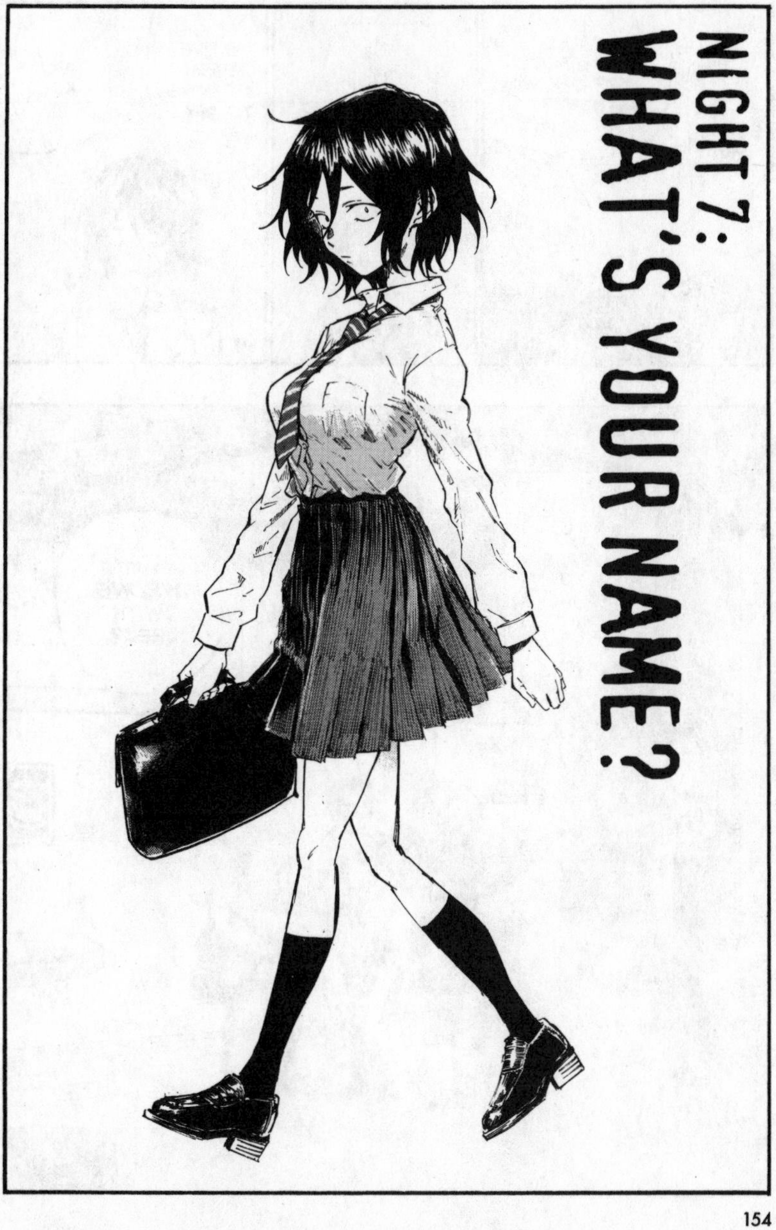
NIGHT 7:
WHAT'S YOUR NAME?

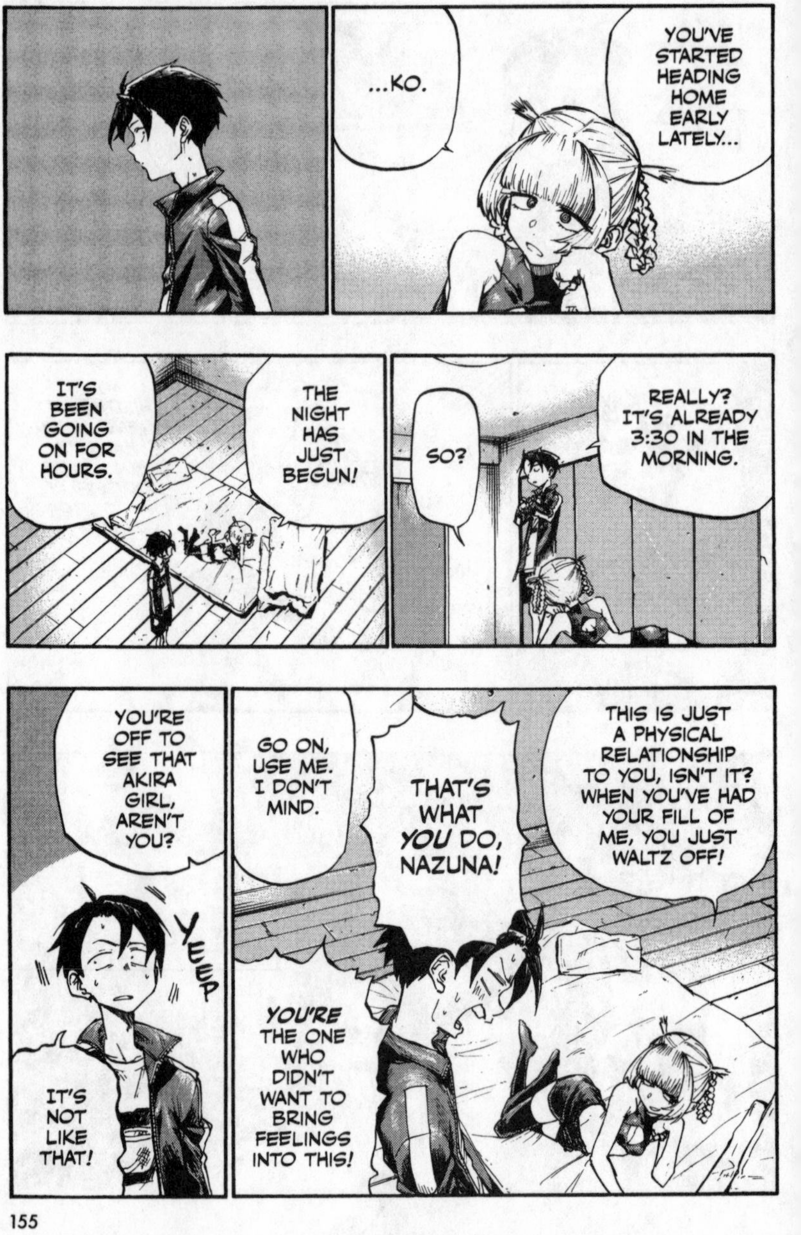
YOU'VE STARTED HEADING HOME EARLY LATELY...
...KO.
REALLY? IT'S ALREADY 3:30 IN THE MORNING.
SO?
THE NIGHT HAS JUST BEGUN!
IT'S BEEN GOING ON FOR HOURS.
THIS IS JUST A PHYSICAL RELATIONSHIP TO YOU, ISN'T IT? WHEN YOU'VE HAD YOUR FILL OF ME, YOU JUST WALTZ OFF!
THAT'S WHAT *YOU* DO, NAZUNA!
GO ON, USE ME. I DON'T MIND.
YOU'RE THE ONE WHO DIDN'T WANT TO BRING FEELINGS INTO THIS!
YOU'RE OFF TO SEE THAT AKIRA GIRL, AREN'T YOU?
YEEP
IT'S NOT LIKE THAT!

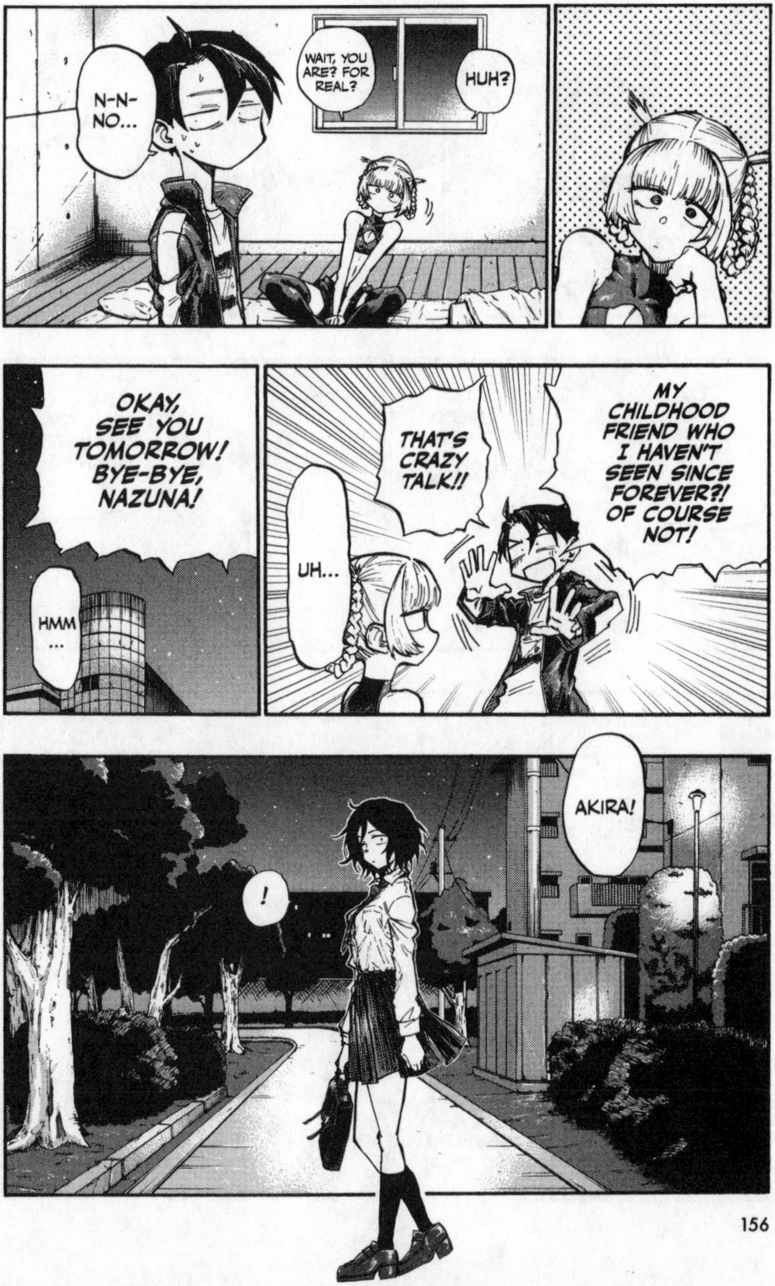
HUH?
WAIT, YOU ARE? FOR REAL?
N-N-NO...
MY CHILDHOOD FRIEND WHO I HAVEN'T SEEN SINCE FOREVER?! OF COURSE NOT!
THAT'S CRAZY TALK!!
UH...
OKAY, SEE YOU TOMORROW! BYE-BYE, NAZUNA!
HMM ...
AKIRA!
!

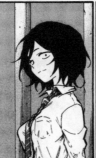

HFF
HEY.
HFF
YOU RAN HERE?
UH... WELL...
HFF
HFF
I'VE STARTED MEETING WITH AKIRA ON HER WAY TO SCHOOL AFTER MY NIGHTLY HANGOUTS WITH NAZUNA.
BUT IT'S KINDA AWK-WARD.
WE DON'T TALK MUCH. SOMETIMES WE SHARE A LITTLE SCHOOL GOSSIP.
I REMEMBER HER BEING FULL OF ENERGY AND TALKING A MILE A MINUTE.
MAYBE I'M IMAGINING IT, BUT...SHE SEEMS LIKE A TOTALLY DIFFERENT PERSON.
WHAT?
OH, UM...

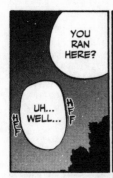

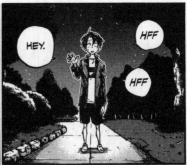

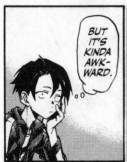

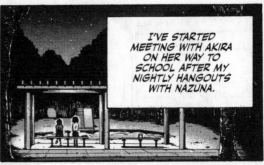

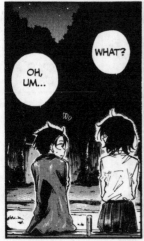

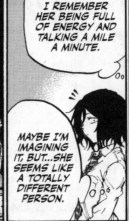

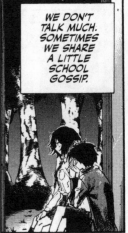

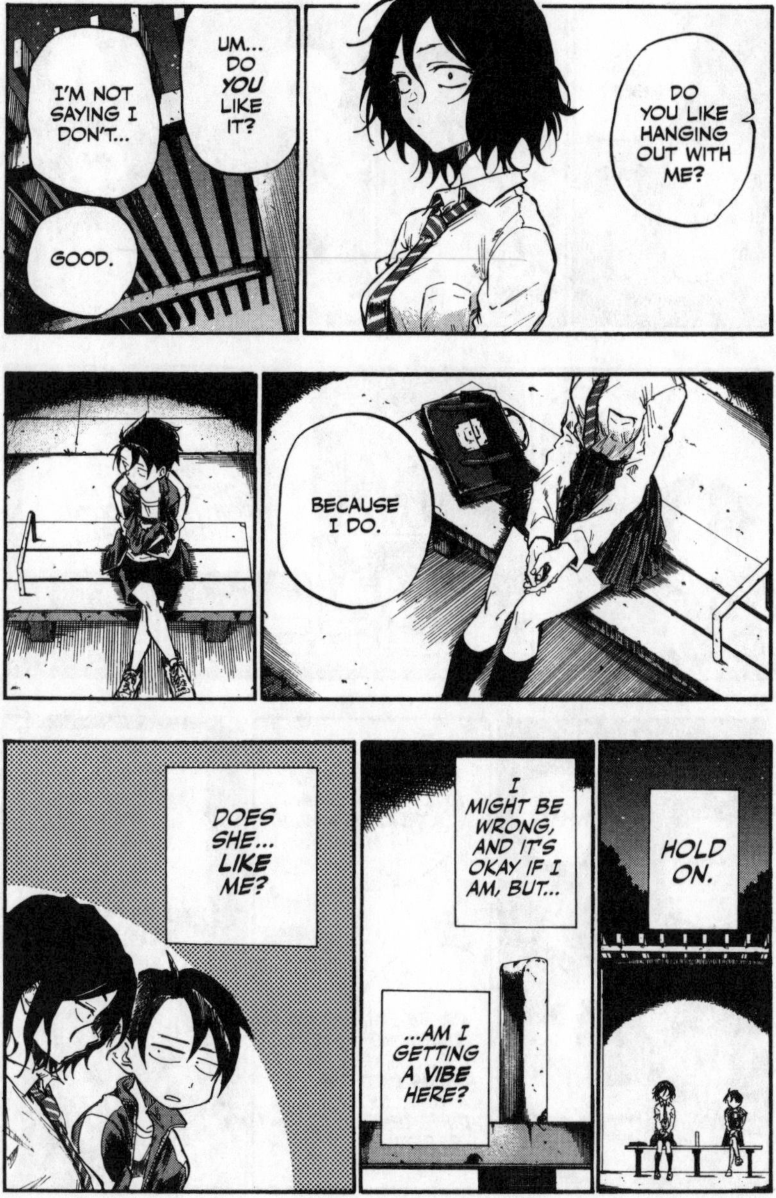
DO YOU LIKE HANGING OUT WITH ME?
UM... DO YOU LIKE IT?
I'M NOT SAYING I DON'T...
GOOD.
BECAUSE I DO.
HOLD ON.
I MIGHT BE WRONG, AND IT'S OKAY IF I AM, BUT...
...AM I GETTING A VIBE HERE?
DOES SHE... LIKE ME?

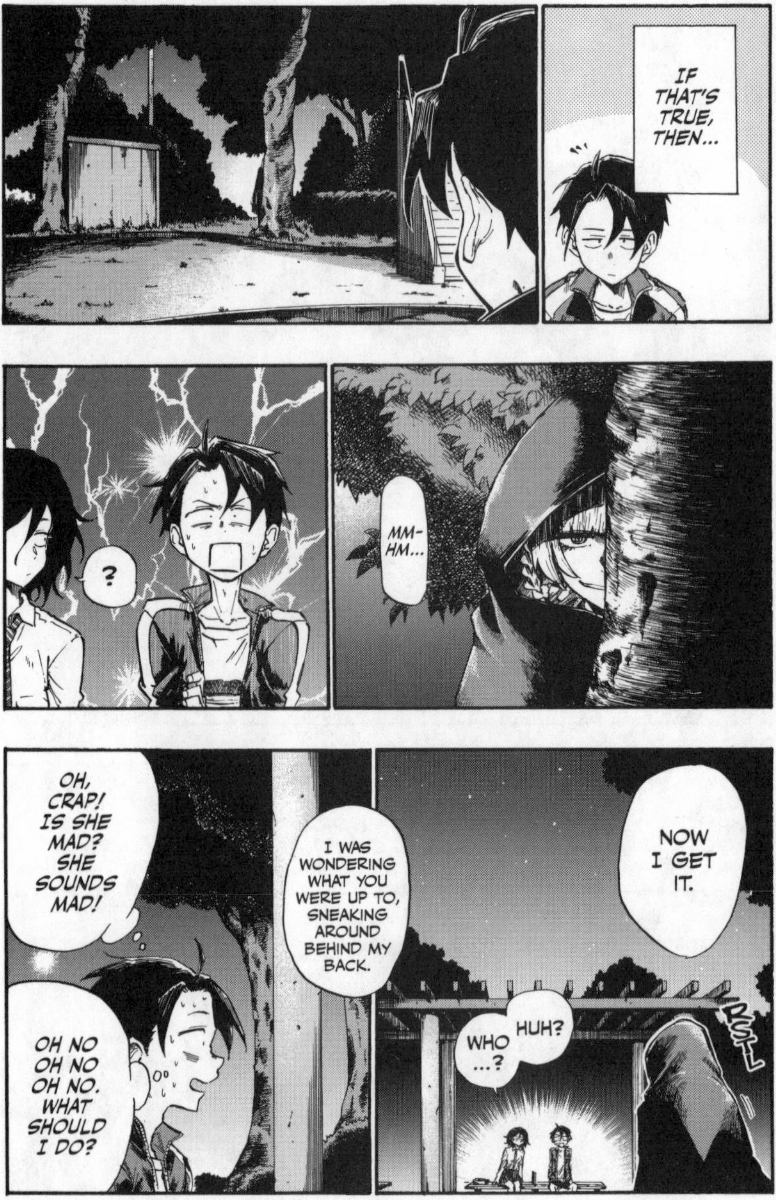
IF THAT'S TRUE, THEN...
MM-HM...
?
NOW I GET IT.
I WAS WONDERING WHAT YOU WERE UP TO, SNEAKING AROUND BEHIND MY BACK.
HUH?
WHO ...?
RSTL
OH, CRAP! IS SHE MAD? SHE SOUNDS MAD!
OH NO OH NO OH NO. WHAT SHOULD I DO?

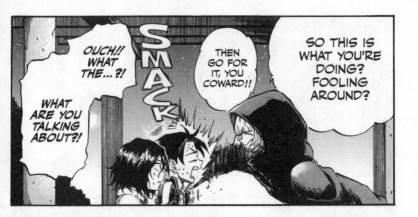

SO THIS IS WHAT YOU'RE DOING? FOOLING AROUND?
THEN GO FOR IT, YOU COWARD!!
SMACK
OUCH!! WHAT THE...?!
WHAT ARE YOU TALKING ABOUT?!
WHAT ELSE WOULD A GUY AND A GIRL BE DOING TOGETHER AT THIS HOUR? GO ON, FOOL AROUND!
I DON'T KNOW WHAT YOU MEAN!
PHEW! SHE ISN'T ANGRY AFTER ALL.
IS THIS YOUR FRIEND, KO?
OH, DON'T MIND LITTLE OLD ME.
UM...
YOU'VE GOT NOTHING TO WORRY ABOUT. OUR RELATIONSHIP IS PURELY PHYSICAL.
WORK ON YOUR PHRASING!!
...
KO, SKIPPING SCHOOL IS ONE THING, BUT I HOPE YOU'RE NOT MIXED UP WITH A BAD ELEMENT.
IT'S NOT WHAT YOU THINK...
OOH, I'M A BAD ELEMENT!
NAZUNA, WOULD YOU PLEASE SHUT UP?!

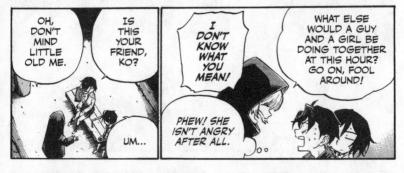

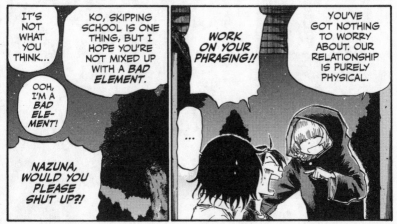

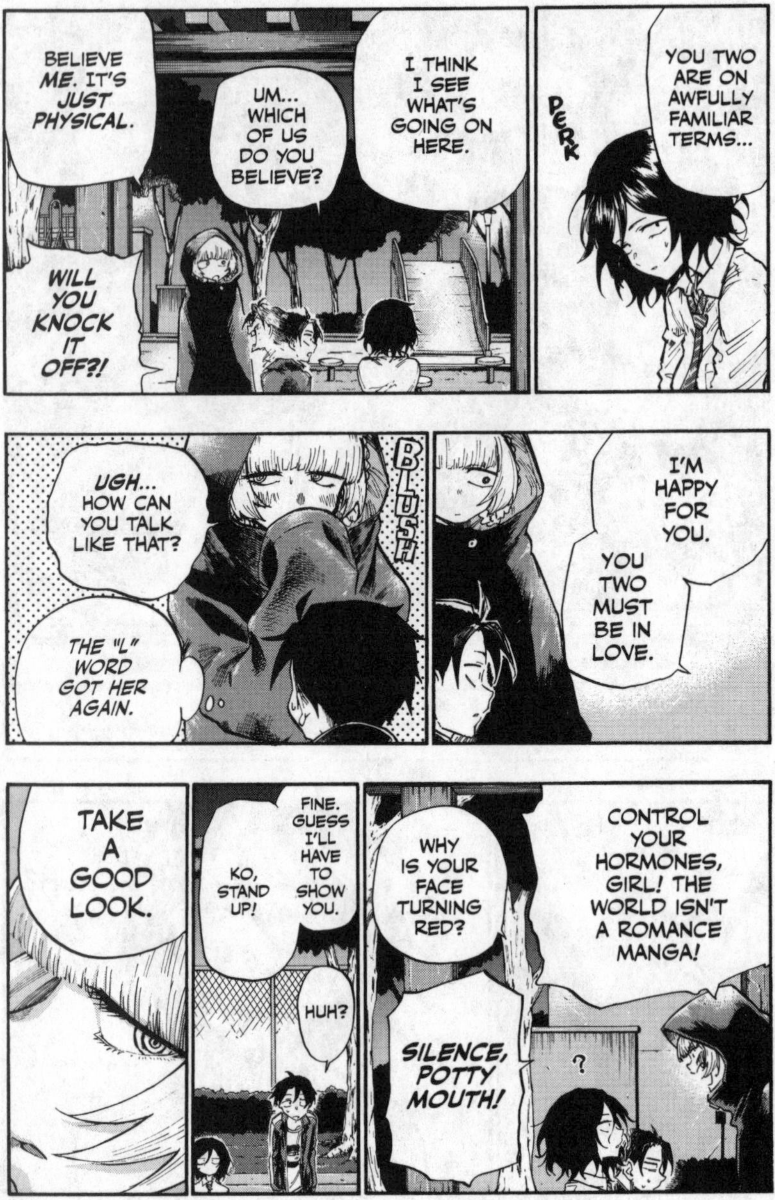
YOU TWO ARE ON AWFULLY FAMILIAR TERMS...
PERK
I THINK I SEE WHAT'S GOING ON HERE.
UM... WHICH OF US DO YOU BELIEVE?
BELIEVE ME. IT'S JUST PHYSICAL.
WILL YOU KNOCK IT OFF?!
I'M HAPPY FOR YOU.
YOU TWO MUST BE IN LOVE.
BLUSH
UGH... HOW CAN YOU TALK LIKE THAT?
THE "L" WORD GOT HER AGAIN.
CONTROL YOUR HORMONES, GIRL! THE WORLD ISN'T A ROMANCE MANGA!
WHY IS YOUR FACE TURNING RED?
?
SILENCE, POTTY MOUTH!
FINE. GUESS I'LL HAVE TO SHOW YOU.
KO, STAND UP!
HUH?
TAKE A GOOD LOOK.

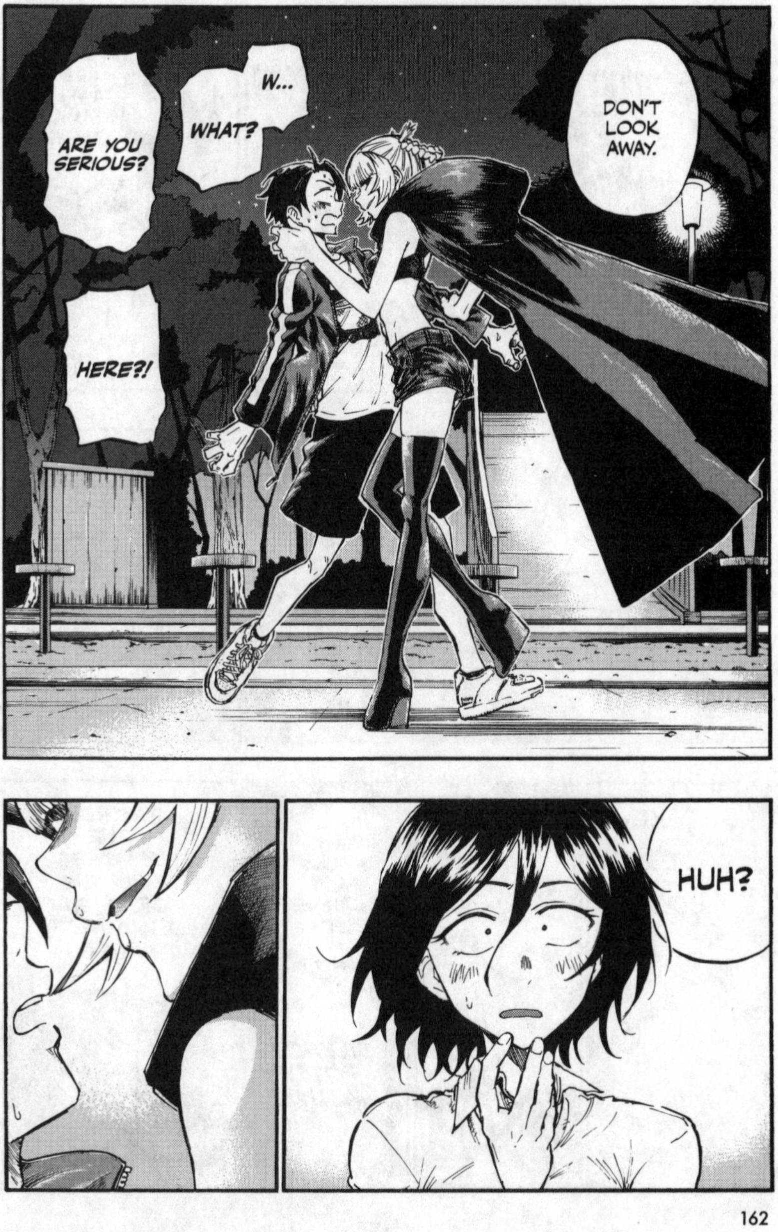
DON'T LOOK AWAY.
W... WHAT?
ARE YOU SERIOUS?
HERE?!
HUH?

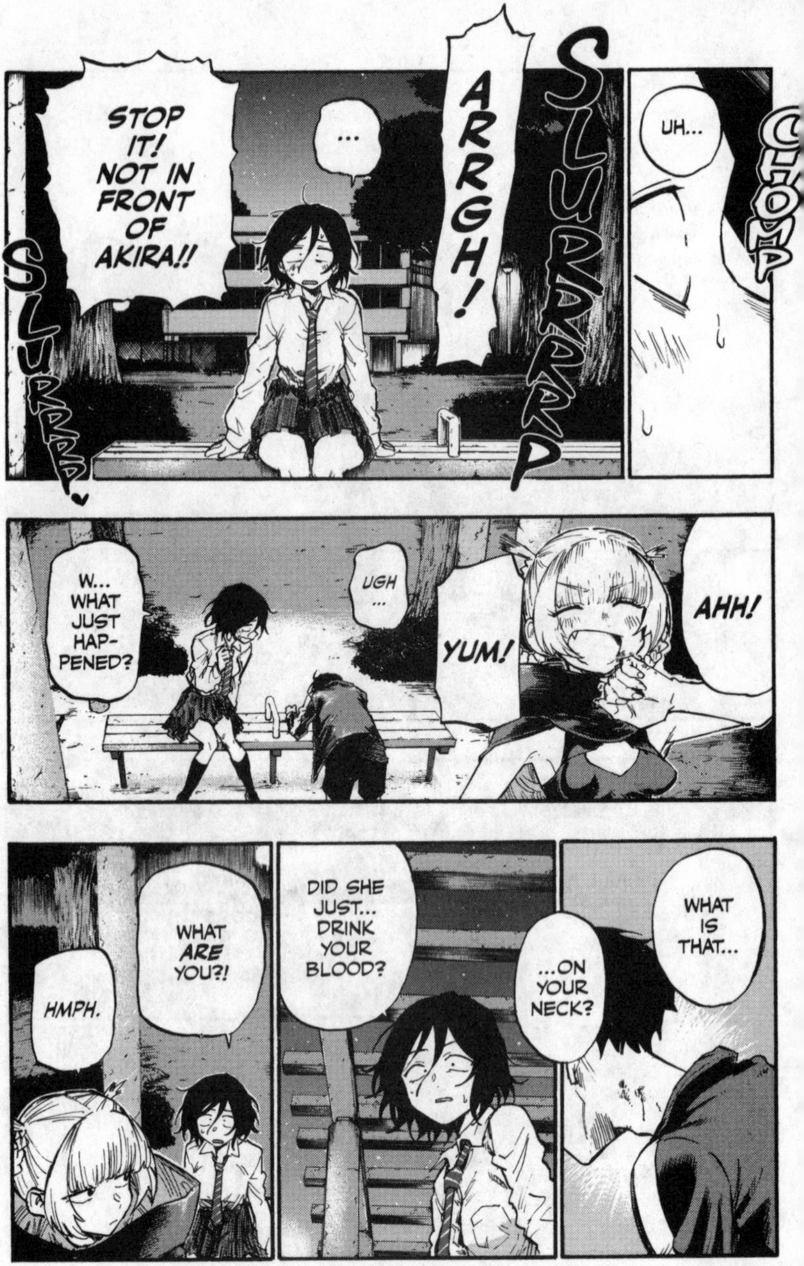
UH...
CHOMP
SLURRRRP
ARRGH!
...
STOP IT! NOT IN FRONT OF AKIRA!!
SLURRRP!
AHH!
YUM!
UGH ...
W... WHAT JUST HAP-PENED?
WHAT IS THAT...
...ON YOUR NECK?
DID SHE JUST... DRINK YOUR BLOOD?
WHAT ARE YOU?!
HMPH.

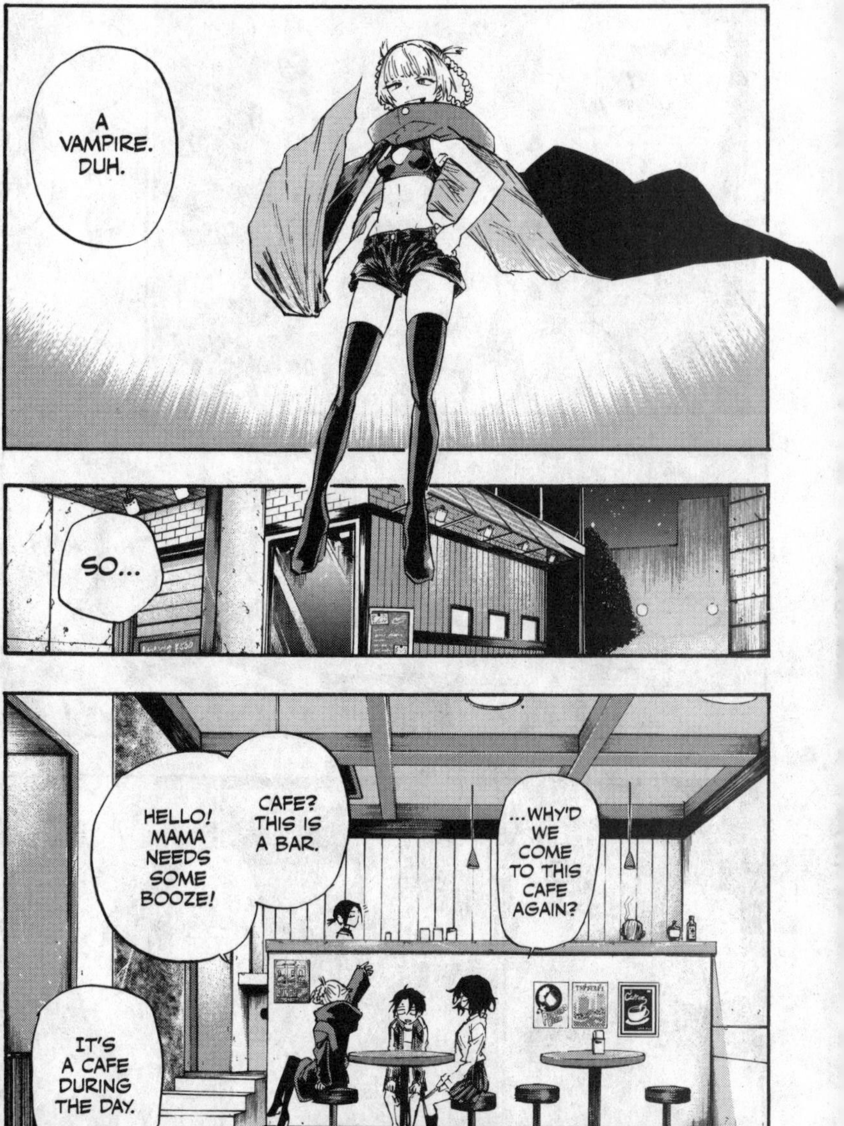
A VAMPIRE. DUH.
SO...
...WHY'D WE COME TO THIS CAFE AGAIN?
CAFE? THIS IS A BAR.
HELLO! MAMA NEEDS SOME BOOZE!
IT'S A CAFE DURING THE DAY.

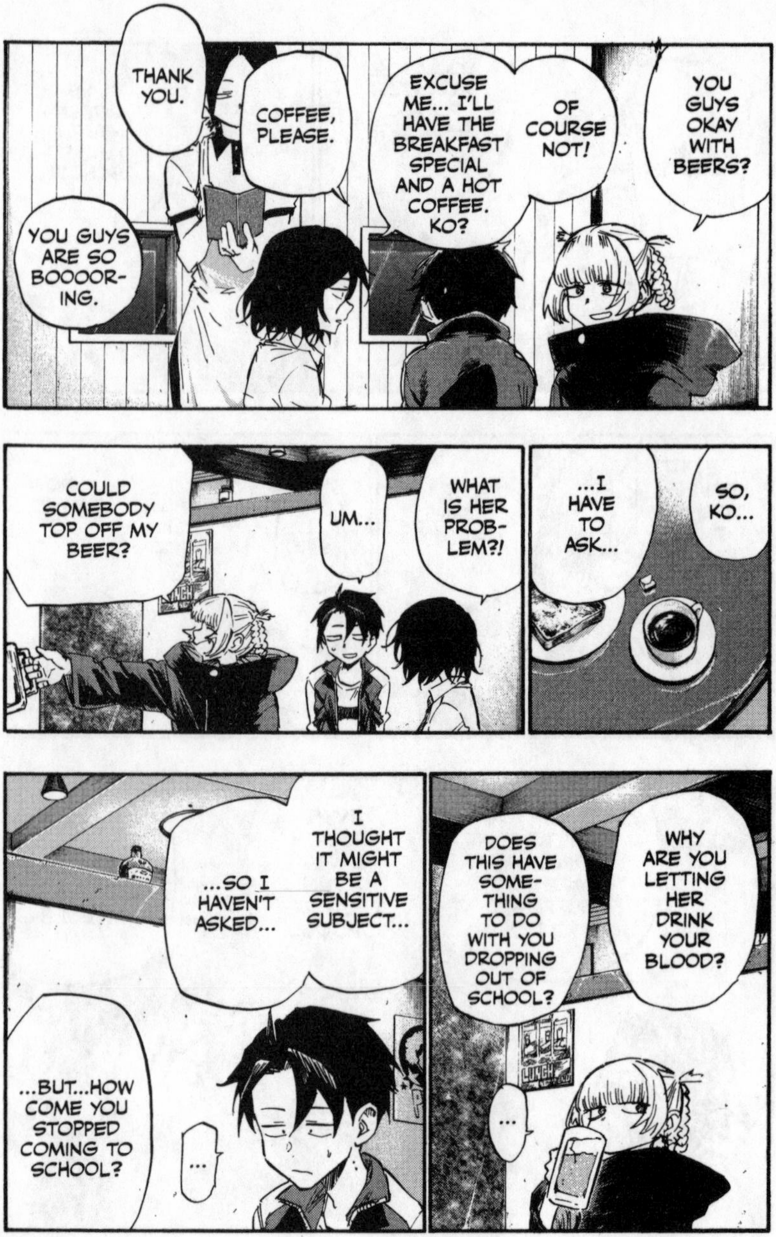
YOU GUYS OKAY WITH BEERS?
OF COURSE NOT!
EXCUSE ME... I'LL HAVE THE BREAKFAST SPECIAL AND A HOT COFFEE. KO?
COFFEE, PLEASE.
THANK YOU.
YOU GUYS ARE SO BOOOOR-ING.
SO, KO...
...I HAVE TO ASK...
WHAT IS HER PROB-LEM?!
UM...
COULD SOMEBODY TOP OFF MY BEER?
WHY ARE YOU LETTING HER DRINK YOUR BLOOD?
DOES THIS HAVE SOME-THING TO DO WITH YOU DROPPING OUT OF SCHOOL?
...
I THOUGHT IT MIGHT BE A SENSITIVE SUBJECT...
...SO I HAVEN'T ASKED...
...BUT...HOW COME YOU STOPPED COMING TO SCHOOL?
...

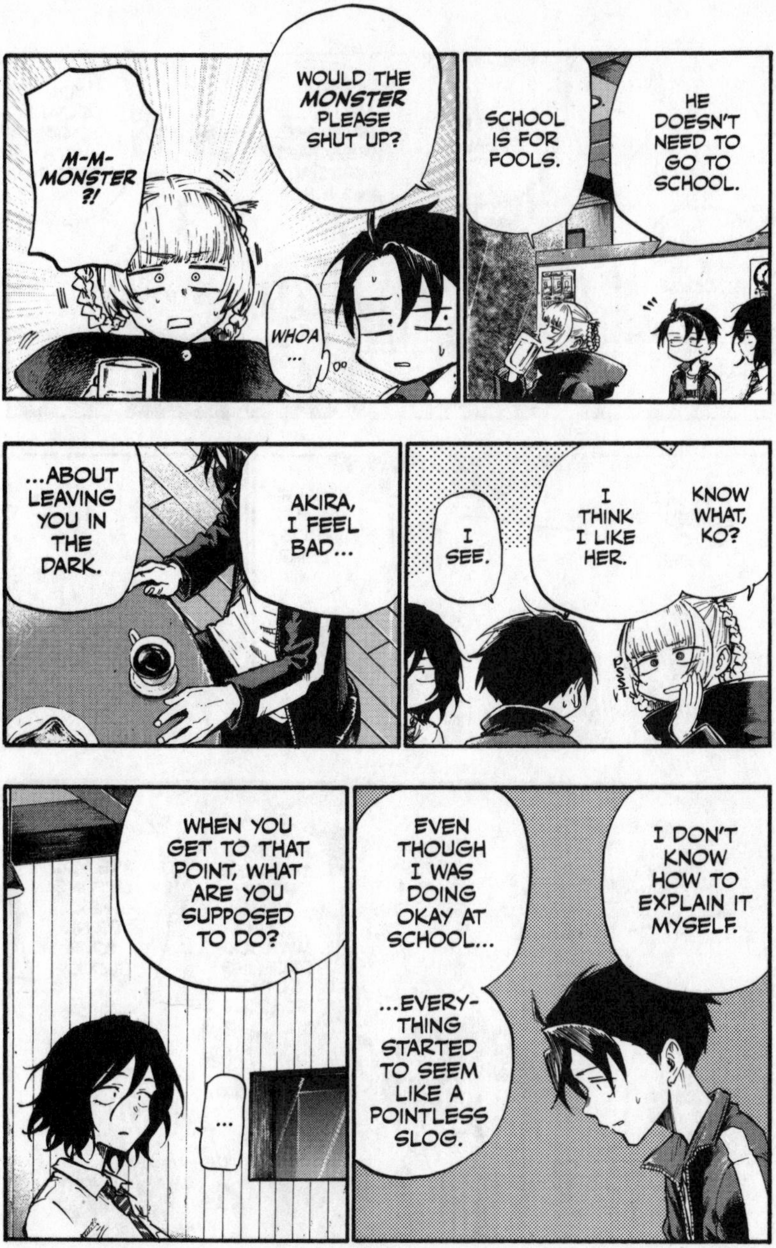
HE DOESN'T NEED TO GO TO SCHOOL.
SCHOOL IS FOR FOOLS.
WOULD THE *MONSTER* PLEASE SHUT UP?
M-M-MONSTER?!
WHOA...
KNOW WHAT, KO?
I THINK I LIKE HER.
I SEE.
PSST
AKIRA, I FEEL BAD...
...ABOUT LEAVING YOU IN THE DARK.
I DON'T KNOW HOW TO EXPLAIN IT MYSELF.
EVEN THOUGH I WAS DOING OKAY AT SCHOOL...
...EVERY-THING STARTED TO SEEM LIKE A POINTLESS SLOG.
WHEN YOU GET TO THAT POINT, WHAT ARE YOU SUPPOSED TO DO?
...

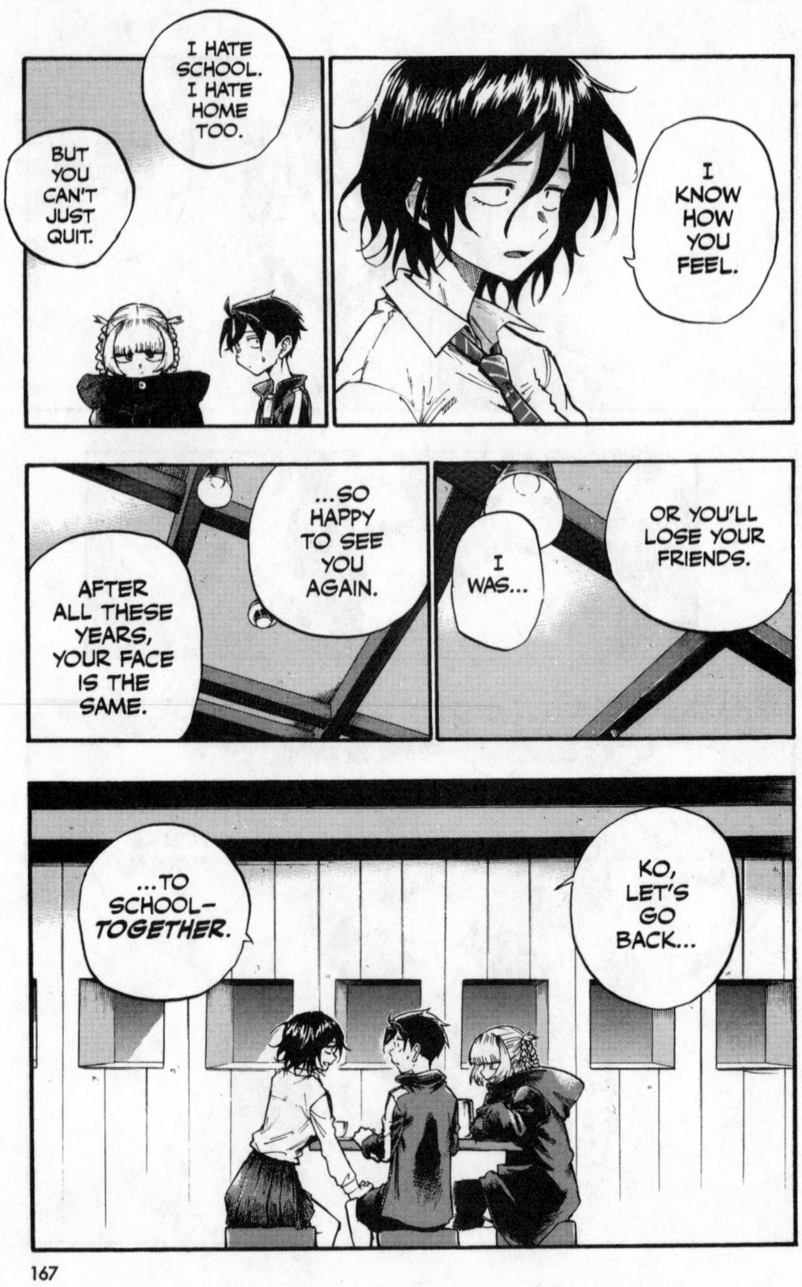
I KNOW HOW YOU FEEL.
I HATE SCHOOL. I HATE HOME TOO.
BUT YOU CAN'T JUST QUIT.
OR YOU'LL LOSE YOUR FRIENDS.
I WAS...
...SO HAPPY TO SEE YOU AGAIN.
AFTER ALL THESE YEARS, YOUR FACE IS THE SAME.
KO, LET'S GO BACK...
...TO SCHOOL—*TOGETHER*.

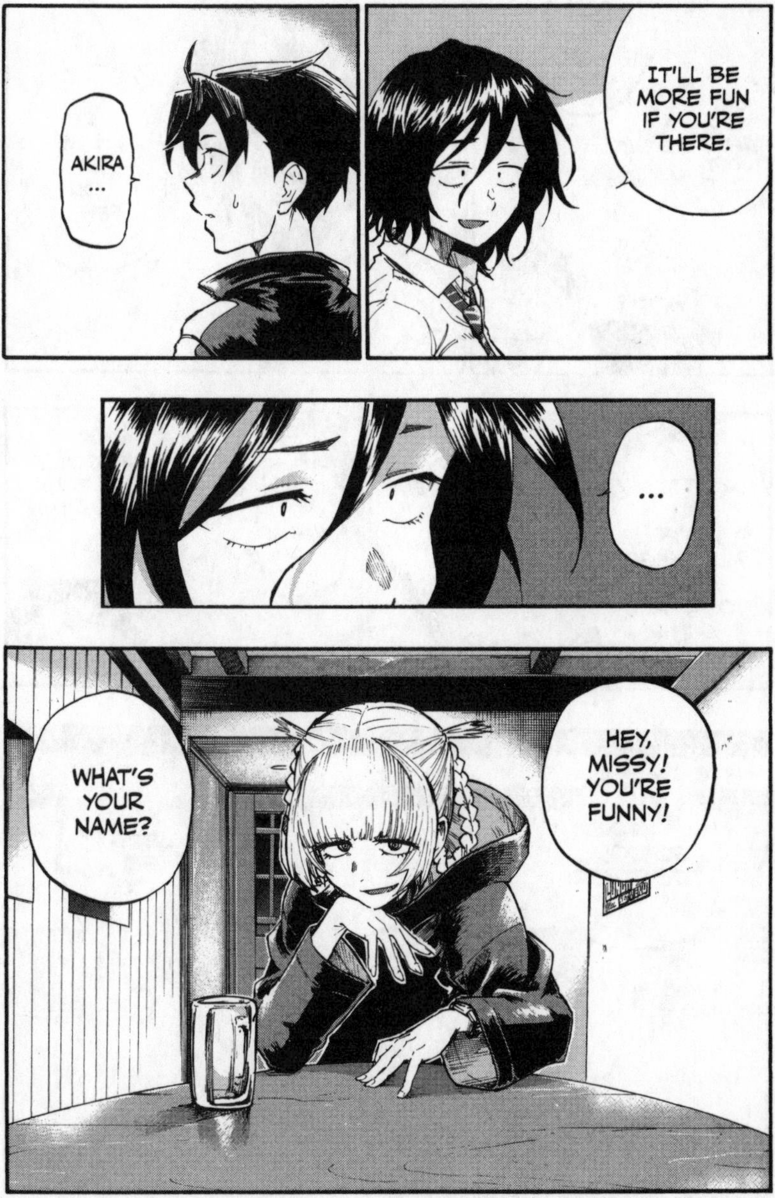
IT'LL BE MORE FUN IF YOU'RE THERE.
AKIRA ...
...
HEY, MISSY! YOU'RE FUNNY!
WHAT'S YOUR NAME?

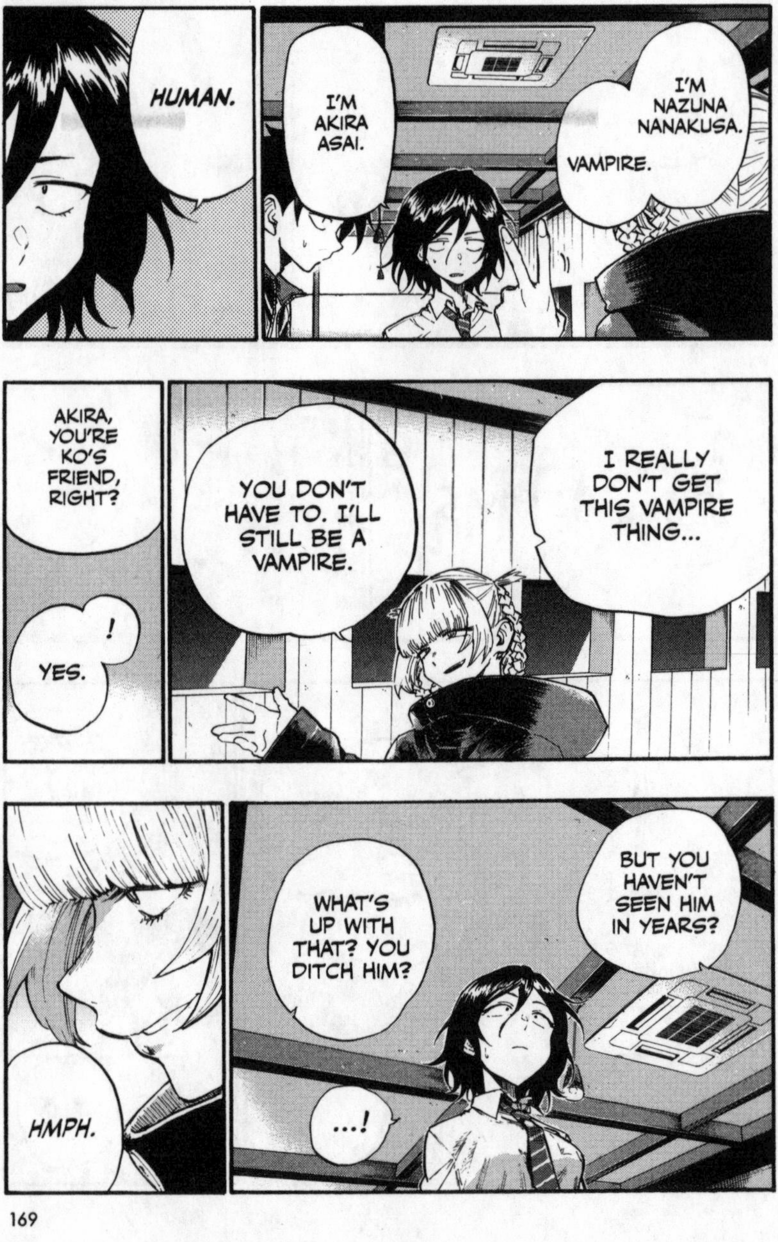
I'M NAZUNA NANAKUSA.
VAMPIRE.
I'M AKIRA ASAI.
HUMAN.
I REALLY DON'T GET THIS VAMPIRE THING...
YOU DON'T HAVE TO. I'LL STILL BE A VAMPIRE.
AKIRA, YOU'RE KO'S FRIEND, RIGHT?
!
YES.
BUT YOU HAVEN'T SEEN HIM IN YEARS?
WHAT'S UP WITH THAT? YOU DITCH HIM?
...!
HMPH.

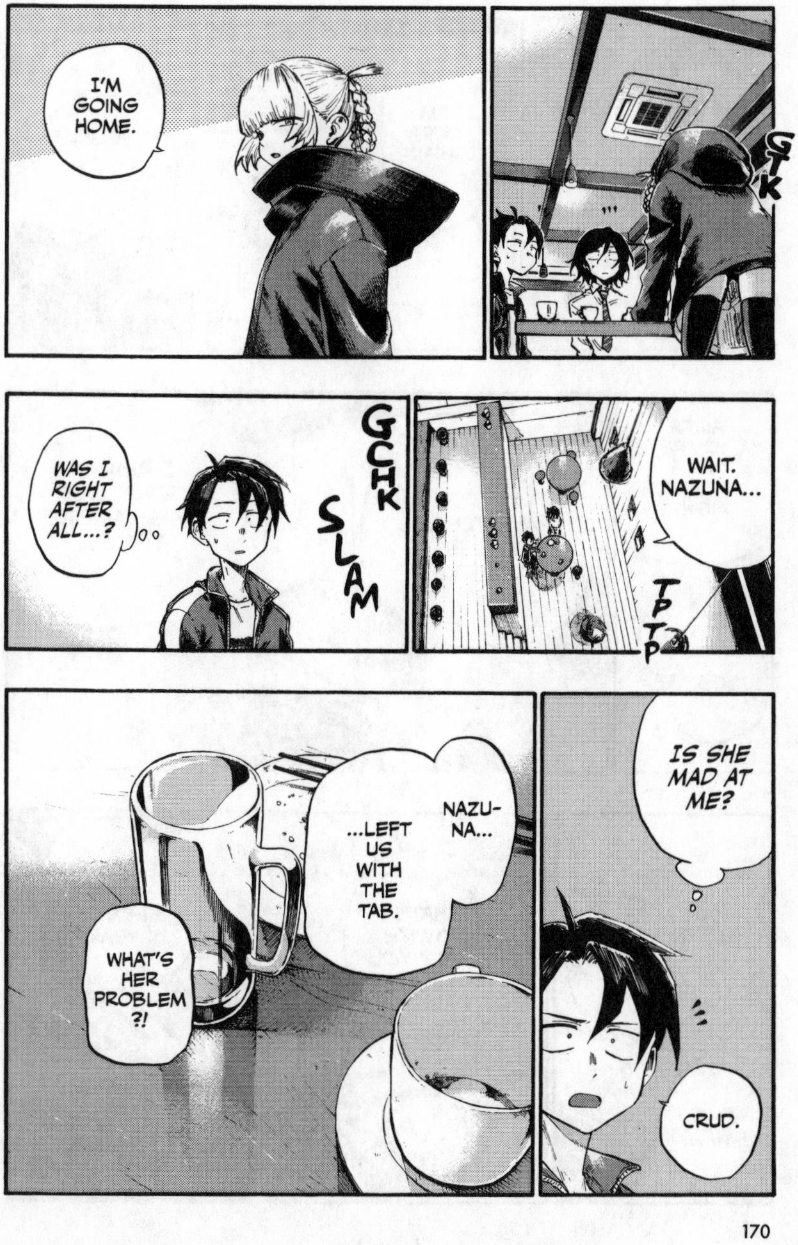
GTK
I'M GOING HOME.
WAIT. NAZUNA...
TPTP
GCHK
SLAM
WAS I RIGHT AFTER ALL...?
IS SHE MAD AT ME?
CRUD.
NAZUNA...
...LEFT US WITH THE TAB.
WHAT'S HER PROBLEM?!

NIGHT 8: A LOT CAME OUT

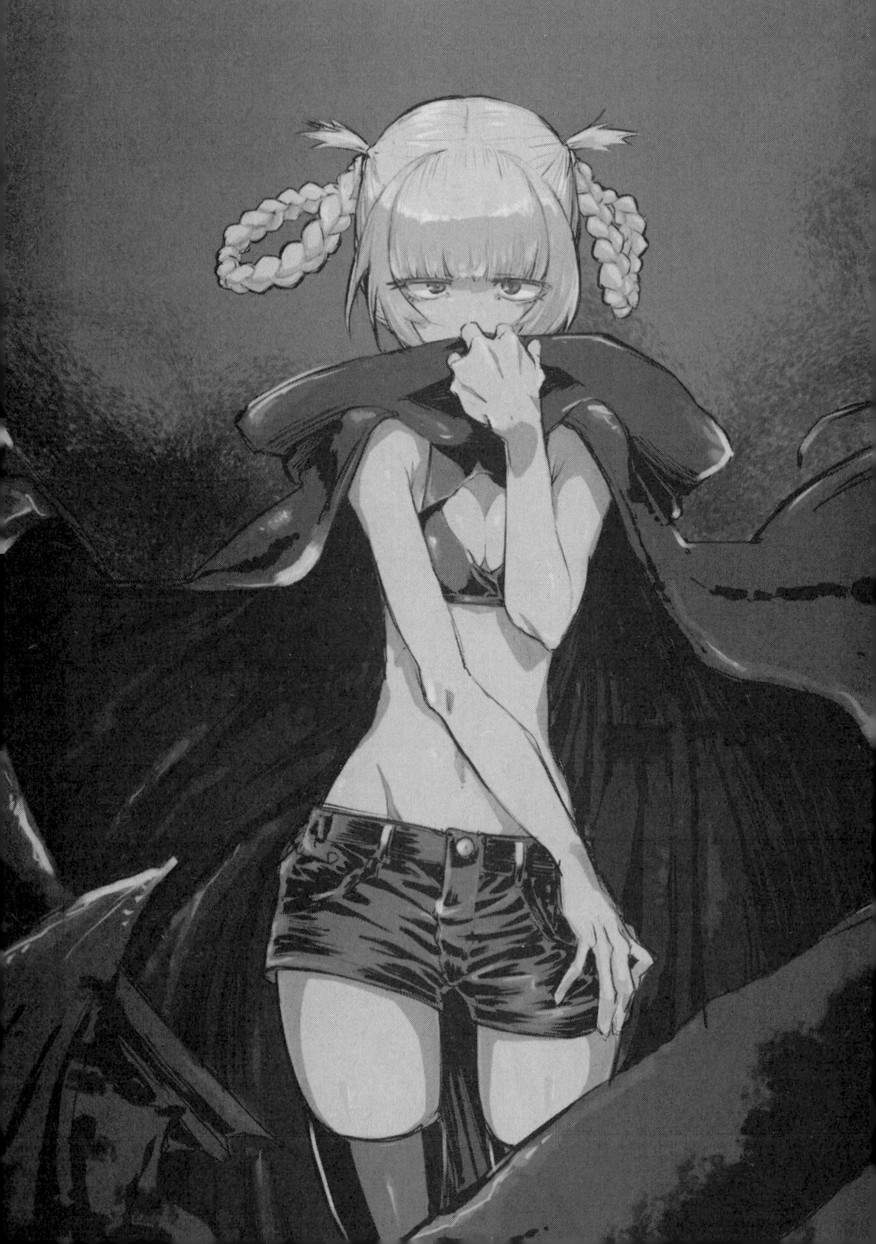

Call of the Night

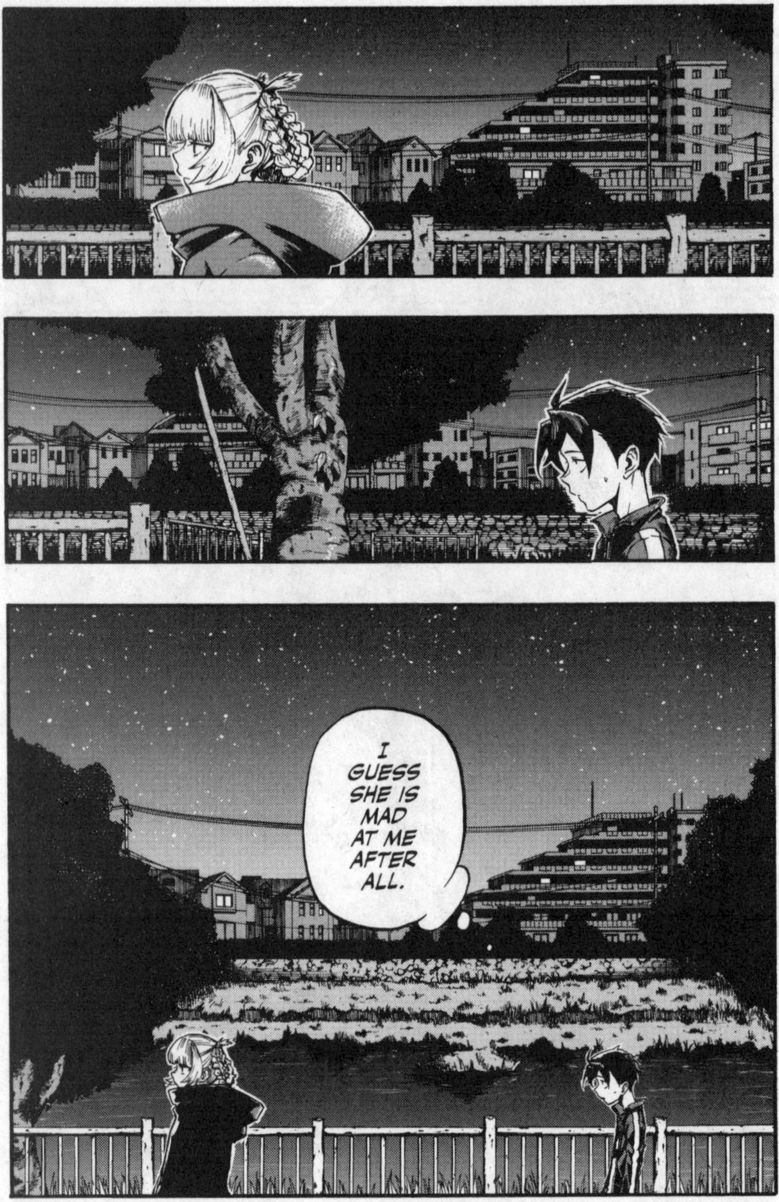
I GUESS SHE IS MAD AT ME AFTER ALL.

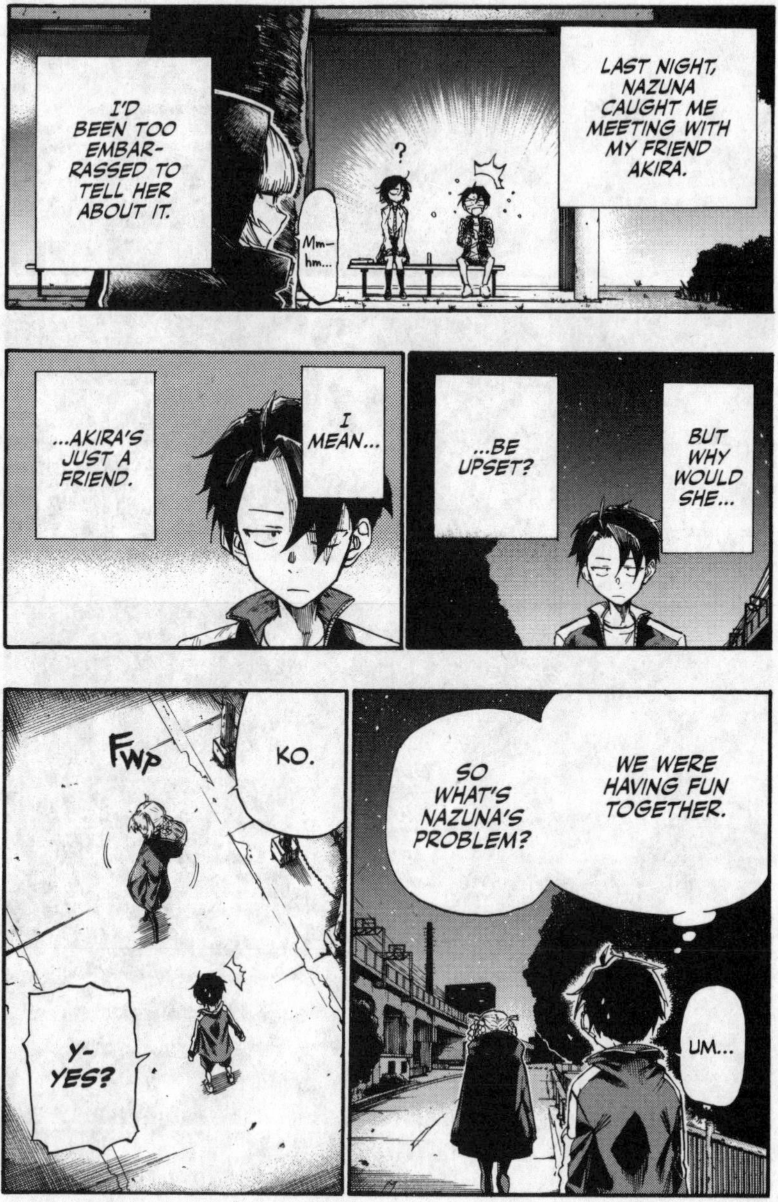
LAST NIGHT, NAZUNA CAUGHT ME MEETING WITH MY FRIEND AKIRA.
I'D BEEN TOO EMBAR-RASSED TO TELL HER ABOUT IT.
Mm-hm...
BUT WHY WOULD SHE...
...BE UPSET?
I MEAN...
...AKIRA'S JUST A FRIEND.
WE WERE HAVING FUN TOGETHER.
SO WHAT'S NAZUNA'S PROBLEM?
UM...
KO.
FWP
Y-YES?

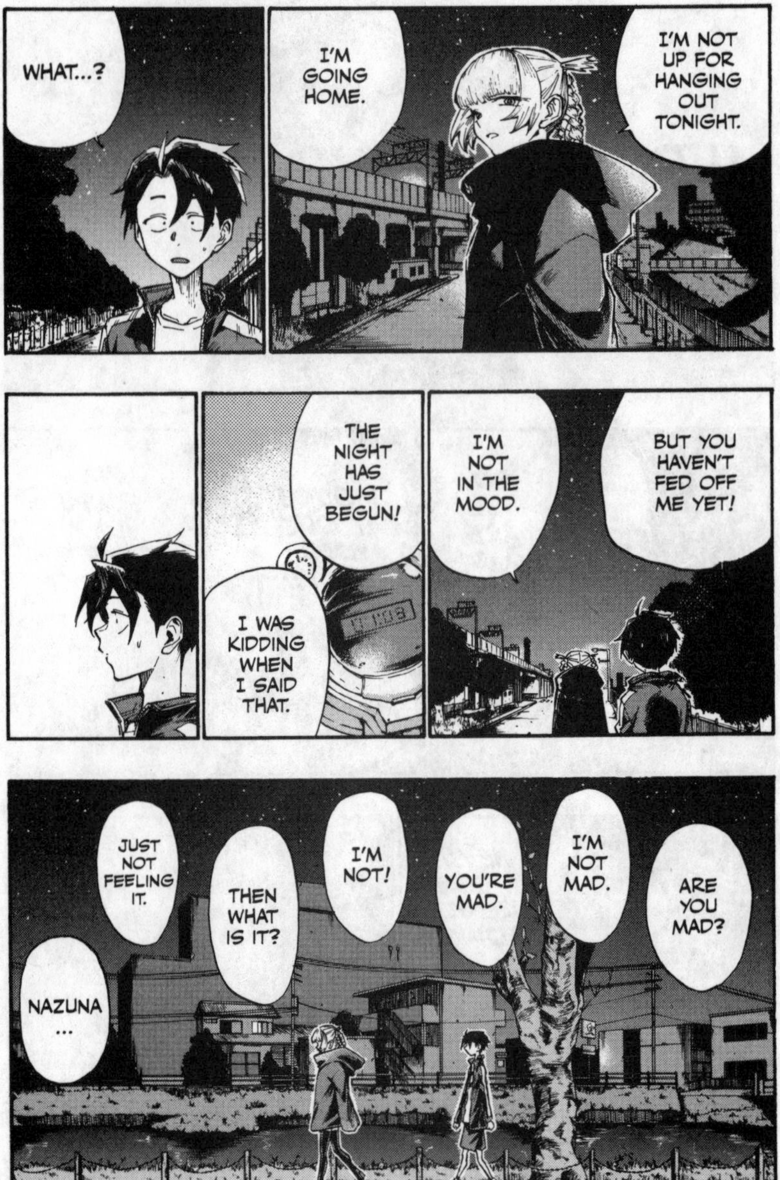
I'M NOT UP FOR HANGING OUT TONIGHT.
I'M GOING HOME.
WHAT...?
BUT YOU HAVEN'T FED OFF ME YET!
I'M NOT IN THE MOOD.
THE NIGHT HAS JUST BEGUN!
I WAS KIDDING WHEN I SAID THAT.
ARE YOU MAD?
I'M NOT MAD.
YOU'RE MAD.
I'M NOT!
THEN WHAT IS IT?
JUST NOT FEELING IT.
NAZUNA...

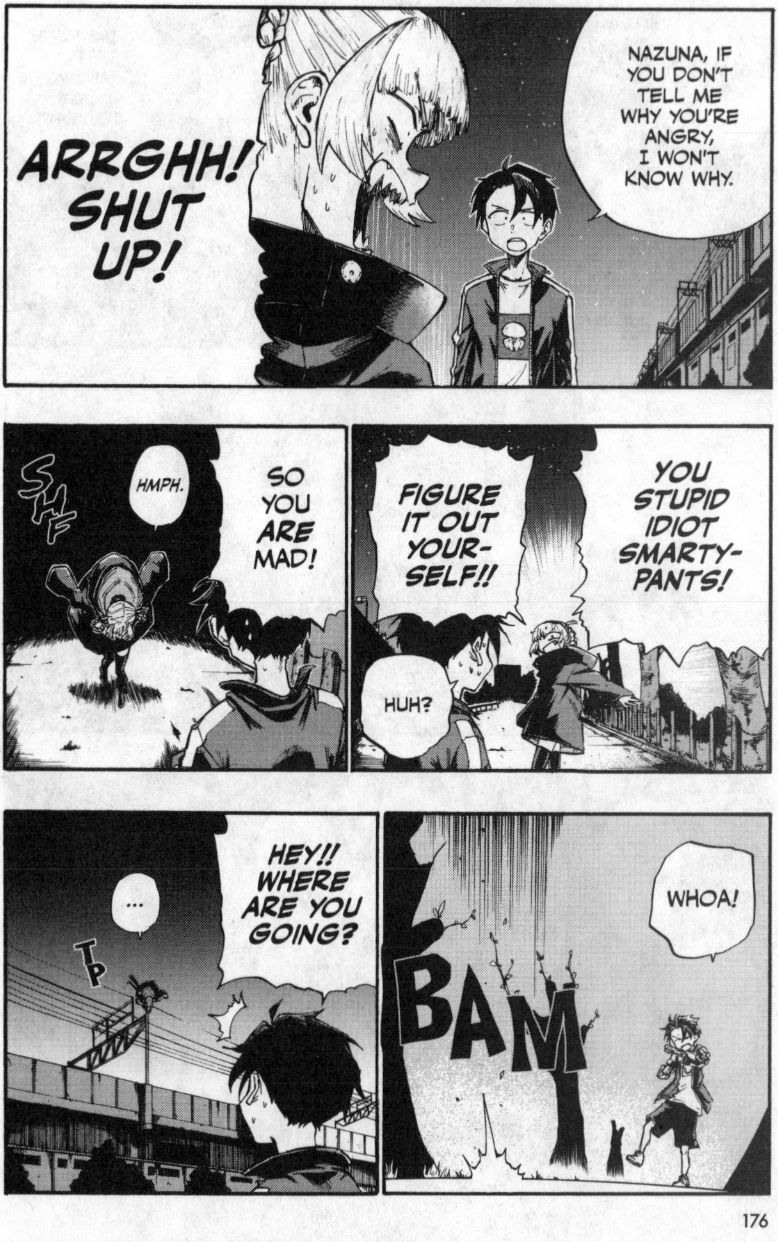
NAZUNA, IF YOU DON'T TELL ME WHY YOU'RE ANGRY, I WON'T KNOW WHY.
ARRGHH! SHUT UP!
YOU STUPID IDIOT SMARTY-PANTS!
FIGURE IT OUT YOUR-SELF!!
HUH?
SO YOU ARE MAD!
HMPH.
SHF
WHOA!
BAM
HEY!! WHERE ARE YOU GOING?
...
TP

HMPH.
WHAT THE...?!
DAM-MIT!
DAK
NAZU-NA!
WHAT ARE YOU...
...MAD ABOUT ?!
DAMMIT, NAZUNA! YOU'RE TOO FAST!!
I WON'T LOSE SIGHT OF YOU!
HFF ...
HFF ...

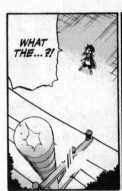

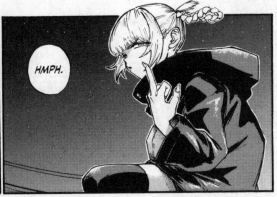

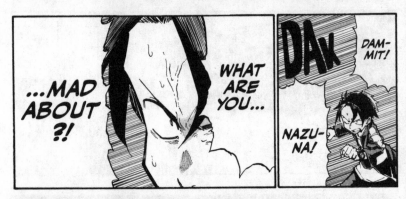

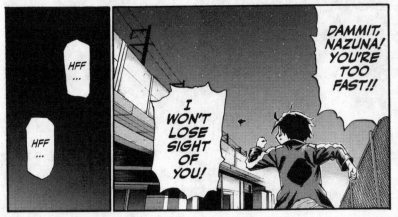

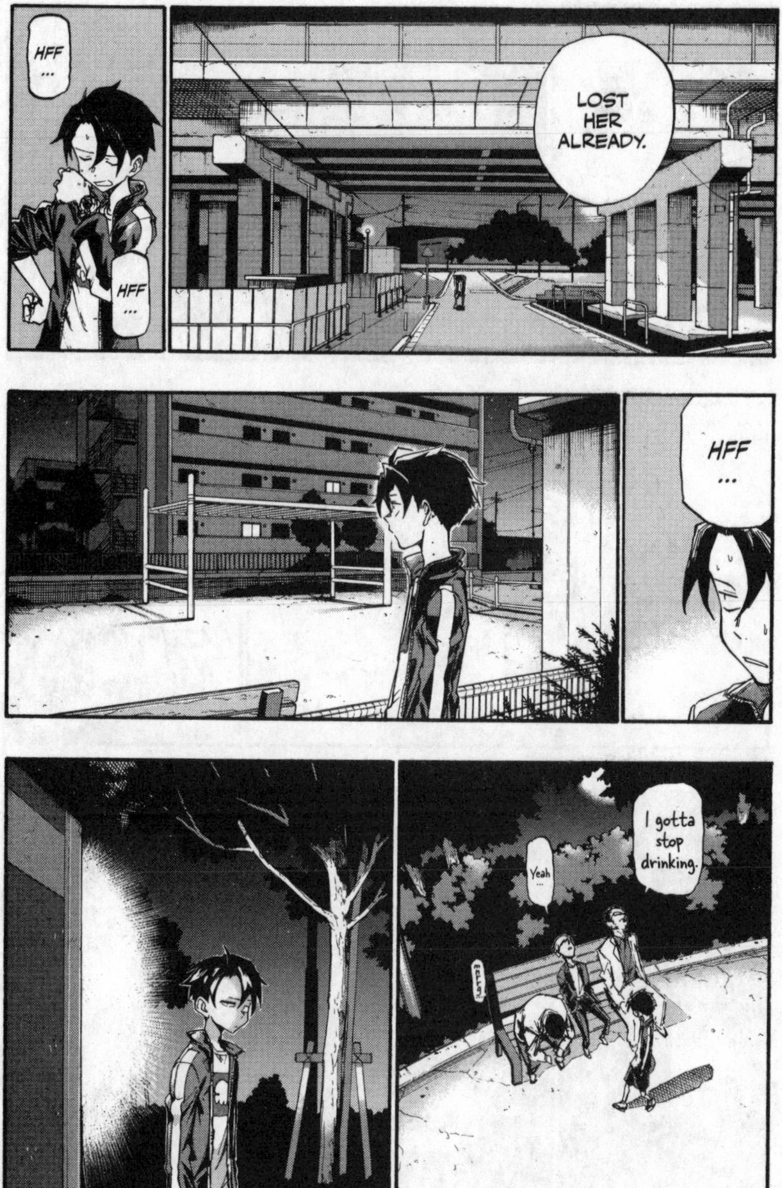
LOST HER ALREADY.
HFF ...
HFF ...
HFF ...
I gotta stop drinking.
Yeah ...

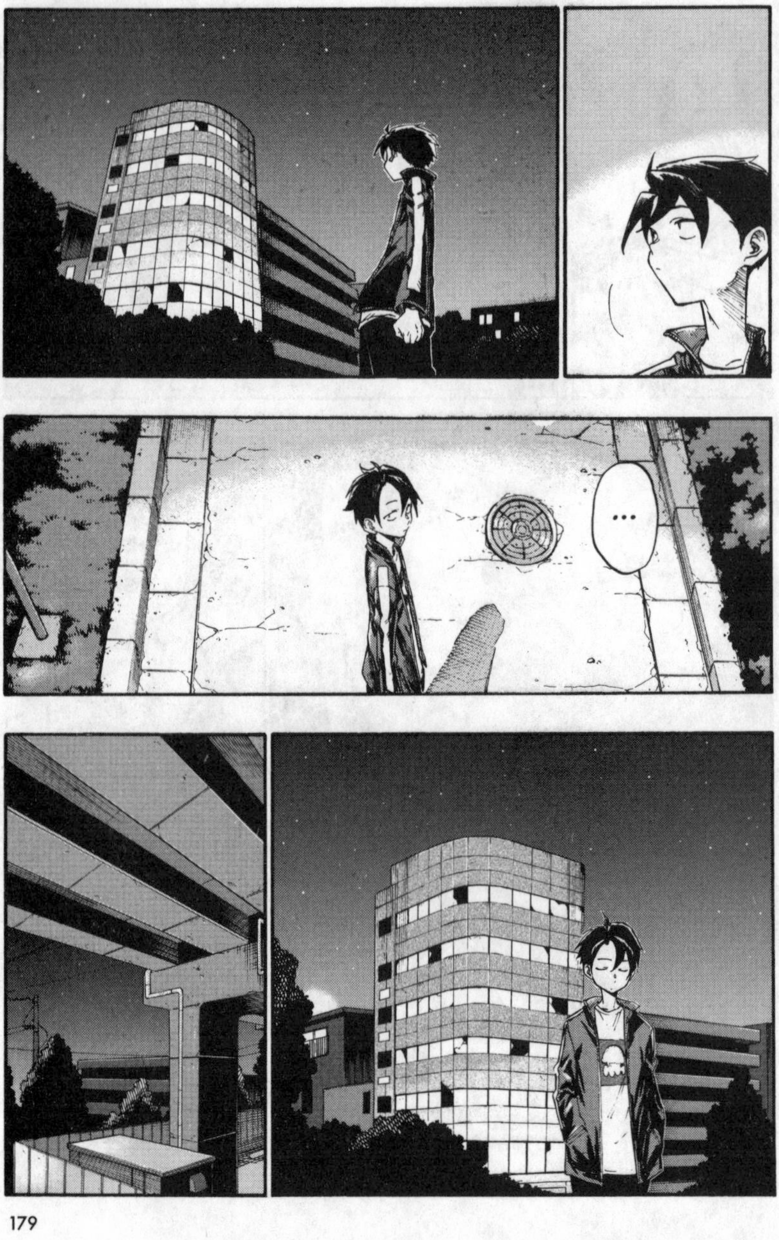
...

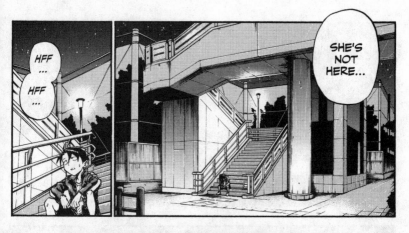

SHE'S NOT HERE...
HFF ... HFF ...
MAYBE I'LL GET A GLIMPSE OF HER FROM HIGHER GROUND.
GRP
WHEW.
WHY IS SHE SO ANGRY?!
ARE WE HAVING A FIGHT?
!
TRIP

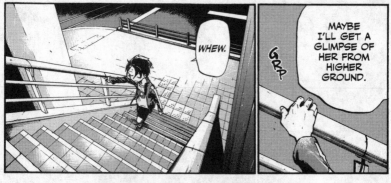

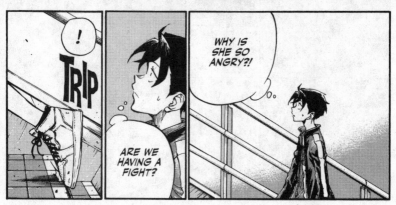

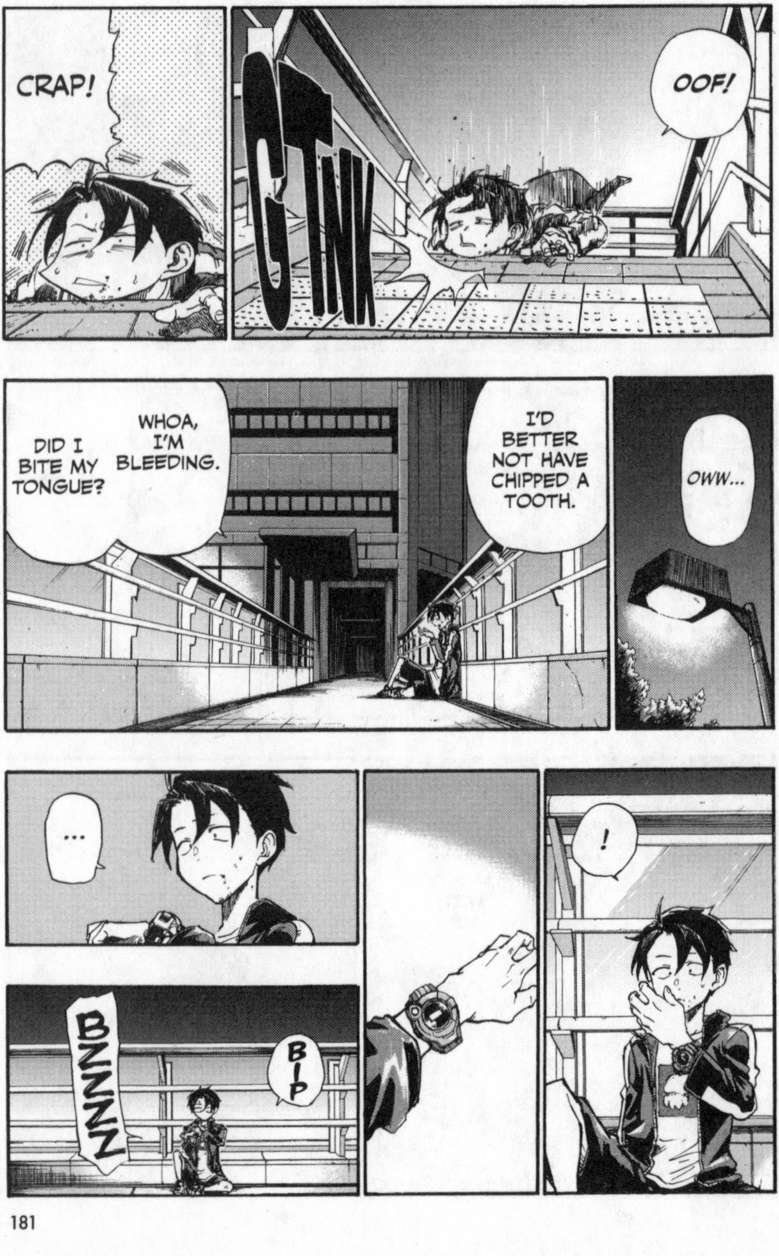
OOF!
GTINK
CRAP!
OWW...
I'D BETTER NOT HAVE CHIPPED A TOOTH.
WHOA, I'M BLEEDING.
DID I BITE MY TONGUE?
!
...
BIP
BZZZZ

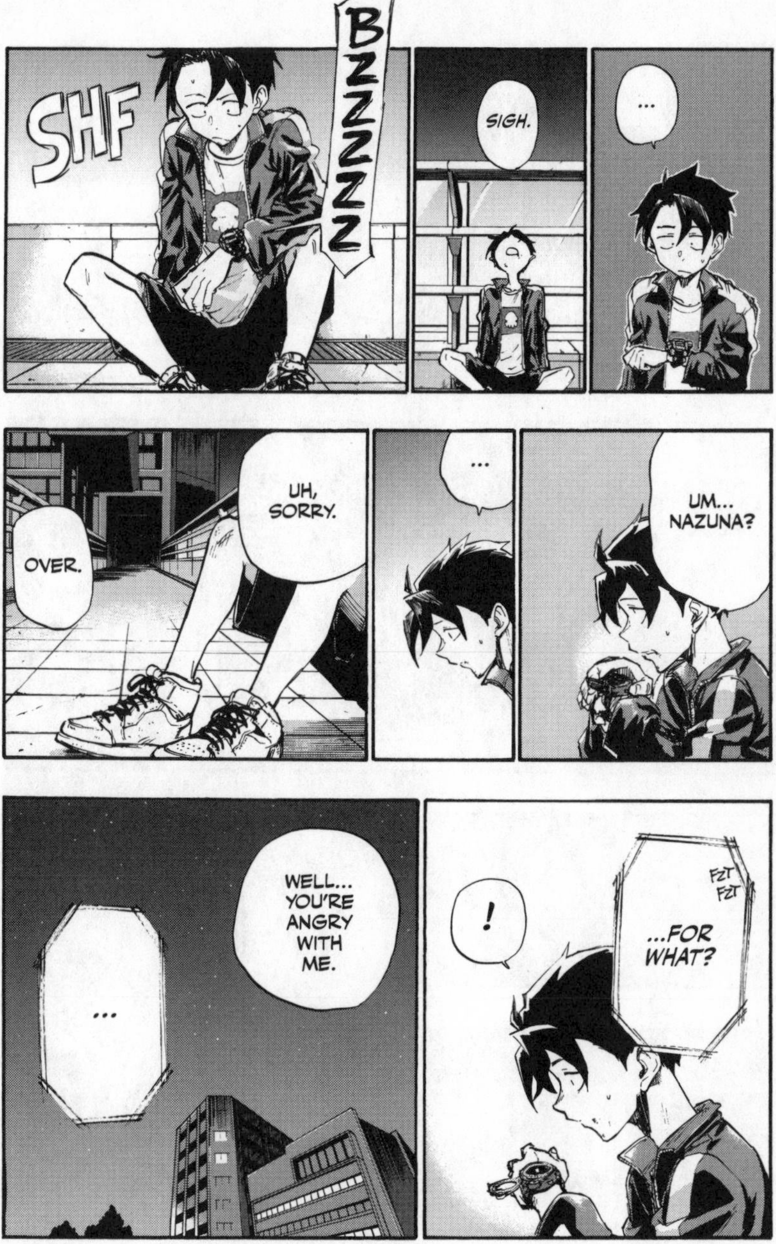
...
SIGH.
BZZZZZZ
SHF
UM... NAZUNA?
...
UH, SORRY.
OVER.
FZT FZT
...FOR WHAT?
!
WELL... YOU'RE ANGRY WITH ME.
...

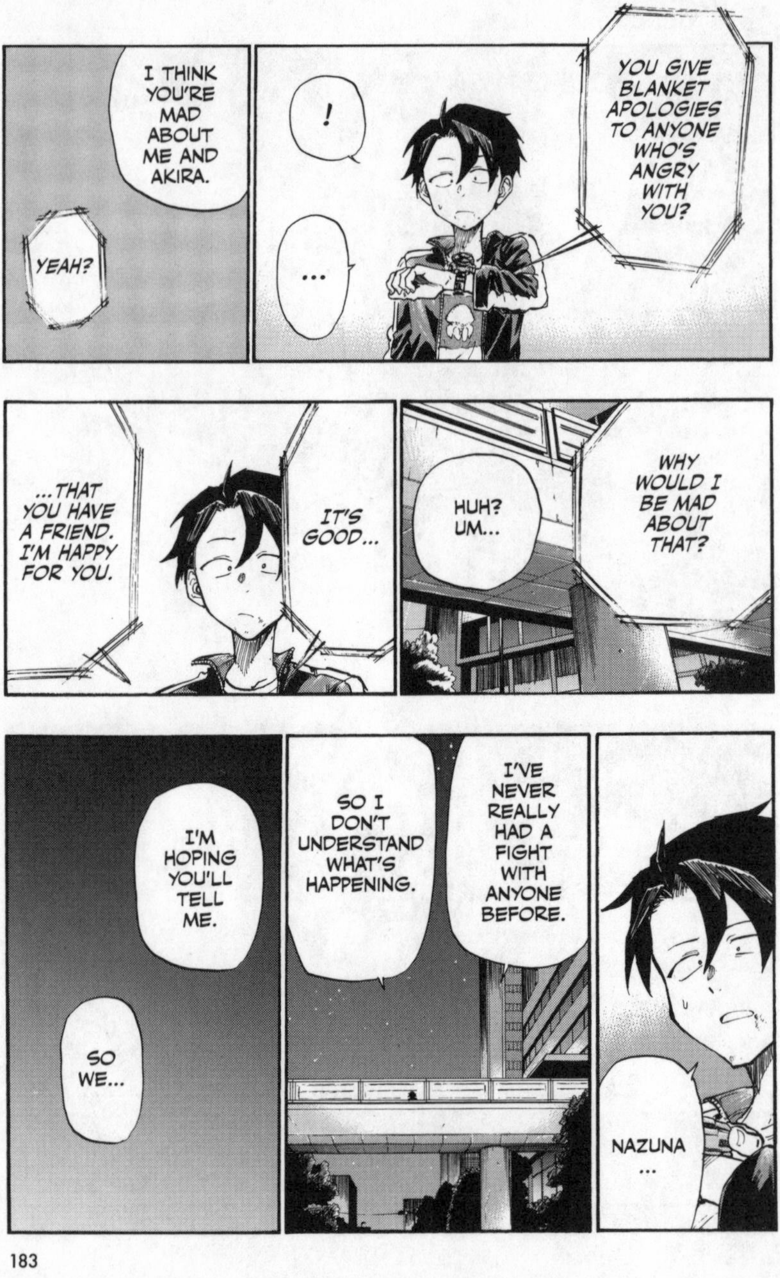
YOU GIVE BLANKET APOLOGIES TO ANYONE WHO'S ANGRY WITH YOU?
!
...
I THINK YOU'RE MAD ABOUT ME AND AKIRA.
YEAH?
WHY WOULD I BE MAD ABOUT THAT?
HUH? UM...
IT'S GOOD...
...THAT YOU HAVE A FRIEND. I'M HAPPY FOR YOU.
NAZUNA ...
I'VE NEVER REALLY HAD A FIGHT WITH ANYONE BEFORE.
SO I DON'T UNDERSTAND WHAT'S HAPPENING.
I'M HOPING YOU'LL TELL ME.
SO WE...

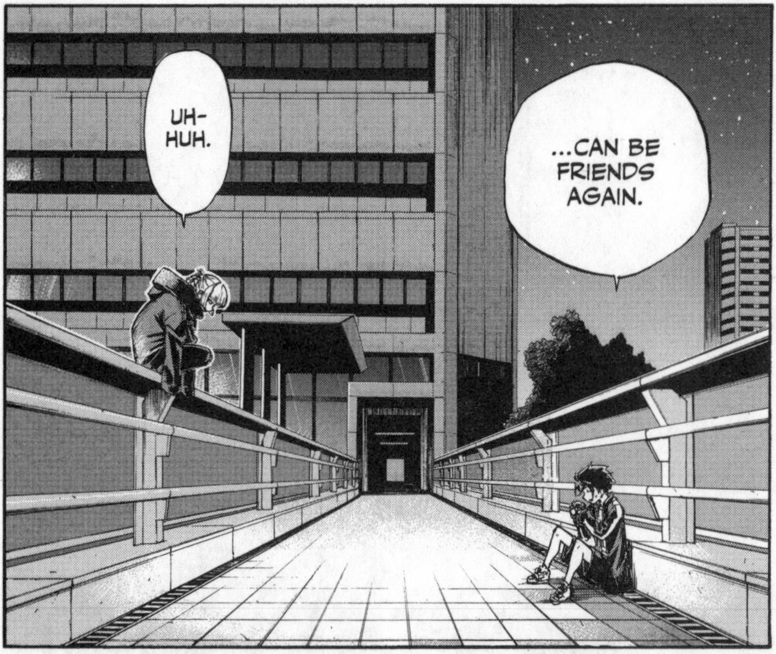
...CAN BE FRIENDS AGAIN.
UH-HUH.

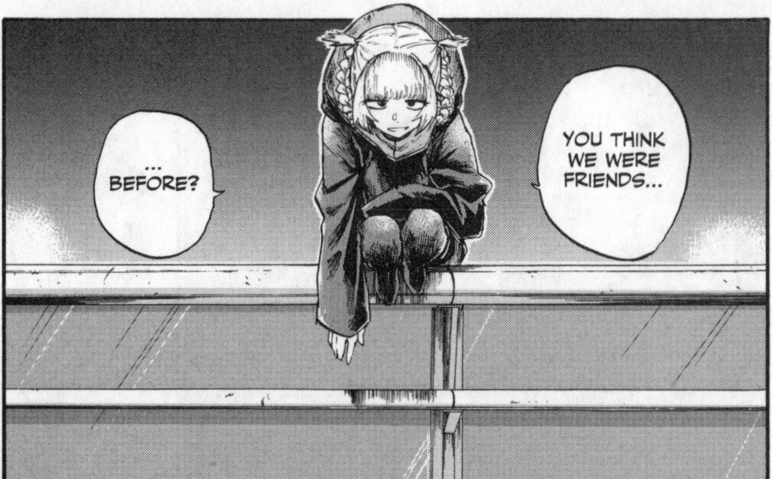
YOU THINK WE WERE FRIENDS...
... BEFORE?

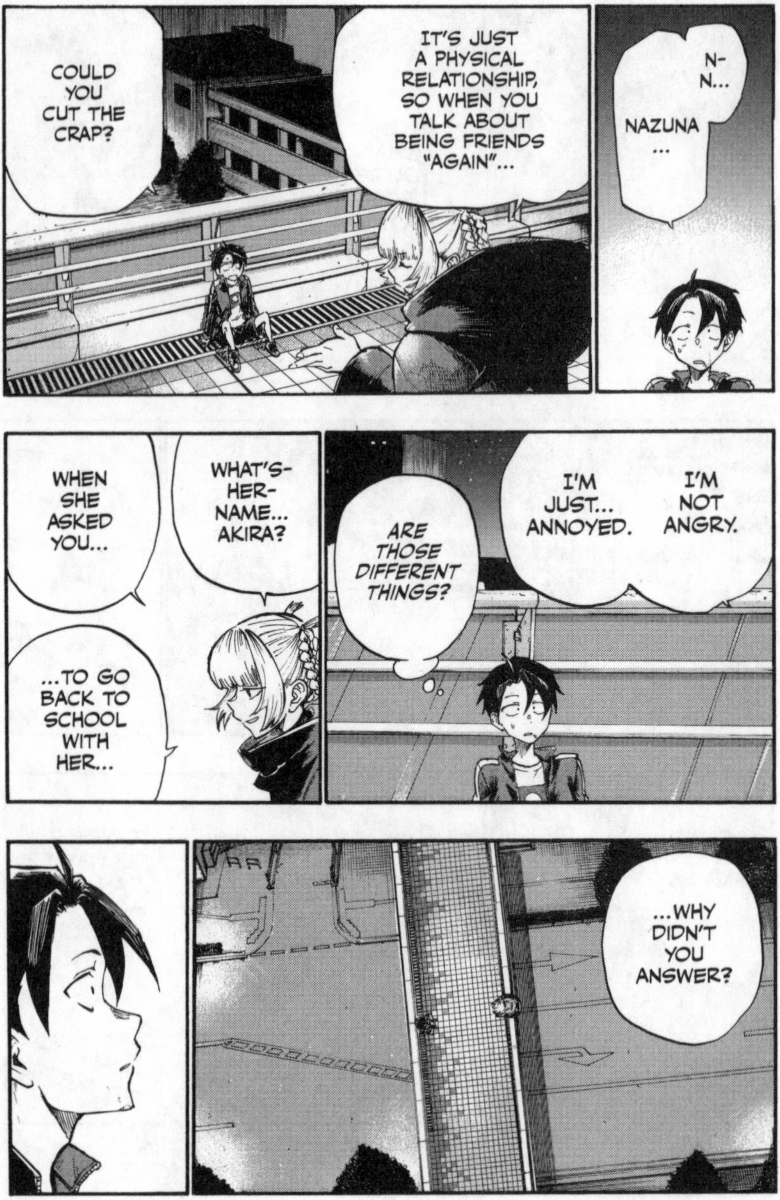
N- N...
NAZUNA ...
IT'S JUST A PHYSICAL RELATIONSHIP, SO WHEN YOU TALK ABOUT BEING FRIENDS "AGAIN"...
COULD YOU CUT THE CRAP?
I'M NOT ANGRY.
I'M JUST... ANNOYED.
ARE THOSE DIFFERENT THINGS?
WHAT'S-HER-NAME... AKIRA?
WHEN SHE ASKED YOU...
...TO GO BACK TO SCHOOL WITH HER...
...WHY DIDN'T YOU ANSWER?

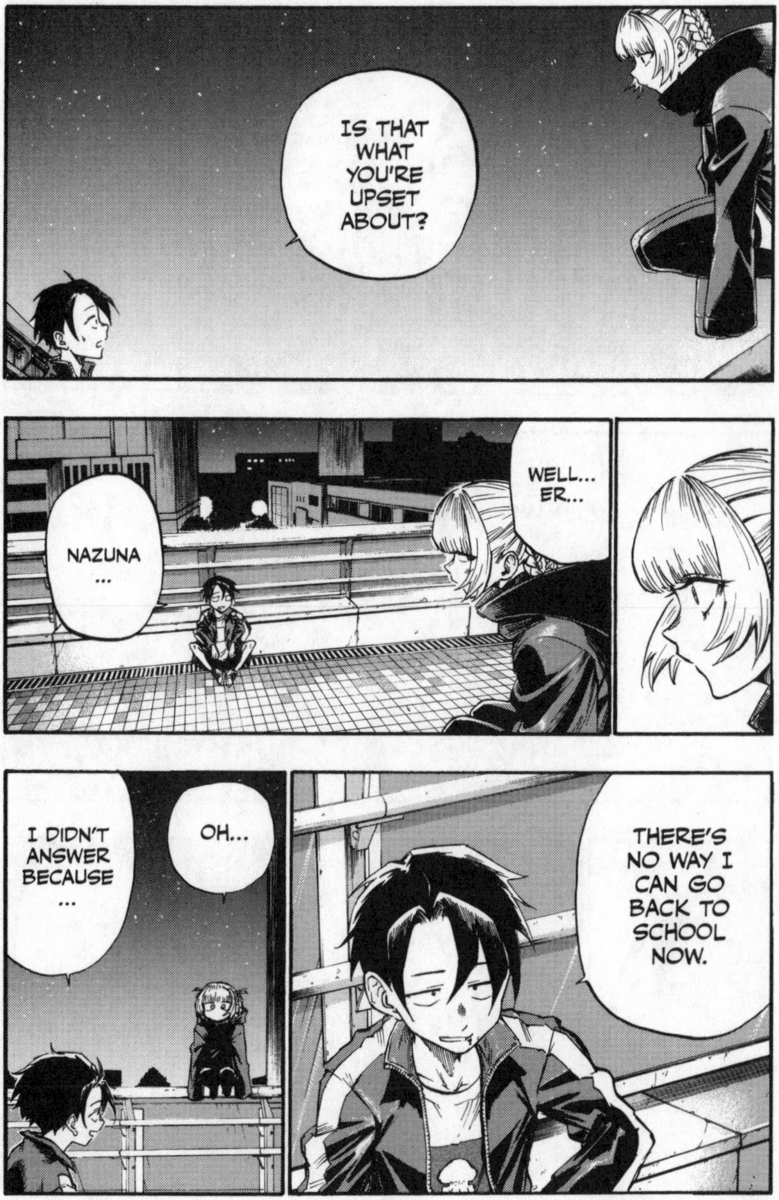
IS THAT WHAT YOU'RE UPSET ABOUT?
WELL... ER...
NAZUNA...
THERE'S NO WAY I CAN GO BACK TO SCHOOL NOW.
OH...
I DIDN'T ANSWER BECAUSE...

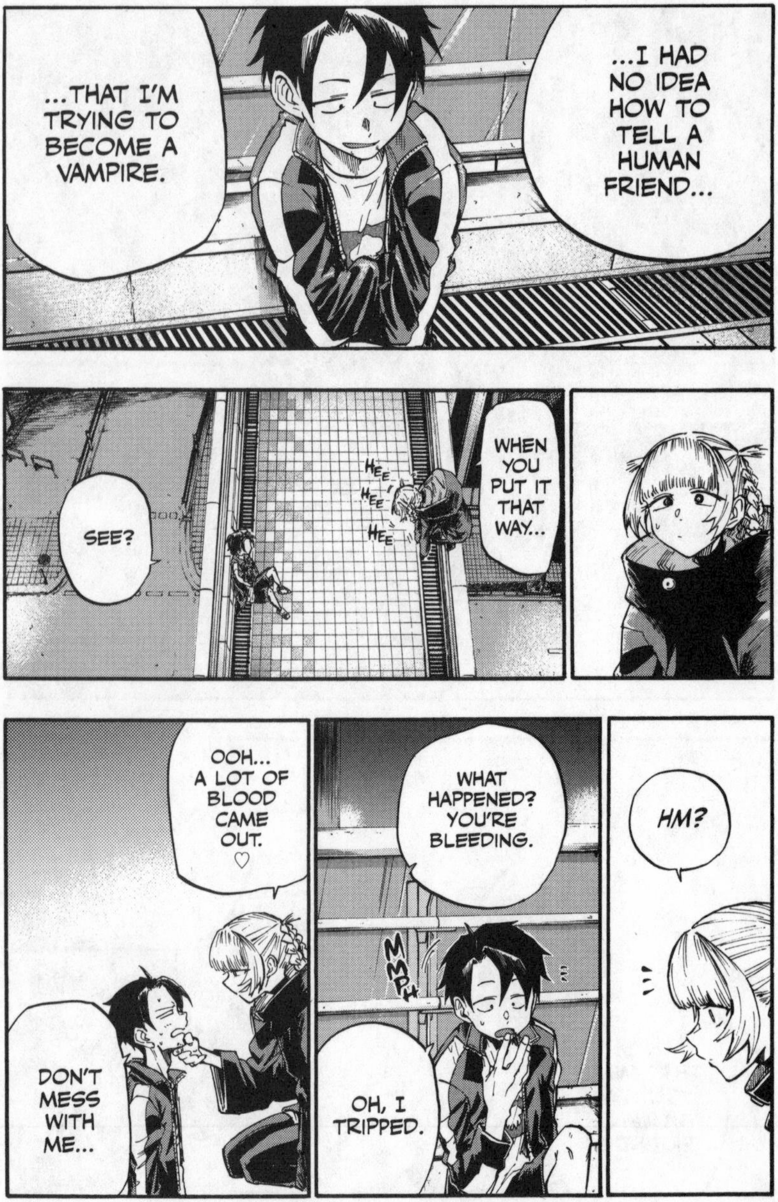
...I HAD NO IDEA HOW TO TELL A HUMAN FRIEND...
...THAT I'M TRYING TO BECOME A VAMPIRE.
WHEN YOU PUT IT THAT WAY...
HEE HEE HEE
SEE?
HM?
WHAT HAPPENED? YOU'RE BLEEDING.
MMPH
OH, I TRIPPED.
OOH... A LOT OF BLOOD CAME OUT. ♡
DON'T MESS WITH ME...

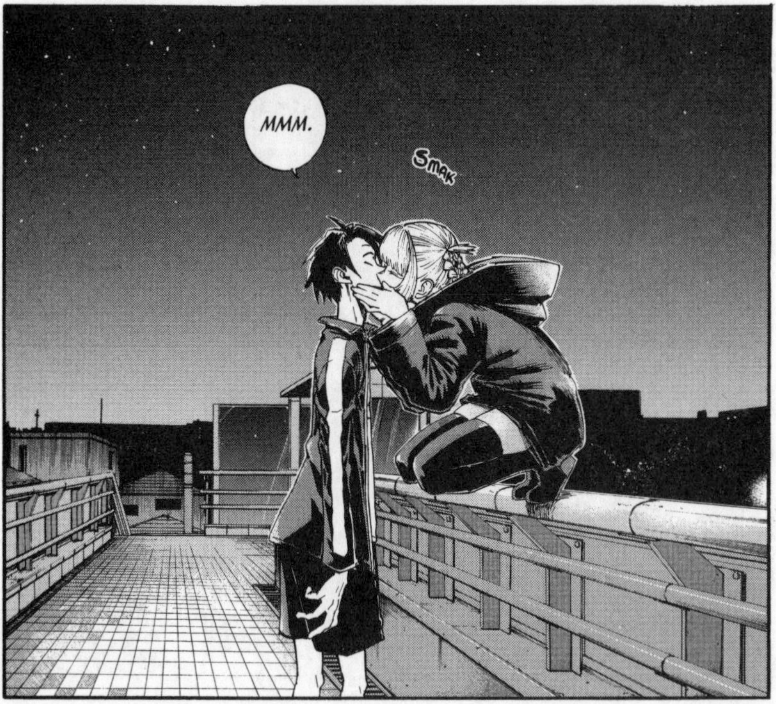
MMM.
SMAK
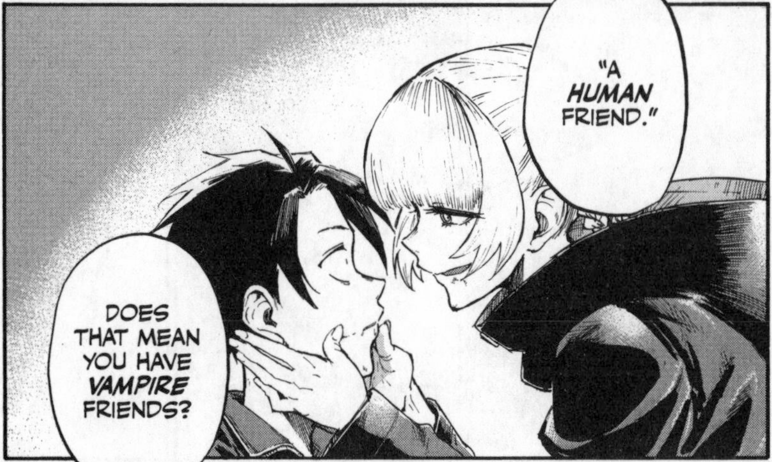
"A HUMAN FRIEND."
DOES THAT MEAN YOU HAVE VAMPIRE FRIENDS?

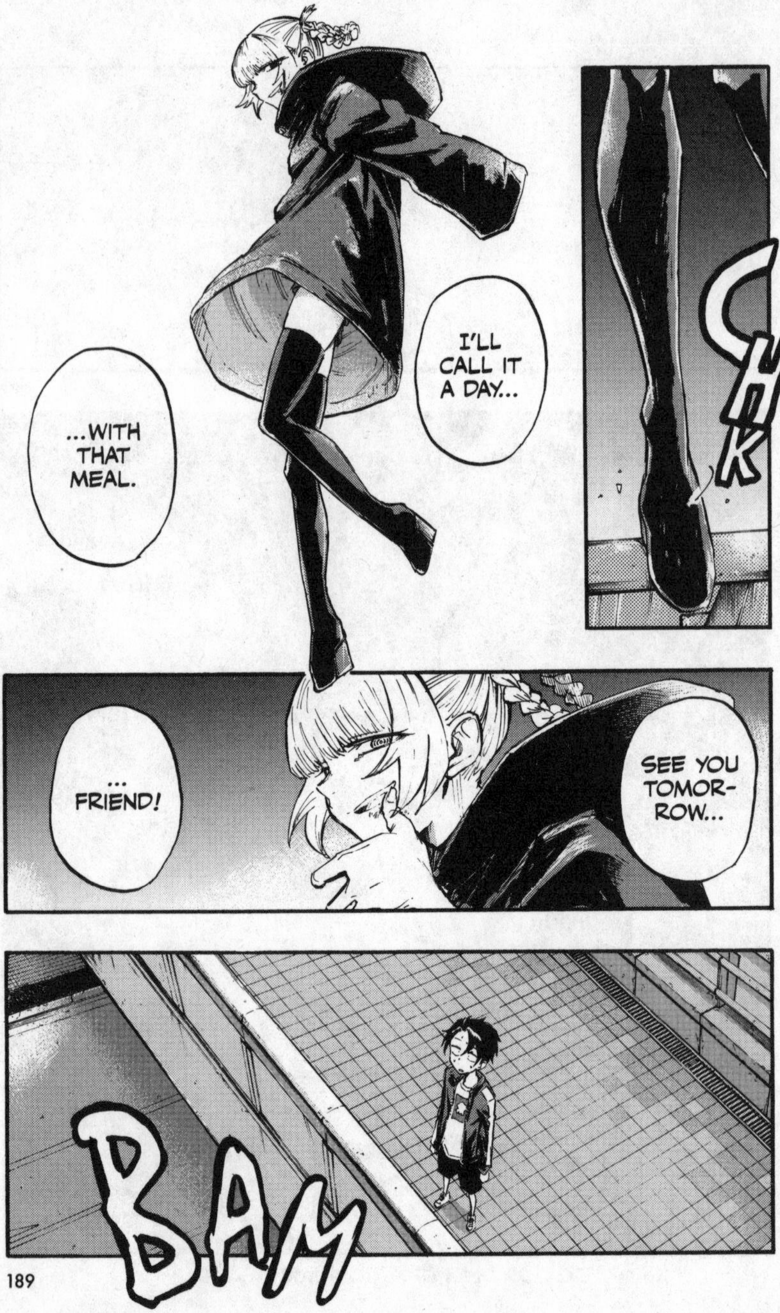
CHK
I'LL CALL IT A DAY...
...WITH THAT MEAL.
SEE YOU TOMOR-ROW...
... FRIEND!
BAM

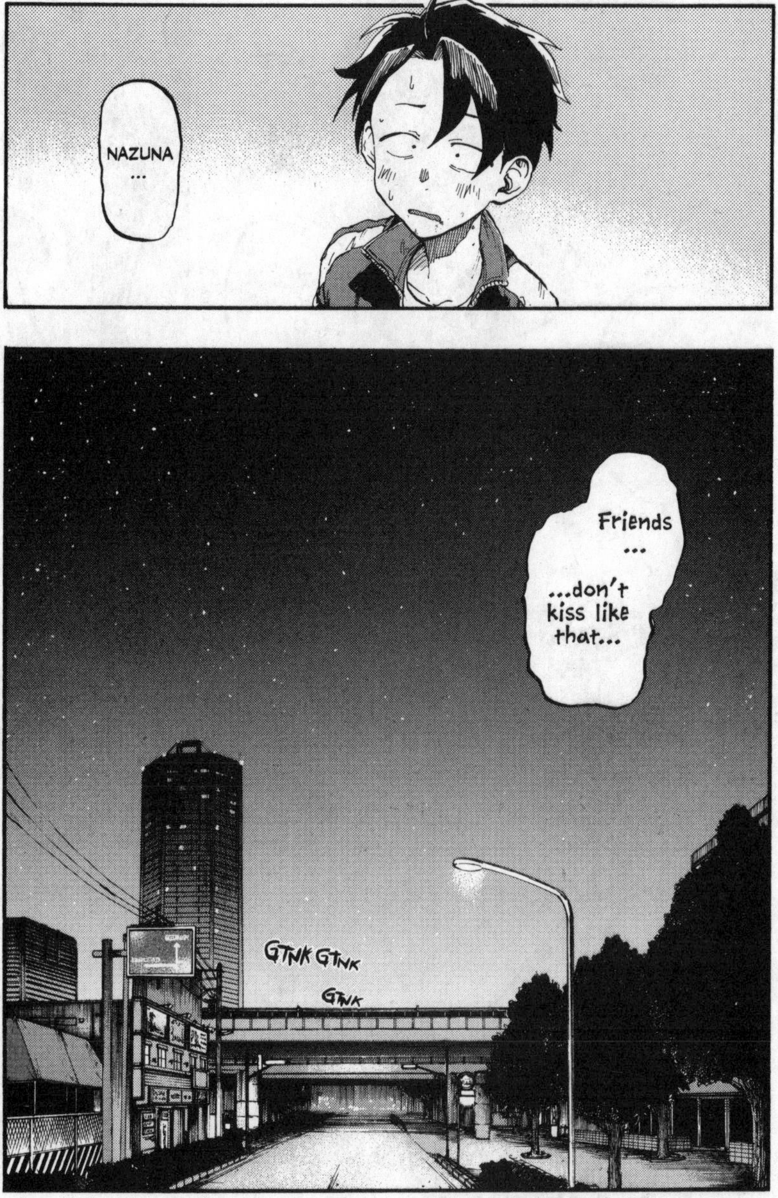
NAZUNA ...
Friends ...
...don't kiss like that...
GTNK GTNK
GTNK

CALL OF THE NIGHT • TO BE CONTINUED...

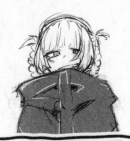

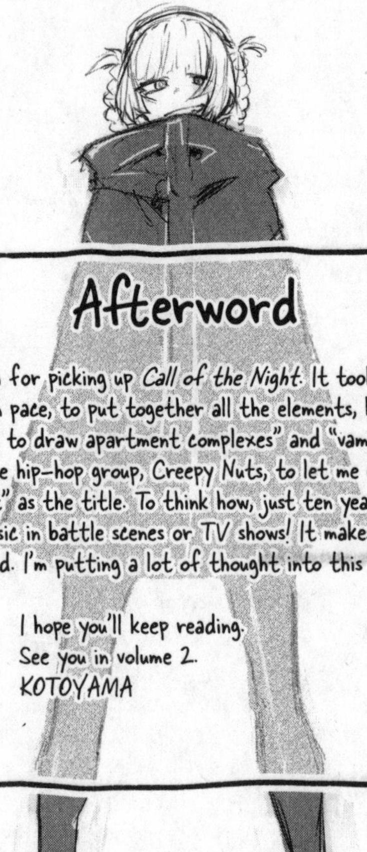

Afterword

Thank you so much for picking up *Call of the Night*. It took about a year, working at an even pace, to put together all the elements, brainstorming stuff like, "I want to draw apartment complexes" and "vampires are cool." I asked my favorite hip-hop group, Creepy Nuts, to let me use their song "Call of the Night" as the title. To think how, just ten years ago, you'd never hear rap music in battle scenes or TV shows! It makes me happy how things have changed. I'm putting a lot of thought into this manga.

I hope you'll keep reading.
See you in volume 2.
KOTOYAMA

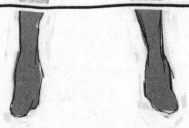

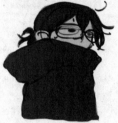

I like baggy clothes.
But they're hard to draw.

Welcome to *Call of the Night*, vol. 1.
I hope you like it.

—KOTOYAMA

KOTOYAMA

In 2013, Kotoyama won the Shonen Sunday Manga
College Award for *Azuma*. From 2014 to 2018,
Kotoyama's title *Dagashi Kashi* ran in *Shonen Sunday*
magazine. *Call of the Night* has been published
in *Shonen Sunda*y since 2019.

Call of the Night

⟨ 1 ⟩

SHONEN SUNDAY EDITION

Story and Art by
KOTOYAMA

Translation — **JUNKO GODA**
English Adaptation — **SHAENON K. GARRITY**
Touch-Up Art & Lettering — **ANNALIESE "ACE" CHRISTMAN**
Cover & Interior Design — **ALICE LEWIS**
Editor — **ANNETTE ROMAN**

YOFUKASHI NO UTA Vol. 1
by KOTOYAMA
© 2019 KOTOYAMA
All rights reserved.
Original Japanese edition published by SHOGAKUKAN.
English translation rights in the United States of America, Canada, the United Kingdom,
Ireland, Australia and New Zealand arranged with SHOGAKUKAN.

Original Cover Design — Yasuhisa KAWATANI

Printed in the U.S.A.

Published by VIZ Media, LLC
P.O. Box 77010
San Francisco, CA 94107

10 9 8 7 6 5 4 3
First printing, April 2021
Third printing, November 2021

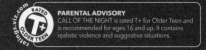

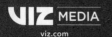

viz.com   shonensunday.com

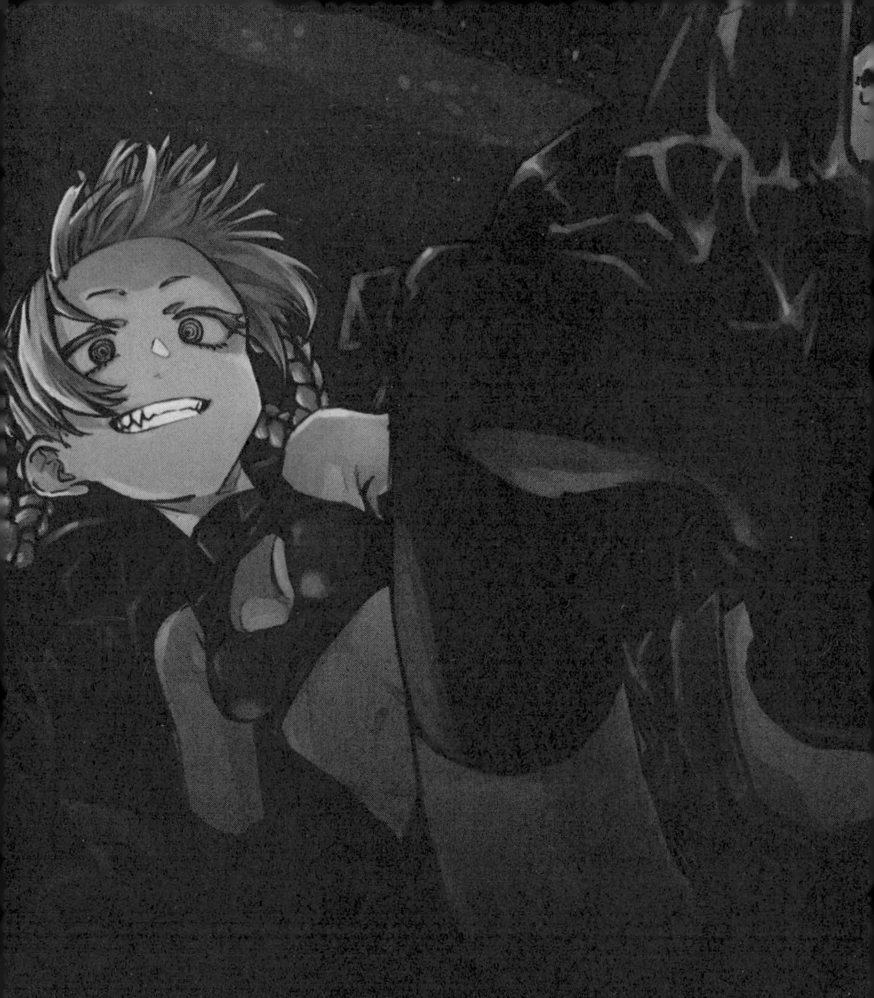

VOLUME 2

What's the difference between desire and love? Does Nazuna know any better than Ko? What about Ko's childhood friend Akira? Unable to answer these romantic questions, Ko and Nazuna go swimming. Turns out bathing beauties at pools are just as hot at night as in the blazing sunshine at the beach... Then, Ko gets jealous when he learns about Nazuna's night job. But when she drafts him into temping for her, the two of them join forces to save a client from her boss—and herself.

Kidnapped by the Demon King and imprisoned in his castle, Princess Syalis is...bored.

Sleepy Princess in the Demon Castle

Story & Art by
KAGIJI KUMANOMATA

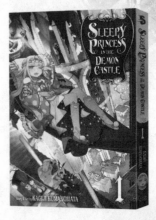

Captured princess Syalis decides to while away her hours in the Demon Castle by sleeping, but getting a good night's rest turns out to be a lot of work! She begins by fashioning a DIY pillow out of the fur of her Teddy Demon guards and an "air mattress" from the magical Shield of the Wind. Things go from bad to worse—for her captors—when some of Princess Syalis's schemes end in her untimely—if temporary—demise and she chooses the Forbidden Grimoire for her bedtime reading...

FLY ME TO THE MOON

STORY AND ART BY
KENJIRO HATA

First comes marriage, then comes an earthbound love that is out of this world!

From the day his parents named him, Nasa Yuzaki has felt connected to outer space...whether he likes it or not. His efforts to outperform the space program veer off course when an accident introduces him to Tsukasa, a mysterious girl with strange powers. Is she an alien, a moon goddess or something else? Since she insists on marrying him, Nasa will have plenty of chances to find out!

FLY ME TO THE MOON
1
STORY AND ART BY
KENJIRO HATA
FLY ME TO THE MOON
1
STORY AND ART BY KENJIRO HATA
VIZ

VIZ

RATED T+ OLDER TEEN

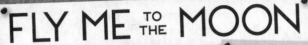

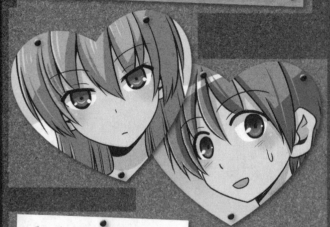

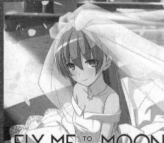

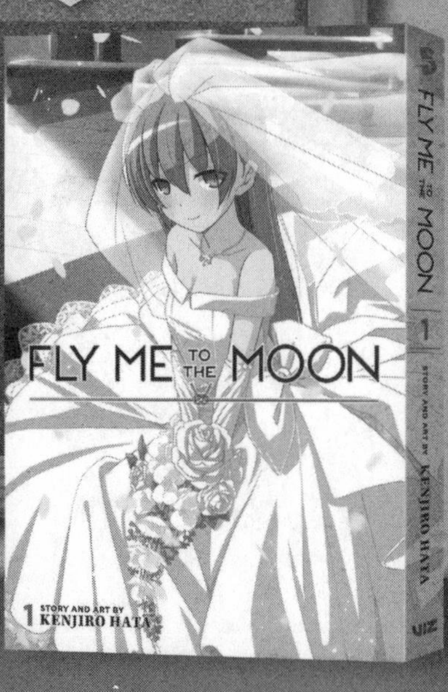

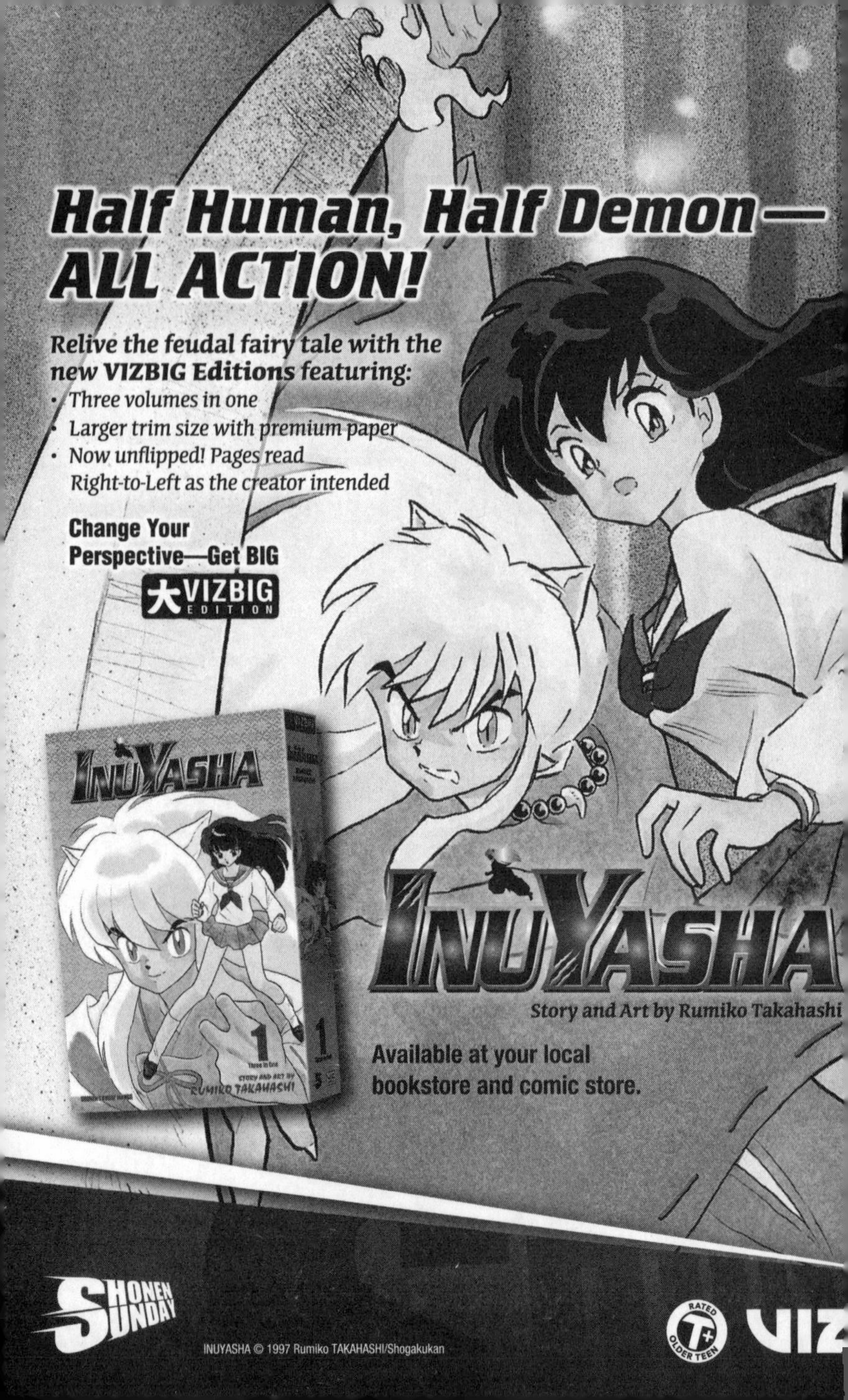
Half Human, Half Demon—
ALL ACTION!
Relive the feudal fairy tale with the new VIZBIG Editions featuring:
• Three volumes in one
• Larger trim size with premium paper
• Now unflipped! Pages read Right-to-Left as the creator intended
Change Your Perspective—Get BIG
VIZBIG EDITION
INUYASHA
1
STORY AND ART BY RUMIKO TAKAHASHI
INUYASHA
Story and Art by Rumiko Takahashi
Available at your local bookstore and comic store.
SHONEN SUNDAY
INUYASHA © 1997 Rumiko TAKAHASHI/Shogakukan
RATED T+ OLDER TEEN
VIZ

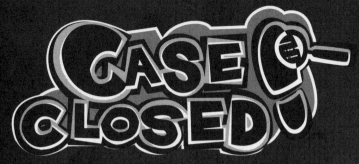
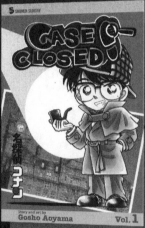

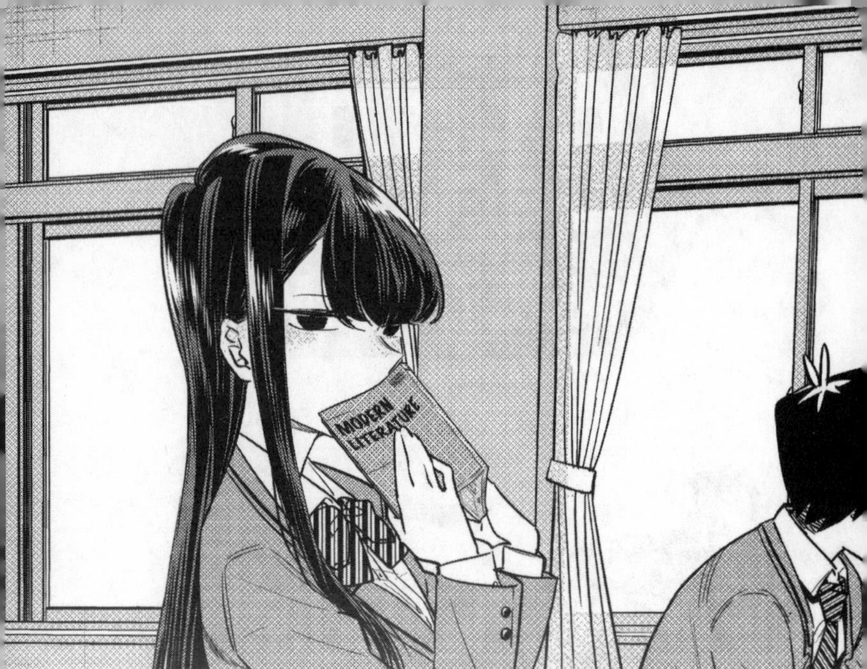
MODERN LITERATURE

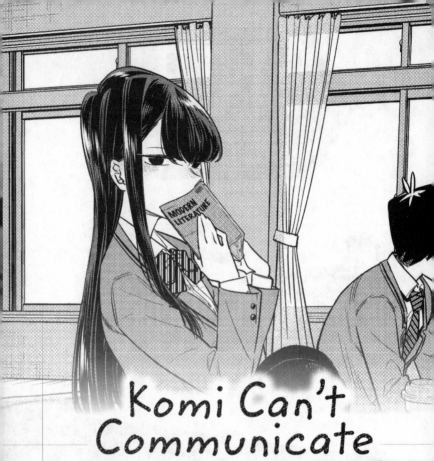

Komi Can't Communicate

Story & Art by Tomohito Oda

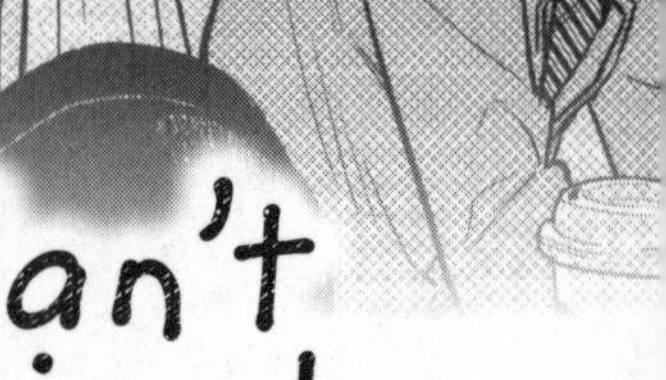

The journey to a hundred friends begins with a single conversation.

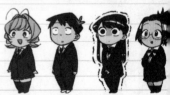

Socially anxious high school student Shoko Komi's greatest dream is to make some friends, but everyone at school mistakes her crippling social anxiety for cool reserve. With the whole student body keeping its distance and Komi unable to utter a single word, friendship might be forever beyond her reach.

VIZ

RATED T TEEN

STOP!

YOU MAY BE READING THE WRONG WAY!

READ THIS WAY

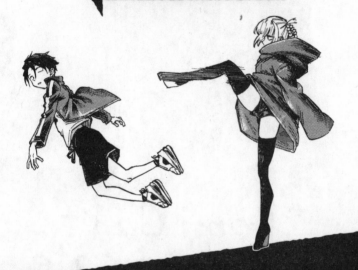

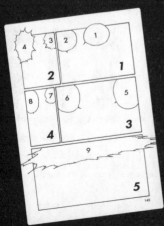

In keeping with the original Japanese comic format, this book reads from right to left—so action, sound effects and word balloons are completely reversed to preserve the orientation of the original artwork.

Check out the diagram shown here to get the hang of things, and then turn to the other side of the book to get started!